Melancholic Freedom

AMERICAN ACADEMY OF RELIGION

REFLECTION AND THEORY IN THE STUDY OF RELIGION SERIES

SERIES EDITOR
James Wetzel, Villanova University

A Publication Series of The American Academy of Religion
and Oxford University Press

LESSING'S PHILOSOPHY OF RELIGION AND THE GERMAN ENLIGHTENMENT
Toshimasa Yasukata

AMERICAN PRAGMATISM
A Religious Genealogy

M. Gail Hamner

OPTING FOR THE MARGINS
Postmodernity and Liberation
in Christian Theology

Edited by Joerg Rieger

MAKING MAGIC
Religion, Magic, and Science
in the Modern World

Randall Styers

THE METAPHYSICS OF
DANTE'S *COMEDY*

Christian Moevs

PILGRIMAGE OF LOVE
Moltmann on the Trinity and Christian Life

Joy Ann McDougall

MORAL CREATIVITY
Paul Ricoeur and the Poetics of Moral Life

John Wall

AMERICAN ACADEMY OF RELIGION

Melancholic Freedom

Agency and the Spirit of Politics

DAVID KYUMAN KIM

OXFORD

UNIVERSITY PRESS

OXFORD
UNIVERSITY PRESS

Oxford University Press, Inc., publishes works that further
Oxford University's objective of excellence
in research, scholarship, and education.

Oxford   New York
Auckland   Cape Town   Dar es Salaam   Hong Kong   Karachi
Kuala Lumpur   Madrid   Melbourne   Mexico City   Nairobi
New Delhi   Shanghai   Taipei   Toronto

With offices in
Argentina   Austria   Brazil   Chile   Czech Republic   France   Greece
Guatemala   Hungary   Italy   Japan   Poland   Portugal   Singapore
South Korea   Switzerland   Thailand   Turkey   Ukraine   Vietnam

Copyright © 2007 by The American Academy of Religion

Published by Oxford University Press, Inc.
198 Madison Avenue, New York, New York 10016

www.oup.com

First issued as an Oxford University Press paper back, 2008

Oxford is a registered trademark of Oxford University Press

Library of Congress Cataloging-in-Publication Data
Kim, David Kyuman.
Melancholic freedom : agency and the spirit of politics / David Kyuman Kim.
p. cm.—(Reflection and theory in the study of religion series)
Includes bibliographical references and index.
ISBN 978-0-19-531982-8 ; 978-0-19-537246-5 (pbk.)
1. Liberty.   2. Agent (Philosophy)   3. Conduct of life.
4. Motivation (Psychology)   I. Title.
B105.L45K56 2007
128'.4—dc22   2006027831

9 8 7 6 5 4 3 2 1

Printed in the United States of America
on acid-free paper

For my family whose love sustains,

My parents, Charles Jae Heub Kim and Anne Young Ok Kim

My sister, Helen Gyulsun Kim

My children, Noah Joonho Hoffman Kim and Josiah Hanul Hoffman Kim

And my wife, Diane Hoffman-Kim, whose hope carries us all forward.

Acknowledgments

From a very young age, I was taught the importance of reciprocity as a personal and social value. In the Confucian-infused household of my childhood, reciprocity was not considered a utilitarian exchange of favors. Instead, my family viewed the practice of reciprocity and mutual responsibility as a measure of moral character. Despite my commitments to radical democracy, I find that I still maintain a strong commitment to reciprocity. And frankly it is an honor to have an opportunity to make account to friends, family, and colleagues who have taken the time and energy to help me think through the myriad strands of this project.

Many friends and colleagues have shown me great generosity in reading and commenting on individual chapters. Let me thank Tom Arnold, Lawrie Balfour, Courtney Bickel Lamberth, Craig Calhoun, Sarah Coakley, Tom Dumm, Francis Schüssler Fiorenza, Edward Hoffman, Russell Jeung, Gordon Kaufman, Kwok Pui Lan, David Lamberth, Kimerer LaMothe, Steve Marshall, Fumitaka Matsuoka, Richard Niebuhr, Jock Reeder, Doris Sommer, David Tracy, and Jim Wetzel. Rom Coles read the entire manuscript after its completion and responded with what I have come to expect of this extraordinary scholar: a critical yet receptive generosity and affirmation. Jane Iwamura and Rudy Busto have been consistent buoys to my spirits as well as voices of conscience that have helped me keep a hand if not my whole mind (at times) in Asian American studies. Judith Butler offered well-timed and much-appreciated words of encouragement as I began the process of finding a publisher. As I hope will be evident and clear to those who read this book, my admiration for Judith's work as a theorist and philosopher is deep and genuine. I am indebted to the editorial staff at Oxford University Press: Cynthia Read, executive editor; Julia Ter Maat, assistant editor; Daniel Gonzalez, editorial assistant; Suzanne Austin, copyeditor; and Gwen Colvin, production editor. It was an honor and a pleasure to work with this group of top-notch professionals. I want to extend particular thanks to Jim Wetzel, the editor of the American Academy of Religion series on Theory and Reflection in the Study of Religion, for including this book in the series. Jim is a terrific reader and critic. No doubt, I was able to write an immeasurably better book by working with a first-rate philosopher of religion like Jim. I am especially grateful to Wayne Proudfoot and Mark Cladis, the official readers of the manuscript for Oxford University Press, both of whom gave insightful, challenging, and constructive criticisms and suggestions. I hope that I have rendered due service to the serious attention these readers have given this text. It remains, nonetheless, that I am wholly accountable for the conclusions and, alas, the shortcomings of the book.

A word of thanks goes to the members of the Theology Colloquium at Harvard who read and commented on early versions of chapters 2 and 3. I am also deeply appreciative to the Department of Religious Studies at Brown University and to the Department of Religious Studies at Connecticut College for the opportunity to develop courses that were critical for my thinking about the problem of agency. I can think of no better initiation into the vocation of teaching than the time I spent at Brown and my ongoing work at Connecticut. The students at Brown and Connecticut who took the various versions of my courses "Freedom and the Discontents of Modernity" and "The Spirit of Politics" were exacting in their intellectual demands and challenges. Their enthusiasm and openness to our collective intellectual experiments speak volumes about the high quality of their minds and their sense of adventure. Connecticut College has been an auspicious place for me to teach. My colleagues in the Department of Religious Studies—Roger Brooks, Gene Gallagher, Gary Green, Lindsey Harlan, and Nora Rubel—have been marvelous in their support and collegiality. I am especially indebted to Gene, one of our nation's master teachers, for his generosity in team teaching with me when I first arrived at Connecticut College and for being an exemplary colleague, and to Roger for his consistent and thoughtful counsel. Fran Hoffman, dean of the faculty at Connecticut College, has been a terrific advocate, perhaps most clearly evident in the faith she showed in appointing me the inaugural director of the Center for the Comparative Study of Race and Ethnicity at the College—a position that has afforded me invaluable experiences and insights. Other colleagues at Connecticut—most notably Armando Bengochea, Sunil Bhatia, Dave Canton, Patricia Dallas, David Dorfman, Teja Ganti, Simon Hay, Candace Howes, Andrea Lanoux, Cybele Locke, Merrilee Mardon, Jackie Olvera, Andy Pessin, Julie Rivkin, Mab Segrest, Catherine Spencer, Cathy Stock,

Derek Turner, Larry Vogel, and Abby Van Slyck—have shown me great conviviality and friendship.

Sharon Krause, Ron Thiemann, Tu Weiming, and Cornel West each read the entire manuscript and offered incisive and invaluable comments and criticisms. I remain humbled and amazed that people of such deep and broad intelligence and creativity not only have shared a consistent interest and enthusiasm for the development of my intellectual life but also have been unflagging in their insistent reminders to me that "the work" is important. Sharon and I continue to share a long and abiding concern for the problem of agency. She has been an indispensable interlocutor and friend, especially in her willingness to hear out my latest intellectual forays, pasta recipes, and rants and raves. Ron has been exceptional in helping me find practical judgment and wisdom in the strange space and time that marks the transition from graduate school to life as a teacher and scholar. His example of good humor and compassion remains a touchstone for me in my ongoing adventures in the academy. My pursuit of the theme of self-cultivation really began years ago in Weiming's classroom. Indeed, he was responsible for reintroducing me to the Confucian world. I am certain that my own Confucian roots would have gone largely unacknowledged and underarticulated if I had not met Weiming and benefited from his singular effort to sustain Confucianism as a living tradition. Cornel has been a mentor, a comrade, and a friend, but I am not certain that even those words capture the spirit of our relationship. I have long since lost count of the thinkers, critics, and artists that he has introduced to me. In thinking back on the countless hours we have spent together talking over the years, I have come to realize that we have been engaged in an ongoing dialogue about philosophy, literature, art, politics, race, religion, and, to my delight, music. I am humble enough to acknowledge that it is at times difficult to keep pace with the intellectual marathon that Cornel has been pursuing. Nonetheless, I keep on running with an appreciative yet exhilarating exhaustion.

This book is dedicated to my family. Among the themes found in these pages is the centrality of courage and integrity. My father, Charles Jae Heub Kim, and my mother, Anne Young Ok Kim, have always been paragons of courage and integrity in my life. They have taught me that, though compromise is inevitable, standing firm in the face of adversity is a premium. For all of the struggles that they have endured, I can, with all honesty, call them the bravest people I know. People often remark how similar I am to my sister Helen. I usually reply that my younger sister has led me more than I have followed. Despite my hardheadedness, she remains good humored and loving toward her brother. My sister Nancy Hoffman is always quick with sincere and genuine care and support. My brother Selçuk Adabag puts the lie to anyone who claims that blood ties are thickest. My nephew Emre and my niece Mina show me that there are always new heights to pursue. My uncle and aunt, Byung Chul and Kyungsoon Lee, and my cousins Moonyoung and Younyoung Lee continue to renew my faith in familial bonds. And my "other" parents, Ed and Esther Hoffman, have shown me that the love of a parent grows as a family grows.

It was once suggested to me that having children during graduate school would only prolong what would already be a protracted process. Surely, those folks were right about the time involved in finishing what, by many estimates, was an overdue text. And yet now that the dissertation has grown into a book, my conviction has only deepened that the intellectual life does not begin and end at the desk but, rather, is organic with the whole of one's life. My sons, Noah and Josiah, have given me more joy than I will probably ever deserve. They have taught me that self-cultivation demands love as much as it requires discipline—focus and attention as well as laughter. They have been constant in reminding me that children always wait with open arms for their father. And it is my wife, Diane Hoffman-Kim, who has been my partner in all the most important things in my life. Diane is an astonishingly complete person of exceptional intelligence and emotional depths. I am, at best, difficult and cranky while immersed in a project such as this book. She has always been remarkably patient and, when appropriate, impatient with me over the twenty years we have been together. Hope can come late, if at all, to the skeptic. And as Diane has shown me time and again, her optimism can always pierce through my most burnished skepticism. She continues to enchant me with her kindness, compassion, and love, and her faith in me saves and sustains.

Contents

Melancholic Freedom

I

Melancholic Freedom

Introduction

> The cry of humanity for salvation is not a matter of any one time or
> faith. The pathos of that cry will become only the deeper when you
> learn to see why it is so universal a cry. The truth, if there be any
> accessible truth, regarding the genuine way of salvation will become
> only the more precious to you when you know by how widely sun-
> dered paths the wanderers in the darkness of this world have sought
> for the saving light.
> —Josiah Royce, *The Sources of Religious Insight*

Among the striking features of our times—whether one calls it modernity, late modernity, or postmodernity—are the ongoing struggles
to feel at home in the world, to live a meaningful life, and to act
with freedom and integrity. Modernity has shown itself to be astonishingly consistent in producing and reproducing paradoxes, contra-
dictions, and inconsistencies that have left these aspirations for home,
meaning, freedom, and integrity under constant assault. In this regard, modernity and postmodernity are marked as much for their
losses as for their achievements. Humanity "discovered" its freedom
in modernity, but it also lost much in the bargain. Human freedom—
which is to say, freedom of movement, speech, and thought—emerges
through the application of critical thinking and reasoning that
continues to render distinctions from the past, authority, and tradition. Modernity finds its pitch and strength in the clasping hands of
discontent and freedom.

And yet anyone who reflects on the ways freedom is augured by discontent must share in the anxiety that the ground on which one stands today may just as surely crack and crumble tomorrow. Paradigms shift, and regimes come and go. It is with this anxiety and uncertainty in mind that I have come to identify a basic problematic of our times that I am calling "agency as melancholic freedom." By framing the challenges of the problematic in terms of "agency" and "melancholy," I am invoking terms that I believe capture the sentiments, dispositions, and experiences of the piety to freedom that have been fundamental to modernity and to late or postmodernity. These are features of late modern or postmodern moral identity that speak to the achievements and losses associated with being an agent. This book focuses on the late modern/postmodern discourse on agency and the dimensions of this discourse that evoke what I identify as a set of religious dispositions, attitudes, and experiences that enables us to operate under conditions in which freedom and agency appear as a paradox, that is, as both achievement *and* loss. In effect, I begin with the question of how and why a sense of loss attaches itself to freedom—which is to ask: are loss and melancholy necessary conditions for understanding the aspirations that bind agency and moral identity together?

The drive for agency—to enact it, to claim it, and to live it—is evident across cultures, races, sexualities, genders, and classes. In acknowledging agency as a central feature of human freedom, emancipation, and liberation, the work of agency becomes apparent in distinctive forms of self-determination, such as political action, cultural expressions and symbolism, and moral reasoning. In the political and global context in which demands for cultural and political recognition are unavoidable, the quest for agency is a focal point for the resistance to domination, the expression of meaningful existence, and the overcoming of experiences of melancholy and symbolic loss. The "Orange Revolution" in the Ukraine, the debate over gay marriage in the United States, and the ongoing struggles to define domestic and international civil and human rights agendas all exemplify the conjunction of social and political recognition with projects of regenerating agency. A major argument of this book contends that at the core of contemporary quests for agency lie dimensions of the religious and spiritual life, the heart of which is to transcend circumstances and conditions of constraint and limitation of varying kinds. I take as a hermeneutical horizon for this argument a diagnosis that concludes that our age is marked by conflicting expectations about realizing life and political possibilities. To be an agent in our times is to live a life of melancholic freedom. Increasingly, we are pressed to acknowledge that the work of fulfilling individual and collective projects of freedom requires the ability to see possibility where there is foreclosure, to discern opportunities for care and regard for the self when choices appear to be diminishing, and to sustain hope in the face of despair.

With these conditions in mind, I identify in this book features and qualities of religiosity in contemporary aspirations to realize freedom and agency.
The analytic device I employ to uncover these features and qualities of religiosity is a critical and comparative examination of the work of two figures
who have been enormously influential in shaping the contemporary discourse
and debates on agency and the self/subjectivity: namely, Charles Taylor and
Judith Butler.[1] I draw on the work of Taylor and Butler in order to analyze the
problem of agency, on the one hand, as a mode of action and freedom and,
on the other hand, as constitutive of moral, cultural, political, and spiritual
identities. The critical trajectory I am following asks what it would mean to
stress the religious, moral, and spiritual motivations that underpin an understanding of agency as meaningful action. The religious dimensions and qualities of agency that I seek to uncover lie where the quests for meaning and
freedom intersect. To wit, I am asking the following: In a predominantly secular political and social culture, what remains of a spiritual heritage that had
tied together the fates of freedom and meaning? Does the persistence of this
heritage—found in the remnants of a Romantic legacy in contemporary culture that celebrates the interplay of authenticity and irony—amount not to
a reversion to one particular religious tradition or another but rather to a
transformed spiritual condition that finds within the quests for agency a connection between freedom and the affirmation of value and meaning?

Let me be clear: by calling agency "melancholic freedom," I am not attempting to integrate a full-blown psychoanalytical approach into religious
theory. Instead, I am gesturing toward and borrowing from Freud's "Mourning and Melancholia" by arguing that melancholy is a state or condition of
the self and the soul in which we cannot let go of something that we love
even if it has become lost to us through death or some other kind of annul-
ment, such as experiences of supercession, obsolescence, or nostalgia.[2] In
other words, melancholy/melancholia is a condition in which the self is unable to mourn. Taking Freud's formulation of melancholy as a point of departure, I identify values such as moral and political ideals of freedom and
justice as candidates for lost objects that are not fully mourned for the modern and postmodern self. By associating these values and ideals with melancholy, I am arguing that the aspiration and desire for freedom—as liberation,
emancipation, and autonomy—have not been lost entirely, but neither are
they as clearly "with us" as they had once been. The sense of loss correlated
with agency is found in historical claims by philosophers such as Taylor who
argue that there is a price the self pays for freedom in a secular age, as well
as with theorists like Butler who identify agency as derivative from the conditions that attempt to deny freedom and humanity to the abject, marginalized, and denigrated of society. By defining experiences of loss as constitutive
of freedom and the self, I characterize the approaches to agency developed
by Taylor and Butler as "projects of regenerating agency." Furthermore,

I maintain that by proposing projects of regenerating agency, Taylor and Butler are also putting forward distinctive calls for human flourishing, self-cultivation, and self-transformation.

These respective projects of regenerating agency run cross-grain to the dominant ethos of both modernity and postmodernity. For Taylor, the need to regenerate agency is induced by a resistance to the detachment and lack of moral clarity found in naturalism, political liberalism, and secularism—which is to say, a resistance to the dominant schools of political theory and moral philosophy in the modern west since the Enlightenment. For Butler, regenerating agency requires working with *and* against the dominant social identity norms that dehumanize differences of gender, race, class, culture, and sexuality. In this respect, a project of regenerating agency such as Butler's finds its inspiration and motivation not in a moral realist orientation to the good as Taylor's does, but rather from the experience of difference itself. For those who are in society but not of society, for those for whom *difference* is not an option but rather a fact of being, the charge for undertaking a project of regenerating agency may be considerably different than the one Taylor suggests.

It is worth reiterating and underscoring the rationale for conducting a comparative analysis of Taylor and Butler on agency. The inspiration for writing *Melancholic Freedom* came, in part, from my curiosity with the intriguing invocation of the term "agency" in the literature from a wide variety of disciplines, such as philosophy, political theory, feminist theory, critical race theory, sociology, and religious studies. As I suggested earlier, in these discourses, agency seems to indicate an achievement of sorts, vaguely associated with values of freedom, liberation, and autonomy. Nonetheless, the specific features of these values are, in my estimation, largely under-examined and not well understood. More specifically, while there seems to be a broad consensus that realizing agency is a good thing, it remains the case that there is not much in the literature in question from these various disciplines that indicates what makes agency a valuable and even virtuous achievement. My sense was and remains that an effective way of interrogating this situation is to examine the work of some of the actors who have played a major role in shaping the discourse on agency. This insight drew me to Taylor and Butler, two major contemporary philosophers and theorists who have had a remarkably wide and deep influence on the discourse on agency. In short, a central concern I had in mind while writing *Melancholic Freedom* is the influence that Taylor and Butler each have had on shaping how contemporary moral philosophers, critical theorists, social theorists, political theorists, and religious theorists have approached the relationship between identity/subjectivity and political and moral agency. This book is not an attempt simply to map some of the conceptual terrain among academic disciplines. More significantly, I take what Taylor and Butler have to say about agency as representative of the changes in the moral, political, and spiritual conditions that unfold in late modernity through the transition into postmodernity. In this regard, I read and interpret the pictures of agency rendered through Taylor's powerful genealogical interrogation of the moral impoverishment of the modern western self and Butler's incisive poststructuralist analysis of the persistent constraints on social and cultural norms and conventions of identity as forms of melancholic freedom. Which is to say, I understand these approaches to the problem of agency as indicative of a set of laments, as well as hopeful anticipations, over the possibilities and available options for living a meaningful life in late modernity and postmodernity.

As with any comparative enterprise, the challenge I face in this book is to identify similarities as well as differences between Taylor and Butler on the question of the meaning of agency. Taylor and Butler do not share the same object of loss for their respective forms of melancholic freedom. Nonetheless, there is a formal similarity in orientation I identify in Taylor and Butler, albeit developed in distinctive ways, in regard to the tragicomic sensibility they present as the necessary responses to the challenges of realizing agency as a (if not *the*) measure of meaningful subjectivity and human flourishing. In effect, the motivational ends and aims for cultivating a flourishing self is the terrain on which I will highlight the commonalities and distinctions between Taylor's and Butler's projects of regenerating agency.

It is reasonable to ask here if there is a specific feature or set of characteristics common to projects of regenerating agency. The dimension I have chosen to focus on is the work of *the religious imagination*. At the service of a project of regenerating agency, the religious imagination engenders new modes of cultural, social, psychological, and political possibilities, which is to say that the religious imagination is an engine of *hope*. As modes of resistance to dominant social imaginaries, I am arguing that both Taylor's and Butler's projects of regenerating agency involve the cultivation of the work of the religious imagination: a faculty that buoys moral, political, psychic, and spiritual motivations to realize the values of one's moral identity. The religious imagination is the faculty that envisions and enables a willingness to risk conceiving of life chances and possibilities for the self under conditions in which these chances and possibilities are neither fully evident nor apparent. In identifying the work of the religious imagination in Taylor's and Butler's projects of regenerating agency, I am stressing the critical role of the Romantic tropes of authenticity and irony that operates for both theorists. More specifically, my interest is in the centrality of the practices of critique that Taylor and Butler deploy as engines for imagining and subsequently creating possibilities of living a life of moral integrity. This work of the religious imagination entails cultivating openness and attunement to the possibilities of realizing agency through a willingness to risk conceiving of life in unfamiliar, disquieting, and even unnerving ways—an unsettling role, I argue, played by the sublime. At the same time, the religious imagination also evokes aspirations and possibilities for the self that are otherwise obscured or negated by codes, conventions, and norms of legitimacy. In other words, the religious imagination affects the possibility of a vocation for the self that would not otherwise exist under conditions of melancholy and loss. Vocation is the tie that binds identity and agency, which is to say that vocation speaks to a care of and for the self that has experienced disempowering forces and life conditions, as well as a lost sense of purpose and meaning. As Robert Merrihew Adams has recently written, vocation "is a matter of who and what one is called to be."[3] My contention is that framing agency as a vocation affirms the connection between intention and outcome that marks one's moral identity as an effective agent in the world. The religious imagination regenerates agency by enabling the will and the self to respond to calls or vocations made available through experiences with the sublime. These experiences make particular moves possible: from concept to action; from the limitations and constraints of all-too-worldly immanence to the possibilities of realizing modes of transcendence and emancipation; and from despair to hope.

It perhaps makes sense here to back up for a moment and ask a basic question: What does agency mean? And why should we associate agency with the melancholic loss of moral and political ideals and values? The first thing to note is that agency, in its most basic sense, is the capacity for self-initiated, intentional action, that is, the ability of an agent (self, consciousness, ego, or even representative body, people, or community) to determine for itself acts and consequences in the world. For example, in modern western philosophy of religion, questions about human agency are often framed in terms of the problems of free will, such as whether our intentions are our own or are actually initiated by God or history. This is to ask, in particular, whether the freedom of the will hinges on the effects of external forces, such as the divine, nature, history, or the passions.[4] With the aim of identifying the religious significance of contemporary intellectual approaches to questions of agency as meaningful action, I have chosen to focus on the dynamic relationships between questions of ultimacy and commitment, as well as the connection that exists between identity and the formation and motivation of values and norms. As such, I am examining the problem of agency at the intersection of a series of theoretical discourses, namely, through the philosophy of religion, moral philosophy, political theory, literary and cultural theory, as well as psychological approaches. As I noted earlier, a review of the contemporary literature in philosophically and theoretically oriented disciplines reveals a lively interest in the problem of agency. This is not to say that agency is by any means a transparent concept, in the sense of having a universal or common usage and idiom. Indeed, as I have already indicated, this book is responding, in part, to the ways that agency is often deployed as a conversation-stopper, that is, as an indication that some kind of positive value has been achieved or demonstrated without any need for further inquiry. And yet it still remains to be determined if agency is an end or value in itself. Just as freedom is widely taken to be the consummate value of modernity, agency appears to have an analogous standing for late or postmodernity. In this regard, agency is at the same time continuous with yet distinct from freedom. The current debates on agency rarely address the topic in such terms but tend, rather, to restrict the analysis of agency to questions of political action and participation.[5] This approach has merit and is indeed critical for our times. Nonetheless, I argue that it is necessary to enrich these analyses of agency and the political through an engagement with religious categories and modes of religiosity that are discernable in quests for agency, or what I am calling projects of regenerating agency. In short, while agency is evident in all moral as well as political deliberations and decisions, there remains a need for a critical and substantive interrogation into the external and internal conditions that reflect the aspirational qualities of the self as agent—which is to say, the material, political, social, psychic, and spiritual conditions that engender agency. I contend that implicit in the struggles to generate and engage in political life, as expressed in Taylor's communitarianism or Butler's poststructuralism, lies a dedication to human flourishing, which I read as a commitment that reflects a deep and abiding religiosity. Furthermore, this commitment necessitates the possibility for realizing modes of self-cultivation and self-transformation that respond to the needs of the self who experiences the loss of the grounds of her/his moral identity. This holds, I would maintain, as much for the tragic states of minds of post-9/11 Americans and wartime Iraqis as it does for the sanguine yet morally difficult context of post-apartheid South Africa. In each of these cases, fundamental questions about the conditions for the possibility of surviving and flourishing arise from experiences of loss and the desire for change.

Characterized as an aspiration for transcendence, political and moral agency often reflect acts of the religious imagination, where "transcendence" means discontinuity with the ordinary, the everyday, the "normal," the taken-for-granted, and all the qualities of life that elude easy, reflective verification.[6] For example, if my moral identity and citizenship are shaped *and* constrained or limited by conditions of *normalized* racism, are my freedom and agency in overcoming this racism reflections of an aspiration to transcend these oppressive and constraining conditions? The realization of these kinds of aspirations requires the work of the religious imagination to conjure and evoke a hope that brings together political, moral, and religious or spiritual quests for well-being and human flourishing. A political agent, democratic or otherwise, is constantly reflecting on the spiritual and existential values that sustain the ongoing pursuit of an ethical and good life, whether this is defined as the pursuit of life, liberty, and happiness or as engaging in the public life of the social world. As part of a quest for human flourishing, political *and* moral agency have innate connections to religious and spiritual concerns about meaning, purpose, and significance.[7] Another way of framing this relationship is to ask if there is a connection between political life, moral deliberation/reasoning, and agency, on the one hand, and the factors that make a meaningful life possible, on the other hand. Projects of regenerating agency engage the religious imagination to synthesize the aims and aspirations of the political, the existential, and the moral, as well as the yearning for "the next self."[8]

Let me offer two examples of the contemporary discourse on agency to underscore these points. The first example is from political theory; the other is from literary theory—arguably the two most prominent theoretical discourses in contemporary academics.

In political theory, the dominant schools of thought have been and continue to be political liberalism and the work on democratic deliberation. More specifically, it is a discourse that remains largely shaped by the work of John Rawls and Jürgen Habermas.[9] Among the defining features of political liberalism and democratic deliberation is the commitment to establishing justice and equality through the protection of the rights of the minority against the tyranny of the majority. And yet the major challenges to political liberalism over the last two to three decades have been from communitarians such as Michael Sandel, Michael Walzer, and Taylor, on the one hand, and, on the other hand, from proponents of the so-called politics of difference or "postmodern political theory" such as Iris Marion Young, William Connolly, and Butler.[10] The common critique levied by communitarians and the advocates of difference is that political liberalism—in its conviction that justice, rights, and political participation are best protected through an increasingly value-neutral or value-thin public sphere—has diminished the energy and reasons that had once inspired people to become politically active, engaged, and invested, that is, to become political agents and actors.[11] If the terms of legitimate political action as defined by liberalism prohibit or at least strongly discourage, for example, *explicit* invocations of religious values *or* seek to limit public and political expressions of "thick" features of identity, such as race, gender, sexuality, and class, then, the communitarians and postmoderns ask: what sort of politics and ethical life will result?[12] What kind of connection to a society's common and political life will its constituents have? Do the achievements of political liberalism and attendant forms of rationalist democratic deliberation come at the price of diminishing the life and political possibilities of democracy itself?[13]

Another example of the prevalence of "agency talk" in intellectual/academic discourse is found in the confluence of Lacanian psychoanalysis and poststructuralism in literary theory. The preoccupation of the psychoanalytical and poststructuralist approaches has been with the possibility of realizing agency in light of or in the face of overwhelming forces of systemic oppression *and* the symbolic ordering of lives and consciousness through language, media, representations, and other cultural, political, and psychic influences. Poststructuralists express skepticism about the possibility of agency, especially given a held belief they maintain in the thoroughgoing effects of systemic oppression and the denial and annihilation of the self/subject. And yet this skepticism is tempered by a conflicting, even paradoxical preoccupation with agency as a persistent and necessary concern. Lacanians persist with their own contemplations about the possibility of realizing agency, despite what they see as the unpredictable influence of the subconscious, on the one hand, and the regulation of thought and action of the self, on the other hand, through the retrievals from "the Symbolic Order." In both cases—that is, in poststructuralism and Lacanian psychoanalytical theory—despite skepticism and even cynicism about the possibility of realizing agency, there is, at minimum, an implicit sense that agency is something we have to hold out hope for even if we believe it no longer remains a viable option.[14]

An overlapping interest between these discourses about agency in political theory and literary and cultural studies is an abiding concern for the notion of agency as a political aspiration. After all, agency and identity, as found in political projects of recognition and legitimation, are among the most pressing issues in contemporary public life. At the forefront of research in the humanities and the social sciences, in general, and in the study of religion, in particular, is the exploration of the moral orientations, values, and ideals found in forms of social solidarity that inspire action, that is, forms of social solidarity such as ethnicity and race, religious fundamentalism, and nationalist and social movements. In considering the relationship among values, beliefs, and action or agency, I maintain that it is necessary to understand how collective identities—especially when framed in terms of "difference" and not in essentialist terms—*and* their associated values, beliefs, and ideals animate individual lives and affect what kinds of actions and forms of participation people take in civil society. In sum, in the cultural and political debates over multiculturalism, transnationalism, race relations, and fundamentalism, what constitutes agency is an open question. Agency *can* be about recognition, but it is also about deeper existential struggles that affect individuals as well as collective bodies.

With these struggles in mind, let me elaborate on the questions I raised earlier, especially as they pertain to my consideration of the religious significance of different forms of agency. Are the struggles of individuals and groups for the full enjoyment of their rights instances of agency? From a political standpoint, does agency mean something beyond intentionality? What are the religious implications if our understanding of agency is enlarged beyond the political? To what extent does the religious quest for transcendence support or inspire human agency? To what extent is it a necessary condition for agency? What can an analysis of agency tell us about the character of the commitments and the moral psychology of late modernity, where "moral psychology" means the study of motivations and inspirations for action? How does secularism affect the character of agency? Does agency or the aspiration for agency approximate something categorizable as religious experience? Does a political life replete with commitments to transcendent goods, such as God, justice, and freedom, implicate political and moral agency with the religious and the spiritual? At the forefront of my inquiry is the question: what kinds of religious insights and sources can one find in expressions of political and moral agency?

The main point I am stressing here is one I introduced earlier: even with its common usage and invocation across the theoretical disciplines, agency is hardly a transparent concept. For example, vaguely populist sentiments that accompany declarations such as "Getting their voices heard is a sign of the protestors' agency" rely on a rhetorical move that effectively uses agency as a conversation stopper. While such a claim about agency may be true, declaring as much still requires further substantiation as to why this is *necessarily* a good thing. It is not always entirely clear how or why agency comes to constitute an end or value in itself, which is to say that more needs to be said about the significance and need for cultivating agency as an end or value.[15]

Agency as the Spirit of Politics

Politics has been called the "art of the possible," and it actually is a realm akin to art insofar as, like art, it occupies a creatively mediating position between spirit and life, the idea and reality.

—Thomas Mann, speech delivered before
the Library of Congress, May 1945

There are philosophical as well as religious precedents, even time-honored ones, that have uncovered organic relationships between agency and the religious or spiritual, and between the political and the moral that are analogous to the ones I am identifying in the contemporary discourse on agency. For example, Confucianism is exemplary in this regard, especially given the pride of place it grants to practices of self-cultivation and the continuity it seeks between the different realms of the ethical life.[16] Another example is the critique of modernity Hannah Arendt offers in *The Human Condition*. This critique relies largely on the differences Arendt identifies between the modern and ancient epochs of the west. In modernity, so Arendt maintains, the overdeveloped separation of life into different spheres of existence delimits the possibilities of agency as public action. This contrasts with the world of ancient Greece that valued overlapping and mutually constitutive spheres of the political/public, private, and social realms.[17]

To illustrate this relationship between the religious/spiritual and other spheres of action, consider a specific example from western thought that identifies the political with particular attributes that speak to the passions, the soul or psyche, and the moral. In Plato's *Republic*, Socrates identifies the notion of "spiritedness," or *thymos*, as "the psychic origin of distinctively political action."[18] According to Socrates, spiritedness is a reflection of the psychological origins and/or manifestations of the political. Socrates likens the division of the soul to the structural order of the city. This sociopolitical order designates these corollary hierarchies: the money-making class finds its counterpart in the desiring part of the soul; the "auxiliary" class is responsible for the care of the *polis*, likening it to spiritedness; the guardian classes are akin to utilitarian and calculating reasoning. In the city and the soul, the spirited parts maintain order and unity by checking against the divisive effects of unjust desires, that is, the threat of tyranny in the city/soul as well as the threat of aggression from without. As Catherine H. Zuckert suggests in her excellent commentary on spiritedness: "As the city needs spirited warriors to defend it from external aggression, so individual rulers must be taught to use the spirited part of their soul to control their potentially tyrannous inclinations. . . . [As] the source of protection from both foreign domination and internal oppression, spiritedness appears to constitute the psychological root of political independence."[19] Plato argued that from the "auxiliary" class of soldiers come warriors *and* philosophers. The warriors, on the one hand, have strong, affective attachment to the *polis* and the state and seek to protect both from outside transgressors, as well as maintain order *within* the political body. Philosophers, on the other hand, have a more tenuous, even paradoxical relationship to the political body. The philosopher serves not only the higher good of the state but also the higher good of reason, and is thereby always in a position to be critical of the political. One way to interpret the distinction between the warriors and the philosophers, both of whom are strongly inspired by *thymos*/spiritedness, is to say that the warrior is always ready to act—that is, always ready to be an agent, especially for the sake of order and protection—whereas the philosopher is subject not only to the sovereignty of the state but also to the sovereignty of reason and rational reflection. As such, the philosopher is less willing and thus less able to act with the alacrity of the warrior. This condition is related to what Aristotle says in the *Nicomachean Ethics* when he argues that *thymos* shares in reason while also sharing in the desires, needs, and passions associated with the appetites, the bodily, and the emotions.[20]

Zuckert argues that while the notion of spiritedness has fallen out of use in modern times, it would seem that the phenomenon of spiritedness, or what I call the spirit of politics, persists.[21] Examples abound. Our times are marked by a widespread concern for political order. This is evident in the calls for the United Nations and the United States to intervene militarily around the world. The American war in Iraq is perhaps our most obvious and notorious example. There is also, among progressive *and* conservative political activists, a concern for encouraging political action. Consider American politics. One of the reasons we have lost sight of the spirit of politics is the tendency to economize and segment life into different realms or spheres of value and action, such as "work," "family," "public-civil society," "religion," and so on.[22] A major concern is whether the direct action and responsibility once assumed by political actors for the preservation of liberty, rights, and the like are now taken to be the responsibility of the government. Political orders, in general, and governments, in particular, are the means of establishing the conditions for the pursuit of "our private desires" in regard to our inalienable rights to life, liberty, and the pursuit of happiness. Modern western political orders (which is to say, the political orders that have, for better or for worse, become the political standard-bearers of "legitimacy" globally) tend to be organized around the protection of the conditions that allow for self-preservation (life, liberty, pursuit of happiness), whereas for the ancients—or at least for Socrates, Plato, and Aristotle—political order emerges from the need to defend against domination and to promote the possibility of human flourishing. In short, political order is rarely coincidental with personal desires (that is, unless you are an emperor or Bill Gates), and it therefore requires a higher form of aspiration to realize itself. This higher aspiration or desire is what the ancients meant by the spirit of politics: it connects a love of one's own with a higher-order good such as a stable political order but more important as *a passion for justice*. In sum, for the ancients, the spirit of politics is connected to the soul and to the passions and is not tied exclusively to reason or rationality, as many contemporary political theories of justice and rights would have it.[23] This example is significant since part of the interpretive task I have set for this book is to determine—given the array of presumed continuities and discontinuities between the political, the moral, and the religious—how supposedly suprarational attachments such as values, political ideals, and collective identities shape action and agency, especially when these attachments have become obscure or lost.

Modernity, Agency, and Melancholy

Don't despair, not even over the fact that you don't despair.
—Franz Kafka, journal entry

[F]or my part I indeed imagine that there is design, consent and pleasure in feeding one's melancholy; I mean the ambition that can also be involved. There is some shadow of daintiness and luxury that smiles on us and flatters us in the very lap of melancholy. Are there not some natures that feed on it?
—Michel de Montaigne, "We Taste Nothing Pure"

There are well-known genealogical reasons for the discontinuities that have come to demarcate differences between the political, moral, and religious spheres of life, and these have to do with the prevailing conditions we find in modernity itself, especially the rise of secularism, political liberalism, *and* moral pluralism in western modernity. To wit, modernity is an age shaped by a continuous and vigorous commitment to human freedom, especially as freedom and autonomy are established and constituted by the distinctions *from* religious, traditional, monarchical, and aristocratic forms of authority. In the breaks from the dominance of these sources of authority, one finds an insistence in modernity on the centrality of reason as the faculty that organizes and makes sense of experience. In other words, reason has a newfound authority *and* legitimacy in modernity, meaning that critical reason and rationality become distinctive features of modernity itself. To be modern is, among other things, to be able to question the legitimacy of authority through the application of critical and rational reflection.

This has a lot to do, especially, with reason's association with science and philosophy but also with its complicity in generating doubt and affirming experience, particularly in regard to religious belief. In a manner of speaking, the critical attitude and disposition employed by science, philosophy, and reason have cultivated a secular culture of disbelief in modernity. This culture has viewed human freedom and agency—which is to say, freedom of movement, speech, and thought—as consonant with distinctions from and discontent with the past, authority, and tradition, established especially through the application of critical thought and reason. To borrow Isaiah Berlin's phrase, the "negative liberty" of the religious, political, and cultural revolutions of modernity is found in the flight from authority.[24] The positive values of freedom and agency in modernity manifest in the advocacy of equality, justice, and even democracy.

A question arises with regard to agency and the sources for motivating and inspiring action in light of this picture of modernity I have just sketched. It is a question I raised earlier about the price paid for freedom and agency. The narrative about modernity as secular and as increasingly prone to the demands of rationality is one that attempts to show how the legitimation of freedom and agency is mediated through the demands of and attendant commitments to political liberalism and moral pluralism. These are demands and commitments that seek to restrict the play of overly "thick" political expressions of values, because of a concern for threats to public discourse and objectivity by forces such as tyranny majority. And yet it also seems that modern secularism and political liberalism have marginalized or segmented off value systems such as religion and family outside of the rationally ordered realms of "legitimate" public life and scientific inquiry.[25] This is, of course, part of the Enlightenment inheritance. Political liberalism, moral pluralism, and secularism allow us to take flight from things such as religious or monarchical authority because they see these sources of authority as predicated on illusions, excess, and false necessity. In this vein, as Kant, Marx, Nietzsche, and Freud argued in varying ways, though life may be harder without the consolations and distractions of religion and tradition, the benefits are worth the fight. Relinquishing religious, theological, and metaphysical fictions such as notions of "life" after death or belief in the existence of a benevolent yet omnipotent God will force us to use our own resources. In other words, in giving up on these ideas we will be forced to be self-reliant and hence autonomous. Our freedom and agency come at the price of abandoning these "illusions." The organizing aspiration of *this* version of the modern ethos is to be able to concentrate our liberated energies into the worldly and the immanent rather than to invest in an afterlife or some other transcendent realm of value. The hope, so the argument goes, is to achieve a condition in which life has possibilities for everyone and the discontents of civilization are productive and not oppressive.[26]

The message of liberation and emancipation is, certainly, the upbeat message of modernity. There is, though, what might be called a more sorrowful side to modernity that has to do with freedom and agency's association with a particular crisis of authority—a crisis that is associated with the achievements of self-reliance and autonomy. Robert Pippin identifies this perception of crisis (variously associated with nihilism, atheism, and secularism) as "the melancholy of modernity."[27] I take the notion of "the melancholy of modernity" as coincidental with the rites and responsibilities of freedom and agency, meaning that there is a price to be paid—a loss suffered—for the freedom of individual choice or will, responsibility, and personal autonomy. Part of this price is most certainly gladly paid: namely, giving up on subservience to and reliance on oppressive and/or hierarchical structures of power and authority. Yet there is also another price exacted, one associated with the death of God and the fragmentation of communities and families. Even without ascribing to a thoroughgoing nihilism or to the notion of rampant and rapacious individualism, it is possible to acknowledge that there is a sense of loss in the critiques of religion and other former sources of authority and "tradition," however broadly construed.[28] In other words, the critical effects of skepticism, doubt, and the rational ordering of the world (what Max Weber called "the rationalization of the world") induce the melancholy of modernity, a condition akin to Weber's idea of the "disenchantment of the world."[29] Weber associates modern "advances" in the social world, such as rationalization and secularization, with disenchantment or "de-magification."[30] Among other things, Weber's analysis is a commentary on the loss of a sense of wonder, mystery, and even awe in modernity. The challenge Weber raises (foreshadowed by Nietzsche before him) is to ask whether there is a corresponding loss of options in modernity for living a meaningful life.

As I have already noted, as with most cases of melancholy, there is an experience of loss identified with the melancholy of modernity, namely, the symbolic losses of ideals as well as systems of values and meaning, all of which qualify as objects of deep, passionate attachment.[31] There is a change in the grammar of authority, obligation, and obedience in the ethos of modernity. The normal nihilism of the modern culture of secularism indicates loss. Though Freud characterizes melancholy or *melancholia* as the "inability to mourn" the loss of an object of attachment, it is perhaps more helpful and clarifying to see the melancholy of modernity as a state in which there is a continuous suspension of mourning. Mourning has a teleological quality about it, implying notions of resolution or closure. Melancholy is, in a manner of speaking, a resistance to these kinds of resolutions and closures. As Freud argued, mourning, like closure, symbolizes, on the one hand, an abandonment of the object of one's passionate attachment or love and, on the other hand, letting go of *the idea* of one's love for this object.[32] As such, the melancholy of modernity marks the way that the symbolic loss of objects of attachment—such as religion or the spiritedness found in the emancipation movements that arose around the fights for racial justice in America—remains *and* persists. Even with the institutionalization of the ideals of the Enlightenment and its secular aspirations of establishing rational certainty and truth, we nonetheless find ourselves confronted by phenomena such as the resurgence of fundamentalist Islam *and* Christianity. In other words, historical formations such as fundamentalism and even nationalism suggest how the symbolic losses of religion, values, and meaning continue to haunt us.[33]

This is not to say that authority disappears in modernity. Instead, the *legitimacy* of authority in modernity no longer comes from unquestioned, unassailable sources such as "the church," "the Monarch," or, for that matter, "Mom and Dad," but rather through the agreement and consent of the constituents affected by the will and power of authority. In other words, as moderns and postmoderns, the conditions for the possibility of freedom *and* agency involve the legitimation and mediation of authority through the will of the individual. There is no agency without the individual will. This is the reason theorists such as Taylor *and* Butler see the relationship between agency and identity as fundamental. For example, the necessity of the mediation of authority through human wills holds, on the one hand, for Kant and the formal conditions he establishes for freedom as morality (that is, a freedom that requires the self-legislation of universalizable moral laws *to ourselves*) as it does, on the other hand, for modern democracies that view self-governance and elections as necessary features of government (which is to say that democracies have authority insofar as they are constituted as systems in which people rule themselves).

Thinking the Religious, the Moral, and the Political Together

To see clearly is poetry, prophecy and religion—all in one.
— John Ruskin, *Modern Painters*

Despite a widespread interest in the complex relationships between the religious, the moral-ethical, and the political, explorations of agency tend to favor political or even sociological analyses to the pursuit of religious-existential questions.[34] As a means of addressing this situation, I am highlighting in this book the religious and existential dimensions of agency along with the political, the moral, and the psychic/psychological. There are two compelling reasons for doing so. First, an examination of the possibility of meaningful subjectivity requires an understanding of moral psychology that addresses the states of mind or dispositions produced by the lack and loss of modern *and* postmodern agency, particularly through experiences of fragmentation, melancholy, and anxiety. This line of inquiry is in concert with what might be called a "phenomenology of agency." I do not use the term "phenomenology" here in a technical, Husserlian sense. Instead, by phenomenology of agency, all I really mean is getting a picture of how and why people act and seek to establish their agency. Subsequently, a phenomenology of agency asks: under what conditions is agency possible? Conversely, under what conditions is agency made difficult, even impossible?

Another reason for examining religious and existential concerns along with political and moral ones is to work against a dominant trend in inquiries about the relationships between religion, morality, and politics. Too often, discussions of the relationships between these three aspects of human experience are framed around questions regarding issues of whether particular sectarian and/or religious bodies (churches, mosques, temples, synagogues, cults, and so on) should be allowed to participate in the political culture of a given society—the so-called "church-state" debates. While these questions are of utmost importance, in my view, they rarely move from the procedural issues of how political liberalism and moral pluralism can accommodate the participation and representation of religious organizations and standpoints. In other words, these procedural preoccupations do not necessarily move from the political protocols of public deliberation to questions of how crises of *de*legitimation threaten the possibility of realizing a religious self-understanding for moral agents. *This* scenario suggests the need for a critique of philosophies and theories of agency that prioritize, for example, the drive for public recognition at the expense of religious faith and spiritual well-being.

By way of ending *and* beginning, let me offer some questions—questions that indicate the directions I will be taking throughout this book. The philosophico-religious analysis of the contemporary discourse on agency I am undertaking asks the following: can we think the existential-religious, the ethical-moral, and the political together, that is, as indispensable aspects of a philosophy of agency and action? Would this understanding of agency constitute a mode of religious being-in-the-world? Is political agency or even democratic agency an adequate response to experiences of undeserved suffering, evil, and despair?

No doubt, a political understanding of agency is fruitful for unveiling regulative structures and systems of legitimation such as cultural regimes that shape our attitudes about citizenship, race, gender, and other markers of social identity. Nonetheless, it is not always clear how religious as well as moral aspirations are actualized if our understanding of agency is restricted to matters of the political. For example, does or should the promise of a political account of agency or action help realize and understand existential and religious aspirations? Is there a necessary connection between political agency and ethical and religious commitments? In short, is political action or agency an intensification of beliefs, values, and commitments? Or is it, instead, a way of sublimating and diverting these beliefs, values, and commitments?

The chapters that follow seek to answer these questions through a critical examination of agency as melancholic freedom. In chapter 2, I begin with Taylor's theory of agency, tracing the move he makes from characterizing agency as strong evaluation or judgment to the rich and complex portrait of modern subjectivity presented in *Sources of the Self*, in which he provides a magisterial genealogy of the moral losses that shape the features of the modern self. From my reading of Taylor's genealogy, I identify agency as the consummate, cultural ethic of late modernity. It is an ethic defined by the losses generated by an estrangement, alienation, and detachment from the moral ideals and higher goods (such as justice, benevolence, and freedom) that had figured prominently, Taylor argues, in our ability to make judgments of value, worth, and affirmation. Chapter 3 frames projects of regenerating agency as responses to this condition of loss in the melancholy of modernity. Of particular interest in this exploration of the religious dimensions of agency is Taylor's turn to the recuperative power of the epiphanic sublime. In Taylor's estimation, the epiphanic sublime has the power and potential to reawaken us to our orientation and connection to moral sources.

My interest is less in the substantive moral realist conclusions that Taylor reaches or with Butler's poststructuralist critique of cultural norms in themselves, and more in the ways that it is possible to interpret these projects of regenerating agency as practices of self-cultivation and self-transformation. This is the reason that in chapters 4 and 5 I shift from Taylor's laments over the condition of the modern self to Butler's postmodern, poststructuralist treatment of agency, difference, and melancholy. Butler's is an approach that emphasizes the losses that originate from the social, political, cultural, and even psychic alienation that she argues is at once the common experience of those who suffer the indignities of racial, gender, class, and sexuality discrimination and hatred, as well as the terrain on which agency will be generated. Thus, for those for whom the means of recognition and representation regularly lack precision, and for those for whom the rhetoric and symbolic resources for social existence, at best, forge a rough correspondence to individual and collective experiences, the end result is striving against seeing the world as social and cultural death. This dire possibility is what suggests these experiences and the attempt to overcome them as profoundly religious concerns. I argue that as a project of regenerating agency, the postmodern foregrounding of difference reflects a call for the care and cultivation of the self.

The work on agency by contemporary thinkers such as Taylor and Butler is suggestive of an effort to cultivate a religious disposition that seeks to regenerate moral identities and political energies through the reawakening of an attunement to higher goods and values. In chapter 6 I refer to this awakening as "agency as a vocation." In calling agency a vocation I am recovering a religious category that has, as Weber noted, become dissociated from its spiritual heritage (specifically the Reformation notion of *Beruf,* or divine calling/ vocation) and yet seems to maintain a currency precisely because of its simultaneous dissonance and resonance with this heritage. This moral attunement requires identifying passionate attachments and senses of necessary concern and commitment that are generated by quests for agency. The drive and affirmation of agency found in Taylor's admonition for greater moral articulacy and in Butler's skepticism in regard to norms of identity are expressions of religious aspirations that seek moral well-being and the transcendence of constraints of varying kinds. Agency is a vocation insofar as these elements of the quest for agency also present occasions to reevaluate widespread investments in secularism, liberalism, and cultural agnosticism. With this in mind, I see the work on agency by theorists such as Taylor and Butler as critical engagements with melancholic freedom that provide analytical frameworks to understand the moral psychology and spiritual dispositions required by a late or postmodern age in which visions of agency continue to echo the moral idioms of emancipation and liberation, but in diminished and understated forms. These *sotto voce* forms of agency convey distinctively religious overtones that express a desire to transcend moral, existential, and political conditions of powerlessness, inefficacy, purposelessness, and cynicism. Agency, as I am interpreting it in this book, reflects the conditions of freedom, autonomy, and liberation that are shaped by and in late modernity and postmodernity. The expressions of freedom created in modernity—liberation as revolution, autonomy as morality and political right, and freedom of thought and choice—have become co-opted in late modernity and postmodernity and, in some cases, have lost the sense of urgency and crisis that inspired earlier generations to fight for freedom. Consequently, the corollary of the thesis of agency as melancholic freedom is the banality of freedom: a condition in which the achievements of freedom, such as liberation, emancipatory movements, and autonomy, have become ordinary, even banal, in the sense that they are being taken for granted. The banality of freedom is akin to the banality of evil—the desensitization of our moral sensibilities—that has taken hold in the political and moral landscape of the late and postmodern west.[35] I am attempting to bring to light some of the religious dimensions of projects of regenerating agency, on the one hand, by framing the contemporary discourse on agency as melancholic freedom, and, on the other hand, by uncovering the presence and persistence of Romantic ideas such as expressivism, aspiration, authenticity, alienation, and fragmentation. I conclude that at the heart of agency is a disposition of readiness, or what one might call an openness, in which attunement to a call to act accompanies a commitment to self-transformation through the work of overcoming and transcending loss through the affirmation of guiding ideals and values.

2

Love of the Good among the Ruins

Charles Taylor and the Enchantment of Agency

Introduction

In this chapter, I discuss the philosophical and historical account that Charles Taylor has developed throughout his corpus on agency, identity, and the good, in particular in his collected essays and in *Sources of the Self*.[1] The chapter begins with a discussion of Taylor's theories of agency and language and the philosophical anthropology that he develops. Taylor deploys his general argument about agency as the capacity of choice in light of qualitative distinctions made about the good in response to the deficiencies and unfulfilled potential he sees in the moral culture of western modernity. By and large, this diagnosis draws conclusions analogous to the Weberian thesis on secularization. Taylor's concern is primarily with the widespread experience of secularization and, in particular, with the delegitimation of religious beliefs and strongly articulated moral values. He is responding to the effects of the rise of rationalism, "scientistic" naturalism, and its concomitant social and political philosophies of atomism, political liberalism, and individualism. In this regard, secularization serves as a descriptive account of the moral culture of modernity as well as a metaphor for its social practices and ideals. Of particular concern are how these forces have altered the quality of modern moral life, especially the compromises they have impressed on the capacity for people to find meaning in the world as engaged and embodied agents. I conclude the chapter with an examination of Taylor's retrieval and critique of the ethos of Romantic expressivism and his turn to modernism as a resource for responding to this condition of disenchantment. Taylor identifies the transformative capacity of expressivism as a significant convention and ethos in modern life (most pronouncedly in various espoused commitments to self-fulfillment). Alternatively, expressivism is also a crucial strategy for regaining access to moral sources that provide meaning and significance to otherwise narrow and shallow ways of being in the world. Taylor's solution for the moral and spiritual predicament of modernity is to look to expressive forms, such as modernism (especially poetry), to render a reconnection with what he calls, interchangeably, moral sources, hypergoods, and constitutive goods. In chapter 3, I undertake a critical examination of what I call Taylor's logic of epiphany. There, I test for the plausibility of this logic. In addition, I lay out some of the implications that this appeal to the epiphanic has for what I call projects of regenerating agency and their religious dimensions. In particular, I examine Taylor's implied thesis that modernist forms of epiphany are perhaps the best hope for opening up the possibility of receiving and experiencing grace, or some secularized analogue to grace, which is to say, experiences that have the ability to transform moral vision and thereby re-engage and even re-enchant agency.

Agency, Articulation, and the Good

What does Taylor mean by "human agency"? On Taylor's view, human agency is primarily a matter of moral judgments, deliberations, and conduct. In other words, the self, for Taylor, is fundamentally a moral self who is constituted through taking moral positions. The agent cannot do this by seeking to adhere to some criteria or procedure for doing what is right, or acting, as Kant suggests, according to obligation solely.[2] Instead, for Taylor, agency is about acting and choosing based on what it is good to be, which is to say that agency requires living according to a vision of the good life. Agency is not complete, according to Taylor, if it is expected to adhere to a single criterion, such as the requirement of universalizing the maxims of one's actions or some other monological approach. Taylor constructs a narrative of modern identity and agency, in part, as a polemic against the dominant forms of modern moral philosophy, in particular deontological theories that prioritize conceptions of universal right over the good. In addition to giving priority to the right over the good, these theories also argue, according to Taylor, for various forms of naturalism, including behaviorism. As such, deontological theories tend to insist that moral subjects are moved not by the good but rather by desires; subsequently, these theories are apt to view human behavior as they would any objects of scientific study, namely, as transparent and fully observable phenomena.[3] What these forms of moral philosophy miss, Taylor argues, is how actual moral agents engage in actual situations of choice. In other words, this picture of the moral life offered by deontological ethics, naturalism, atomism, and behaviorism cannot capture or understand engaged and em-bodied agency.

In order to understand what it is to be a fully embodied agent that en-gages in actual situations of choice, Taylor argues that it is necessary to begin with the "moral and spiritual intuitions" that people draw on as agents. Taylor uses the category of "the moral" in the broadest possible terms. The moral thus includes conventional approaches, such as the commitment to justice and respect for the life, well-being, and dignity of others. But it also pertains to that which underlies human dignity, such as questions about what makes life meaningful, fulfilling, and worthwhile.[4] In Sources of the Self, as well as in his other essays on agency, language, and the self, Taylor sets for himself the task of laying out a plausible philosophical anthropology in which questions of the good are of utmost concern for understanding agency.[5] Intuitions are not only moral but also "spiritual," in Taylor's terms, insofar as they require acting in and through judgments or what he calls "strong evaluation." This is to say that "they involve discriminations of right or wrong, better or worse, higher or lower, which are not rendered valid by our own desires, inclinations, or choices, but rather stand independent of these and offer standards by which they can be judged."[6] The agent as embedded in a framework of strong eval-uation is a central doctrine for Taylor. In a Hegelian vein, Taylor intentionally invokes the vague category of the spiritual in regard to strong evaluation because he believes that strong evaluation is indicative of and implies the background against which moral action and choice transpire. In other words, this background is a moral ontology, and thereby real and objective. This background forms a horizon of meaning and a framework in which the moral intuitions and instincts of agents function and make sense. As Taylor puts it, strong evaluation constitutes such a background insofar as it is "a background of distinctions between things which are recognized as of categoric or un-conditioned or higher importance or worth, and things which lack this or are of lesser value."[7] Agency requires a measure of self-understanding in which these backgrounds/frameworks enable the agent/self to make qualitative distinctions among components and features of the good life, or what Taylor calls "life goods."[8]

Whether acknowledged or not, these moral frameworks are unavoidable in any attempt to understand and enact practical agency. Higher-order goods shape these "inescapable frameworks" by providing an orientation and direc-tion that determine the significance of the overall contours of life. These con-stitutive and "hyper" goods are not universal. Instead, Taylor's strong claim in his philosophical anthropology of the agent posits, rather, that having hy-pergoods and constitutive goods is universal. To hold these higher-order values and ideals is a distinctive feature of what it means both to be an agent and to be human. Life goods, such as the value of the loving family or the ide-als of benevolence and compassion, are undergirded and given meaning by constitutive goods. Constitutive goods are ideals or values such as the sanctification of the ordinary life by a loving God or the belief in a providential order that coheres such a vision. As such, constitutive, strongly held goods play a critical role in the moral life. According to Taylor:

> [t]he constitutive good does more than just define the content of the moral theory. Love of it is what empowers us to be good. And hence also loving it is part of what it is to be a good human being. This is now part of the moral theory as well, which includes injunctions not only to act in certain ways and to exhibit certain moral qualities but also to love what is good.[9]

The philosopher has a particular task in interpreting the nature of this relationship, insofar as she/he is responsible for identifying the constitutive moral goods/moral sources that orient life goods. More specifically, the philosopher clarifies and articulates what the constitutive goods are. As Taylor argues, "articulating a constitutive good is making clear what is involved in the life good one espouses. Unreflecting people in the culture, who are drawn to certain life goods, may have nothing to offer in the way of description of constitutive good, but that doesn't mean that their sense of what is worth pursuing isn't shaped by some unstructured intuitions about their metaphysical predicament, about their moral sources being within or without, for example."[10]

As should be clear by now, a great deal is at stake for Taylor's consideration of agency in the ability to articulate the good, in particular in the recognition of the interplay of constitutive goods and life goods. In other words, being able to express one's moral orientation—that is, the self's relation to constitutive goods or moral sources—is crucial for realizing one's agency and identity. What, then, does recognizing a moral horizon or a framework defined by a constitutive good entail?

The determination of higher goods requires that the agent have a "language of qualitative contrasts," that is, a "vocabulary of worth" and value. In the essay "What is human agency?" Taylor takes Harry Frankfurt's distinction between first- and second-order desires as his point of departure. First-order desires are what might be termed nonreflective, even animalistic desires. In contrast, second-order desires reflect a degree and level of self-consciousness and self-evaluation. Taylor breaks down these second-order desires between evaluations that are "weak" and "strong." Only strong evaluations and judgments relate to desires as to worth or significance. Weak evaluations (a term that Taylor drops in Sources of the Self) are not concerned with moral motivation but simply deal with the satisfaction of first-order desires.[11] In calling these distinctions "strong evaluations," Taylor is arguing that they reflect a kind of self who has a vision of what it is to live a meaningful moral life. Strong evaluations involve the use of contrastive language; that is, they involve choices and decisions based upon qualitative distinctions, or what I am calling judgment. As such, the strong evaluator (the agent) engages in a mode of self-reflection, interpretation, and evaluation when deliberating over courses of action by determining the worth of desires based upon whether they resonate with a higher-order value; whereas someone who evaluates on the basis of consequences or quantitative effects, as in pluses and minuses, is only a "simple weigher." The strong evaluator requires not only consciousness of higher goods or other standards of value but also a language of judgment that can articulate contrasts of higher and lower, of better and worse, and, presumably, of good and evil. Agency as strong evaluation employs a "vocabulary of worth." According to Taylor, "[t]he strong evaluator can articulate superiority just because [she/]he has a language of contrastive characterization."[12] Strong evaluation or moral judgment involves greater articulation about preferences and beliefs than ordinary choices require. And with this articulation comes a willingness to deliberate on a "deeper" level. The strong evaluator deliberates not merely because of *de facto* desires or because of unreflective gratification. Rather,

> [a] strong evaluator, by which we mean a subject who strongly evaluates desires, goes deeper, because [she/]he characterizes [her/]his motivation at greater depth. To characterize one desire or inclination as worthier, or nobler, or more integrated, etc. than others is to speak of it in terms of the kind of quality of life which it expresses and sustains. . . . [F]or the strong evaluator reflection also examines the different possible modes of being for the agent. Motivations or desires do not only count in virtue of the attraction of the consummations but also in virtue of the kind of life and kind of subject that these desires properly belong to.[13]

The hermeneutical operation of agency lies in the articulation and interpretation of these distinctions of worth, based upon constitutive goods and the subsequent inculcation of these distinctions into one's self-understanding. The language of contrasts is crucial because constitutive and hypergoods are *incommensurably* higher than other life goods. The claims that moral goals or ends, such as God or freedom, make are incommensurably greater than ordinary desires and purposes or life goods. Again, Taylor's strong claim is that this is not *a* thesis of human agency but is in fact a philosophical anthropology. In other words, this is how ordinary people actually understand themselves as human agents, how they—"we"—engage in moral and practical reasoning.[14]

Taylor insists on providing a portrait of agency as engaged and embodied because he sets his theory directly in opposition to behaviorists, naturalists, rationalists, utilitarians, and political liberals, that is, against conceptions of agency that rely on one notion or another of impartiality, neutrality, and disengagement. Taylor's theory of agency is one that attempts to take up the fullness of identity and not only the machinations of reason. As such, he forges a picture of agency in terms of motivations, significance, and, above all, meaning. And this agency as meaning-making can only take place through the determination of higher goods, that is, through a sense that some goods and desires are of qualitatively higher worth than others. "To be a strong evaluator," Taylor suggests, "is thus to see desires in an additional dimension. And this is in fact essential to our important evaluative distinctions."[15] This "additional dimension" is the way in which higher values move, inspire, and empower. These higher-order goods are constitutive of our identities as moral agents, and are thus qualitatively higher in our estimations than ordinary life goods, insofar as "they command our awe, respect, or admiration."[16] Taylor recognizes that there is a circular relation between life goods and the articulations of the constitutive goods that underlie them.[17] However, he does not see the relationship as deterministic, in the sense of an absolute and transparent causality between constitutive goods and life goods. The relationship is more dialectical than such an interpretation would suggest. For example, the social and cultural changes from which secularization emerges largely issue from a sense that certain life goods would be realized if related to a nontheistic source. However, in transposing from a theistic orientation to a nontheistic one, the quality and even the content of what counts as life goods are reinterpreted. More specifically, the good life regulated by an ethic of benevolence within a theistic worldview will not be identical with the same conception of the good life organized around a secular version of human flourishing. The practices and ways of life in these horizons of meaning will differ because the higher-order, constitutive goods that determine each worldview are different. This is a difference indicated by the distinctions drawn between the moral acts performed because of a belief in divine sanction versus those performed through universal respect according to human-generated laws.

Agency, as an exercise of the will and choice, is a matter of responsibility, according to Taylor, in that choosing among second-order desires also means endorsing them and the existential consequences that follow therewith, such as how one is to live a life and the judgments one makes about worth, respect, honor, and duty. This position is made clear in Taylor's reinterpretation of Sartre's famous allegory of Pierre. The story goes as follows: during World War II, Pierre must choose between staying home to take care of his ailing mother and fighting for the French Resistance. Taylor resists Sartre's existential option of capitulating to radical choice, in which Pierre simply "throws himself one way." Pierre's predicament, according to Taylor, is that he has no terms, no language in which to determine the superiority of one alternative over the other. The alternatives are tragic to Pierre because he does not have a language to mediate the differences between them. If decided by radical choice, Pierre as agent chooses (if one can call it choice) by fiat. In other words, following a path established by fiat would mean that Pierre did not articulate the specific reasons for staying with his mother or for leaving to fight the Germans. Instead, he abandons his role as a reasoning agent by making a leap of faith in the direction of one option rather than that of another. Taylor argues that choices made on such "basic and fundamental issues" are not defined because one is forced into a situation of radical choice; rather "their importance is given, or revealed in an evaluation which is constated, not chosen."[18] To take responsibility for a choice means that I endorse what the consequences of the choice entail, especially in regard to what the choice will mean and say about the kind of person I am, what kind of life I value, and what I understand to be indicative of human flourishing. As Taylor argues:

> [t]he stance of "good faith" is higher, and this is not in virtue of radical choice, but in virtue of our characterization of the human predicament in which radical choice has such an important place. Granting this is the moral predicament of man [sic.], it is more honest, courageous, self-clairvoyant, hence a higher mode of life, to choose in lucidity than it is to hide one's choices behind the supposed structure of things, to flee from one's responsibility at the expense of lying to oneself, of a deep self-duplicity.[19]

As a moral agent, I must not simply be aware of the goods and values I hold, but I must also be able to articulate what they are, specifically as I reflect upon and adjudicate among these goods and values. Thus, Taylor concludes:

> Our identity is therefore defined by certain evaluations which are inseparable from ourselves as agents. Shorn of these we would cease to be ourselves, by which we do not mean trivially that we would be different in the sense of having some properties other than those we now have—which would indeed be the case after any change, however minor—but that shorn of these we would lose the very possibility of being an agent who evaluates; that our existence as persons, and hence our ability to adhere as persons to certain evaluations, would be impossible outside the horizon of these essential evaluations, that we would break down as persons, be incapable of being persons in the full sense.[20]

This example not only shows the significance that articulation and language have in Taylor's conception of agency, but it also indicates the kind of practical reasoning that strong evaluation and moral judgment involve. In accord with his commitment to providing an account of moral identity that begins with the perspective and experience of the agent, Taylor insists on a form of practical reasoning that is historical and embodied. According to Taylor, practical reasoning is reasoning in transitions. It is deployed not to establish the absolute or foundational truth but rather to determine that some position, that some moral stance is superior to another based upon the principle of the "best account" available. As such, practical reasoning deals with "comparative propositions." Comparative claims are well founded when an epistemic gain is demonstrated by a move, that is, in a transition from moral position A to moral position B. Furthermore, this happens when the agent shows, in making the transition to another position or belief, that the new position she/he takes is predicated on making sense of experience, as in the idea of sustaining a continuous effort to reduce error (revealing and eradicating a contradiction, confusion, or unacceptable inconsistency, and so on). The nub of this argument is in the nature of the transition, which is to say, what is involved in the move is a reduction of error and the enabling of life possibilities based upon the rational and qualitative comparison of rival interpretations.[21] Taylor's theory of practical reason is clearly in opposition to forms of moral and practical reasoning that posit formal criteria and procedures that are abstract from moral intuitions, which is to say, that disengage from that which most inspires and moves the self ethically and morally. The only criteria that should apply in practical reason, according to Taylor, are the best accounts available based upon the breadth of human experience.[22]

In fact, Taylor invokes the best account principle as a criterion employed, on the one hand, in the practical reason of individual subjects and, on the other hand, as a principle that can elucidate historical shifts in collective attitudes.[23] In this way, Taylor's version of practical reason is similar to Thomas Kuhn's argument that paradigm shifts occur when a new paradigm supersedes the capacity of an existing paradigm to solve problems of knowledge.[24] For individuals as well as collective bodies, sociocultural forms of practical reasoning, the principle of the best account available to experience, and transitions based upon the reduction of error all count as epistemic gains and thus as marks of advancement and growth. In casting epistemic gain and practical reason in terms of growth and maturity, Taylor explicitly draws on narrative and biography as the proper metaphors and forms according to which identity should be conceived. This goes to what Taylor calls the "inescapable structural requirements of human agency," which is to interpret one's life in narrative form as "a quest" for the good or as a story that shapes one's orientation to the good. By invoking the metaphor of narrative in describing the self, Taylor is also making a rebuff to various postmodern and poststructuralist theories of subjectivity that posit the self as fragmentary.[25] He does this by drawing on the notion of life as narrative that philosophers such as Alasdair MacIntyre, Paul Ricoeur, and Jerome Bruner, among others, have developed (the language of "quest" is MacIntyre's)—which is to say that Taylor sets subjectivity within a phenomenological framework. Thus, the narrative of life is read in terms of unfolding time, as well as the realization of action through the projection of possible futures, goals, and goods. Taylor couples the temporality of the unfolding self in narrative or biography with spatial metaphors of "orientation." Thus, he posits: that the agent is moving in the direction of the good; that moral agency requires being in "contact" with or determining one's "place" or "situatedness" in relation to the good; or that one's life is moving in the direction of the good. In both the temporal and spatial aspects, the critical issue for Taylor is the sense in which an orientation to the good determines the extent to which one is able to live a meaningful life.

In *Sources of the Self*, Taylor deepens his earlier formulation of agency as the strong evaluation of goods by stressing the contextualization of agency within forms of life. In other words, strong evaluation and the invocation of contrastive language make agency and articulation a public and communal matter—one that always involves interlocution, which is also to say it is constitutive of a framework of meaning shared with other people. As Taylor suggests:

> I want to defend the strong thesis that doing without frameworks is utterly impossible for us; otherwise put, that the horizons within which we live our lives and which make sense of them have to include these strong qualitative discriminations. Moreover, this is not meant just as a contingently true psychological fact about human beings, which could perhaps turn out one day not to hold for some exceptional individual or new type, some superman of disengaged objectification. Rather, the claim is that living within such strongly qualified horizons is constitutive of human agency, that stepping outside these limits would be tantamount to stepping outside what we would recognize as integral, that is, undamaged human personhood.[26]

This picture of health—of "undamaged human personhood"—is a critical standard for the argument that I am developing about agency and melancholy. This passage reflects Taylor's ascription of a hermeneutical nature to the self. In addition, it also speaks to his concern for the severe consequences of secularization and alienation on agency as strong evaluation, in that they have produced a situation in which the agent has lost contact with her/his constitutive goods. Subsequently, there is a diminished ability to engage in a vigorous moral life. The effects of the disenchantment of the modern world, as Weber put it, run the gamut from the extreme to the everyday. On one end, there are the limit cases of existential experiences in which there is the loss of a sense of one's moral framework, resulting in disorientation, despair, and meaninglessness. Nihilism and the death of God are the paradigmatic forms here, but certainly other versions of extreme psychic trauma qualify as well. The more widespread phenomenon associated with disenchantment and secularization is moral pluralism. Moral pluralism, as a social and political philosophy, seeks to validate a plurality of goods. Cultural and institutional commitments to moral pluralism generate situations and predicaments, following Taylor's argument, in which everyone runs the threat of losing contact and access to our respective moral sources. Why? Because the tempering effects of the mutual recognition required by moral pluralism diminish the power, intensity, and clarity about what lies behind widely held commitments to social ideals such as justice. This lack of clarity about fundamental goods has such a hold on the moral imagination that it results in moral tentativeness, as well as a weakening of agency and the possibilities of living a good and meaningful life. Taylor clearly laments this scenario. This is not to say that Taylor believes that one or another idealized representation of the good will solve all our problems. He is quite explicit that identity is deeper and more complex than any particular articulation of the good can represent.[27] Nonetheless, this does not mean that one can live well and flourish without these articulations. The connection between identity and moral orientation hinges on the articulation of background pictures. This means that agency transpires against a background of strong evaluations and thereby comes to being through deliberations over "courses of action," which also determine the quality and kind of life one chooses to lead. Agency requires adjudicating among different goods not simply on the basis of rational criteria but through a complex set of conjectures that involve the imagination, which is to say, the ability to see what kind of life follows from adopting one moral vision rather than another. This capacity to evoke visions of the good life is one expression of what I am calling "the religious imagination."

On this score, self-interpretation on Taylor's view is not a matter of clairvoyance. Instead, self-knowledge is a constant struggle.[28] Taylor's sociohistorical diagnosis concludes that "we" now live in an age in which there is a pervasive lack of clarity about constitutive, higher goods and this condition leaves "us" with the impression that moral frameworks are (somehow) optional. In this sense, Taylor's polemic is not simply against the dominant modes of moral philosophy, but it is also aimed at the moral cultures of secularism and political liberalism that correspond to attitudes of disengagement and value-neutral objectivity.[29] Again, the issue is not only the apocryphal story about the disenchantment of the world, but, more urgently, a critical response to the objective reality of moral pluralism. Taylor is quite aware that conflicts, tensions, and clashes of varying ways of life and potentially incommensurable visions of the good give plausibility to the argument that, say, a liberal attitude warrants prescinding from carrying on with thick descriptions of individual and collective moral constitutions. In other words, speaking and acting through the acknowledgment of higher-order goods in various public spheres and other webs of interlocution may be illiberal in modern moral culture. Nonetheless, Taylor sustains the argument that even so-called neutral moral theories are in fact predicated on unacknowledged higher-order goods. For example, the commitments to justice and liberalism gain their moral force through their reliance on the background values of human dignity, that is, the principles of benevolence, freedom, and the respect for the value and dignity of human life. The heart of Taylor's project is to recover a discourse of meaning and significance for human agency. And this involves the kind of expressive articulation about the good that acknowledges moral frameworks as indispensable to identity and human flourishing.

Modern Moral Identity and the Melancholy of Agency

The fate of our times is characterized by rationalization and intellectualization, and, above all, by the "disenchantment of the world." Precisely the ultimate and most sublime values have retreated from public life.
—Max Weber, "Science as a Vocation"

In contemporary secular cultures defined by moral pluralism, is it possible to avoid in the work of understanding and articulating moral frameworks generating a legitimation crisis for moral pluralism? Will the expressions of this work in moral understanding beat the same hasty retreat as the "ultimate and most sublime values" Weber identifies? As a way of beginning to answer these questions, let me now take up Taylor's genealogical narrative of modern identity from *Sources of the Self* at its historical climax, namely, his discussion of Romantic expressivism. In particular, I want to highlight Taylor's characterization of Romantic expressivism as a rebellion against "radical" Enlightenment humanism and rationalism. It is important to note that Taylor is selective in what he takes from the expressivist tradition. He wants to lay claim not to the subjectivist forms of self-expression but rather to the ethic that is committed to the transformation of the ordinary that issues from the creative imagination, or what I am calling the religious imagination. This is, admittedly, a difficult set of qualities to distill. Nonetheless, Taylor's interpretation of this ethic, in particular its valorization of art and the aesthetic, are mediated by his commitment to the idea that these transformations of the ordinary require being able to "see" the good. And this requires being open to the possibility that constitutive goods do in fact condition moral agency. Insofar as that is legitimate, Taylor argues, art and the aesthetic hold forth to disclose forms of affirmation—intellectual, social, cultural, political, *and*, of course, religious affirmation—that have become pervasive and persistent in modernity. Among these sources of affirmation are forms of grace—which, for Taylor, means some thing or some force (e.g., God) that is able to alter one's moral vision. In other words, Taylor posits that grace, or something analogous to it, is available through art in the form of epiphany. To anticipate: the aesthetic serves as a medium between the agent/self and her/his moral sources.

Keeping the theory of agency as strong evaluation in mind, Taylor constructs a history of modern identity in *Sources of the Self* that seeks to uncover the moral sources that underlie dominant values in the modern west, as well as the conditions for the possibility of moral agency as a mode of judgment and choice. In other words, Taylor's historical narrative recounts the individual *and* collective processes that have been paradigmatic for modern identity. The meta-theme that Taylor identifies as responsible for perpetrating the series of transvaluations of values for modern identity is the story of western secularization and the general delegitimation of moral orientations grounded in religious beliefs and other moral sources. Taylor objects to much of modern moral philosophy, such as deontological theories, for assuming that moral deliberation and holding obligations require abstracting from frameworks of meaning. Naturalism and other reductionistic theories that build on principles derivative of science and rationalism, such as the continued effort to establish mastery over nature, see secularization as a form of liberation. In other words, these theories view secularization as a form of human self-reliance and thereby representative of modernity's hallmark achievement: namely, freedom. And yet the freedom that has arisen from the Enlightenment conceit of valuing independence from external sources of moral authority (cosmological, divine, or otherwise) is a negative freedom; it does not point in any particular direction other than "away." In addition, according to the positive take on secularization, the disenchantment of modern culture has allowed for adherence to a plurality of value systems rather than the dominance of one, such as Christianity. Taylor certainly views respect and moral and cultural pluralism as epistemic gains, yet he is equally distressed at the effects of pluralism: in particular by its effects on the ontology of agency of strong evaluation he believes is crucial to moral identity. Consequently, Taylor is incredulous that it is possible to have agency that is meaningful, that makes sense, and that is moral (in the broad use of this term) if frameworks are somehow considered optional. He maintains that "[o]ur evaluations are not chosen. On the contrary they are articulations of our sense of what is worthy, or higher, or more integrated, or more fulfilling and so on."[30]

I read *Sources of the Self* as a performative act on Taylor's part that demonstrates the virtue of being clear and articulate about the moral sources that animate a meaningful sense of self. Methodologically speaking, Taylor enacts the commitment to articulation in *Sources* by revealing—and thereby articulating—the moral sources for "common" modern moral intuitions and reactions such as justice and benevolence. In a quasi-Hegelian fashion, Taylor sets out to demonstrate the necessity of his philosophical anthropology of agency by showing how articulation, historical examination and reflection, and practical reason work in analogous terms for individual agents and for societies at large. In doing so, he is articulating and revealing how the modern understanding of agency must start with our "strongest intuitions, where these have successfully met the challenge of proposed transitions away from them."[31]

Therefore, the history of modern identity is one that reveals different constitutive goods for different eras. In the modern west, the dominant moral sources include God, reason, and nature, among others.[32] With the identification of these three moral sources of God, reason, and nature, it is noteworthy that Taylor is also arguing for his own brand of moral realism.[33] Constitutive goods are real in that they ground and direct moral beliefs and judgments by shaping the moral ontology or background picture that corresponds to our best account of our moral intuitions and experience.[34] On these terms, whatever the best account of moral experience invokes as a moral source—nature, reason, God—is real since these constitutive goods, on this account, must be independent of us. This is what makes them "objectively real"; which is to say, they are not dependent upon our interpretation of them. There are no absolute frameworks or paradigms for moral experience; in fact, best accounts are always partial. However, from the perspective of moral subjects, agency involves evaluations based on standards of values that transcend interests and desires. These frameworks function as "transcendental conditions."[35] The articulation and hermeneutical interpretation of what these standards are have undergone changes and are specific to moral agents of particular eras and particular cultures, in which enduring transitions arise based upon judgments of the best accounts available.[36] A higher-order good—whether it is a Platonic notion of the good, a Christian God, or perhaps a humanist version of justice—is a "moral source" when "it is something the love of which empowers us to do and be good."[37] In the end, this moral love instills a motivation, an imperative to be articulate about the good vis-à-vis one's agency. Articulation, according to Taylor, "can bring us closer to the good as a moral source, can give it power."[38] And on Taylor's diagnosis, clarifying what moral sources are operative is of utmost urgency given the moral and spiritual predicament of the modern agent.

But this raises the question: what is the moral and spiritual predicament that Taylor identifies as a challenge and threat to realizing individual moral identity in late modernity? This moral and spiritual predicament appears to correspond to features that corroborate Taylor's view that modern agency has taken a form that is flattened, narrow, and lacks a deep sense of purpose and significance. In short, the loss of contact with moral sources is the nub of the problem. This is not to say that Taylor argues that moral sources have disappeared altogether. Rather, as I have already indicated, Taylor identifies three important moral sources for modern identity: reason, nature, and God. Reason as a moral source is manifest in the culture that warrants respect for the dignity of rational agents and life. And the dignity of the rational agent derives from her/his capacity for self-determination, as well as from her/his powers of expression and articulation, which is also to say, from the capacity for human freedom.[39] By most accounts, the idealization of reason and freedom reaches its vertex in the Enlightenment. The problematic, on Taylor's account of modernity, is that even with the identification of reason as a moral source, it has left us—"we" moderns—in a condition that no longer requires or acknowledges that close contact with other moral sources and constitutive goods is necessary. This is the rationale that Taylor invokes in seeking out resources to challenge this dominant view.

The immediate historical challenge to Enlightenment rationalism was, of course, the Romantic movement, which sought its moral sources, as Taylor notes, in nature and in the Romantics' abiding faith in the creative imagination.[40] By "nature," the Romantics were referring both to the external "natural" world of forests, mountains, and seas, as well as to the inner ocean of the self. Before discussing the legacy of Romantic expressivism that Taylor pursues, it is helpful to anatomize the belief in nature as a moral source that is central to Taylor's account. The view of nature as a moral source derives from the evolving perception that there is a moral order to the world. This belief, in turn, descends from a variety of theories about the design of nature by a divine author, most particularly in the estimation that there is an interlocking, providential order at hand in the world. Most significant for the culture of modernity, undergirding this belief in nature as a source of morality is the widespread conception of the affirmation of ordinary life. Taylor traces the origins of this central value of modern life to the rise of new orientations in science and religion in early modernity. In science, following Bacon, among others, there is a shift in the guiding ideals of scientific inquiry, from the contemplation of higher truths to a greater emphasis on practical effects. Within western Christianity, especially following the Reformation and later with the Deists, there came a refusal of the mediation of the "priestly" classes and a rejection of the increasingly profane character of life, both of which would eventually lead to valuing and affirming the fulfillment of ordinary human life. In other words, a belief developed that the divine infused the "profane" concerns of work and family as if they were localizations of the sacred. This put work and family—"the ordinary"—on par with the sacraments and the pursuit of certain sanctified ways of life, that is, with the lives of the monk, priest, and nun. Thus, the ordinary takes on unprecedented significance insofar as humanity becomes the stewards of God's creation. Significantly, this shift away from particular "priestly" vocations of higher calling toward the sanctification of the ordinary democratized, in a sense, access to the divine.[41]

The original affirmation of the ordinary extended beyond work and family, especially through the later developments by Locke and Shaftsbury, both of whom developed a belief in the expansion of the goodness of the natural order. This meant diminishing the significance of the Reformation's emphasis on original sin and inculcating human activity as part and parcel of this wider order. The upshot of the latter is that a wider variety of human desires and needs are viewed as divinely conferred and sanctioned. Ethically speaking, the human instinct for the pursuit of pleasure and the avoidance of pain was an indication that God's purposes would be best served through universal human flourishing and procreation. This in turn elevates benevolence as a value. Deists such as Hutcheson further develop the notion of the interlocking, providential order by positing that the instincts, desires, and sentiments that God has implanted within each of us are to be probed as a means of access to the divine. In other words, it is not only nature in the world that provides evidence of God's design but also internal inclinations and sentiments— including the pursuit of happiness—that are now integral to the overall design.[42]

This shift in moral perspective, exemplified here by the Deists, is significant for Taylor's narrative because he identifies the affirmation of ordinary life as crucial to the Romantics. Furthermore, in his reconstruction of the Romantic tradition and its heritage, Taylor identifies Rousseau as pivotal for inaugurating a major change in the belief in nature as norm. This was a shift from seeing nature as an inner tendency to *listening* to it as an inner voice, that is, as the calling of a moral source. Rousseau identifies the voice of nature with a conscience that speaks through language and reason. Regaining contact with this voice "would be to transform our motivation to have a wholly different quality of will."[43] It is not only that one has sentiments accorded by God that are in tune with the universal good, but also that the inner voice of one's true sentiments *defines* what is the good. In other words, the spirit of nature *within* each of us *is* the good. Of course, with Kant, there is a further development of this idea, in which the residence of freedom is within the subject, but it is not *of* nature. Freedom is the capacity to legislate morality to oneself through reason. What is crucial for Taylor's purposes is that Rousseau and Kant are seen as parts of a continuous movement and development in the moral culture of modernity in which access to moral sources are found within the self. Self-knowledge and moral identity are mediated through interiority. For Rousseau, it is the voice within; for Kant, it is the discovery of the moral law within. For both, freedom is inextricably linked to an authentic self: either as a transformed good will (Rousseau) or as a moral and rational agent (Kant). In other words, the consolidation by Kant of radical autonomy, inspired in part by Rousseau's focus on inwardness, is a fundamental transformation in modern moral culture that invests the individual self with the capacity for moral responsibility and freedom.

In addition to Rousseau and Kant, Taylor also emphasizes the Augustinian legacy of interiority as an enduring influence on modern western moral life. Augustinian interiority is found not only in various articulations of human sinfulness and "fallenness," but also in the adoption of the view that the human will is in turmoil because it is beholden to two loves: "the sense that good and evil are in conflict in the human breast."[44] In Taylor's account, this retrieval of the Augustinian view of the conflicted will is a crucial countervoice to the dominant thought and sensibility of the Enlightenment, which was utilitarian in its ethics and atomistic in its social philosophy. Nature and society were, for the mainstream Enlightenment, only of instrumental significance.[45] They were means to the ends that satisfied human desire and interests. The abiding hope was to bring happiness through a perfect mutual adjustment, by training and organizing social practices according to the principles of social scientific engineering. Reason could free humanity of errors that derived from egotistical desires as well as from the illusions of superstition and parochialisms, such as religion and other forms of metaphysics. The promise was deliverance from this natural realm of illusions to a universal order of benevolence and harmony. The legacy of the Enlightenment that Taylor counterposes to what will eventually become Romantic expressivism is based on this belief in freedom as radical autonomy. Furthermore, this transition is only realized through a critique of the scientistic faith in the disengaged rationality of naturalism and humanism. In short, the radical, unbelieving Enlightenment, on Taylor's view, narrowed human pursuits to such an extent that the modern situation is one in which there are diminishing opportunities to pursue *publicly* that which makes life significant and worth fulfilling. This is an indictment reminiscent of the conclusions drawn by other important philosophers of modernity, such as Weber and his laments over the "iron cage" of rationalism and Arendt and her prognosis of the separation of private and public spheres of life and action. The wake of the Enlightenment has been especially devastating, according to Taylor, in the effect it has had on truncating the strong evaluation of goals and desires and the subsequent compromises inflicted on the possibilities for human agency.

Of course, one does not have to wait for late modernity to see a strong response to this compromise of human agency. It was the Romantics, after all, who made the first important incursion against this standard Enlightenment view. In Taylor's genealogy, Romanticism completes a process initiated by Rousseau in which there is an internalization and a consequent location of the moral within the subject/self. With the Romantic movement, there is an attempt to maintain the achievement of human freedom, as conceived in the Enlightenment, but also an elevation of forms of philosophy and aesthetics that give greater credence to the notion of an inner voice or impulse. In other words, Romanticism validated the idea that the truth and the good are within the self, especially in feelings and sentiments. In short, Romanticism recognized that the good and the moral are available both in nature itself and in the vast inner resources within each individual.[46] According to Taylor, the validity of this view issues from the expressivist movement.

"Expressivism" is Taylor's term of art for an *ethos* that emanates from Romanticism, with Herder as one of its founding figures.[47] Herder, a student of Kant and the major theorists of the German *Sturm und Drang* (storm and stress) movement, was an influential critic of the Enlightenment (among those most influenced by Herder was the young Goethe). In addition to Hegel and Humboldt, Herder is a key figure for Taylor from this period. Herder, and Humboldt afterwards, inaugurates a tradition of thought and aesthetics that is deeply concerned with the objectifying tendencies within modern culture, especially the Enlightenment conceit that it is possible to make human nature an object of inquiry. According to the expressivists, this pursuit results in a series of losses, schisms, and estrangements between humanity and nature, between reason and sensibility/feeling, as well as among people. The expressivists aspired to identify a form of freedom predicated on the reconciliation of these dualisms. Expressivism continues in our times, according to Taylor, in the intensification and subsequent democratization of the notion of the inner voice. Though Rousseau originally identified the inner voice with conscience, afterward the ethical dimension of the inner voice takes on greater moral and aesthetic breadth. The Romantics, as expressivists, subscribed to the notion that it is through the inner voice and impulse that one finds access to significance and meaning—that is to say, nature, reason, God, or other sources of the good find expression *within the self*. I make what I hear within me real, so the expressivist says, by working to articulate and speak this voice. The realization of this inner calling through speech, especially in the very idea of having a voice, underscores the necessity of the human to mediate between the natural and the divine, between the worldly and the transcendent. As Taylor writes: "And so among the great aspirations which come down to us from the Romantic era are those towards reunification: bringing us back in contact with nature, healing the divisions between reason and sensibility, overcoming the divisions between people, and creating community."[48]

A clearer sense of the significance of expressivism for Taylor's reformed conception of engaged and embodied agency becomes evident when one takes a closer look at the theory of language that underlies the expressivist movement. The term "expressivism" is, after all, evocative of language. In turn, the moral and existential elements that Taylor discerns within Romanticism in terms of manifestation and creativity are evident in his study of language. Taylor sees an inherent link between agency and language. This is one of the reasons, I believe, that in the concluding sections of *Sources*, Taylor looks to aesthetic forms, especially the poetic and the literary, as the media that best capture the expressivist synthesis of the ethical, the moral, and the aesthetic. The argument is that understanding these connections will greatly advance the agenda of rehabilitating and regenerating modern agency.

The appeal of expressivism for Taylor is that it indicates not only a theory of language but also, and more important, a theory that establishes continuity between experience, embodiment, and agency. The idea here is that there is a synthetic web of connections between the existential and the moral, the cultural and the social/political, and the aesthetic and the spiritual/religious. Part of expressivism's appeal for Taylor derives from its capacious range but also from its ability to preserve language's quality of *mystery*. Expression is mysterious, according to Taylor, because of its inseparability from the medium, since it is only manifest in expression itself. The meaning cannot be understood by pointing to some other phenomenon, but only by and through another expression. As such, expression cannot be fully objective, as scientific linguistic theories presuppose. Expressions are always related to the subjects who manifest them. This reading of language tempers Taylor's self-characterization as a moral realist, to some extent, especially since an expressivist account of meaning is always associated with subject-related properties. An expressivist account of the universe would not intend or even pretend to be an objective one as promised by scientific naturalism; rather an expressivist account always applies properties related and relevant to the self, "that is, properties that things have in the experience of subjects, and which would not exist if subjects of experience did not exist. . . . Expression is the power of a subject; and expressions *manifest* things, and hence essentially refer us to [the] subjects for whom these things can be made manifest."[49] In other words, the mystery surrounding the generation of linguistic expression lies within the self. Expressivism is therefore in opposition to theories of language that see language as instrumental, designative, and representational. This expressivist theory does not see language as mimesis, as a mirror of reality. Instead, it is a "locus of mystery, that is, of anything which might be irreducible to objectivity."[50] As M. H. Abrams formulated the distinction, expressivism does not presuppose that language is a mirror of nature; instead, language is like a lamp that illuminates life, including the inner self.[51]

In Taylor's view, what Herder, Humboldt, and the later Heidegger and Wittgenstein establish is the worldview that language is essential to thought, insofar as it proves to serve the expressive needs of a people's humanity.[52] A language is indicative of the identity and soul of a people. For the expressivists, language has a resource in feeling, which means that it reflects a disposition of the will, such that feeling and thought are inseparable. On this score, true, authentic expression, as generated by the self, is a crucial advancement over the understanding of human freedom put forward by the Enlightenment. This series of connections establishes a moral and ethical continuity between self-reflection, feeling, self-expression, and, most acutely, art. For the expressivists, the most adequate language is that which unites a description of the world *and* the expression of human feeling. In turn, this expression defines what the feeling is and thereby realizes and clarifies what it means to be human. As I noted earlier, Taylor sees Romantic expressivism as a culmination of a long tradition of inwardness and interiority that began with Augustine. "Inwardness" is Taylor's term for the belief and state of being in which moral sources are constitutive *and* transcendent, yet also accessible to the soul, spirit, or mind. Herder, in particular, articulated this sense in which language was not merely reflective of an external, objective reality but was indicative of the human capacity for self-reflection. Hence, language as a species of expressivism is the articulation of the inner states and self-understanding of the person. As such, the individual does not know what her/his moral sources are prior to the attempt to articulate and express them. Realigning this synthetic relationship between interior states and external expressions, between intentions and voice, is a major focal point of what I call in the next chapter projects of regenerating agency.

It is clear that Taylor's philosophy of language is a contrapuntal voice to his theory of agency and that the motif that sustains this counterpoint between the two—between language and agency—is personal identity. As with the theory of agency, Taylor's reading of the expressivist theory of language is mediated through the mutual refraction of a philosophical anthropology and an ordinary language philosophy. In Taylor's view, language is expressive, disclosive, and constitutive. As I noted in the previous section of this chapter, expression and articulation are crucial for realizing the picture of agency that Taylor advocates. By "expressive," Taylor is referring to the manner through which language shows the standpoint of the subject toward reality as well as to other interlocutors. By "disclosure" or "disclosive," he is referring to the capacity of language to articulate a concern or issue and thereby making it publicly available. Language is "constitutive" in that the language that makes sense of experiences is not simply a pattern that one fits into but rather is integral to the experiences themselves. Taylor goes as far as to say that "the expressive dimension seems to be more fundamental: in that it appears we can never be without it, whereas it can function alone, in establishing public space, and grounding our sensitivity to the properly human concerns."[53] This is all by way of saying that in distinction to representationalist or designative theories of language, in which the self is detached and instrumentalist, expressivism always indicates the moral values that support it. Language for the expressivist is dynamic. While designative and representationalist theories of language hide the values that undergird them—especially any aspirations to freedom—expressivism proceeds with the aim of always seeking to reveal and make evident moral sources.

It is this coincidence of foregrounding moral sources, articulation, and expressivism that makes Taylor's expressivist theory of language consonant with his theory of agency. Taylor follows Romantics such as Herder as well as later philosophers such as Wittgenstein, Heidegger, and Gadamer in positing that a language is a world, which is to say, it is a background against which its use and invocation are not separable from an implicit understanding of the whole. This is a holist reading of language in which individual parts and words are only understandable by assuming the whole of language as background. Language is "the capacity to speak (express/realize) the reflective awareness implicit in using words to say something. Learning to use any single word presupposes this general capacity as background. But to have the general capacity is to possess a language."[54] In other words, the expressive theory of language is a synecdochal web in which parts and wholes reflect one another simultaneously. It is a view of language that is in opposition to representationalist and empiricist theories in which language is said to correspond to objects and things in the world as discrete signifiers. The crucial feature of expressivism and expression for Taylor is in the capacity to *manifest*, which in itself is a mark of human creativity and hence the imagination. Taylor lays out the relationship between expression and manifestation as follows:

> Something is expressed when it is embodied in such a way as to be made manifest. And "manifest" must be taken here in a strong sense. Something is manifest when it is directly available for all to see. It is not manifest when there are just signs of its presence, from which we can infer that it is there, such as when I "see" that you are in your office because of your car being parked outside. In this case, there is an implied contrast with another kind of situation, in which I could see you directly.
>
> Now we consider things expressions when they make things manifest in the stronger sense, one which cannot be contrasted with a more direct manner of presentation, one where things would be there before us "in person," as it were. . . .
>
> Expression makes something manifest in embodying it. Of course, a given expression may reveal what it conveys in a partial, or enigmatic, or fragmentary fashion. But these are all manifestations in the above sense, that however imperfect we cannot contrast them with another, more direct, but non-expressive mode of presentation. What expression manifests can *only* be manifested in expression.[55]

Thus, expressive meaning is never fully separable from its manifestation or medium. And the foremost medium that manifests feeling, experience, and freedom for the Romantics was art.

> The expressive view of human life went along naturally with a new understanding of art. If expression defines in a double sense, i.e., both formulates and shapes, then the most important human activity will partake of this nature. The activity by which human beings realize their nature will also define in this double sense.
>
> It is art which comes to fill this niche. In our civilization, moulded by expressivist conceptions, it has come to take a central place in our spiritual life, *in some respects replacing religion*. The awe we feel before artistic originality and creativity places art on the border of the

numinous, and reflects the crucial place that creation/expression has in our understanding of human life.[56]

Taylor is not alone in identifying the Romantics as precursors to contemporary concerns with fulfillment and unity.[57] Nonetheless, his interpretation is unique in the ways he creatively appropriates the Romantic *ethos*, especially in that this retrieval is open to a relegitimation of religion through its capacity to enable agency, especially through artistic expression. Significantly, it is a critical retrieval on Taylor's part. He is quite explicit in *Sources* and elsewhere that a complete and unproblematic return to Romantic expressivism is not possible.[58] In fact, the kind of poetic modernism that Taylor focuses on, which I discuss below, is as much a departure from Romanticism as it is a continuation of Romantic expressivism. Nonetheless, in his discussion of the Romantics and the modernists, Taylor wants to preserve some aspect of the Hegelian aspiration to reconcile freedom and meaningful expression, as well as reason and fulfillment. This task represents the recuperation of situated subjectivity, of engaged and embodied agency.[59]

For the expressivists—and those who followed elements of this stream of thought, such as Schiller, Schelling, and Hegel—access to the good (that is, to the moral sources within the self) is not a matter of finding or recognizing an objective order of being. Instead, the meaning of being is manifest only through the expression and creation that brings it to light. Expressivism is not an orientation that seeks to recover a lost past, for example. Rather, expressivism is about manifestation *and* creation, such that it is not possible to separate the message from the medium, the good from its articulation and expression. Products of the creative imagination—which is to say of artistic expression—thereby take on moral significance. Taylor endorses the expressivist dictum that the world is good only insofar as one can see *and* show it to be good. In his genealogy, this is an equation that issues from the Romantics and finds resonance with the book of Genesis in which God looked upon creation and saw that it was good. For the Romantics—Herder, Schiller, and others—the conviction that one's creation is good derives from a conception of the artist, a vision that Harold Bloom calls "theomorphic."[60] The conceit here is that the poet and the artist create works that are akin to God's creation. The artist as expressivist believes it possible to manifest a unique vision of the cosmos and thereby transform individual as well as universal self-understanding. Herder put it in the most extreme theomorphic terms: "The artist is become a creator God."[61] Within such a worldview, the creative imagination is the faculty through which expression of language and art is made manifest. And as an act of creation, the manifestation of reality does not constitute a form of mimesis but rather the articulation of a previously inchoate vision. The crucial juncture here is the mediating role of the human. The artist is a necessary medium for realizing the good. This is clear, for example, in Hegel's *Lectures on the Philosophy of Religion,* in which he argues that the "economy" of God—God's presence and realization in history—is incomplete without the manifestation and involvement of humanity. The indispensable human element in manifesting and creating the good is essential for Taylor because it speaks to the inextricable link between human freedom, agency, and moral sources. Consequently, Taylor's identification with expressivism is a distinct stance against the nihilistic conclusions of secularization, while also serving as an acknowledgement that, with the advent of modernity, it is not possible to transcend human invention and intervention, even when considering hypergoods such as God.

In defending these aspects of his philosophical anthropology, Taylor makes an essentially theological claim that grace or something analogous to it is required to transform the will and the self's relation to the world. And the experience of grace results in a transformation of vision such that the self can *regain* the ability to see the good.[62] In other words, although "we" are mediators of the good, we need divine love/*agape* or some secularized version of grace—this is Taylor's language here—to recognize the good as such. Grace will flow through that which fills the self with awe, such as Kant's moral law or the Romantics' conception of the sublime's captivation of the creative imagination. According to Taylor, such experiences are necessary in modernity, since the modern self has become blind and deaf to the good. This requires the transformation of the human vision of the world as well as an affirmation of human goodness.[63] This is consonant with the pervasive belief that nature is a moral source whose truth and goodness is found in the inner voice of the human. As Taylor notes: "The source of unity and wholeness which Augustine found only in God is now to be discovered within the self."[64] Thereafter came a succession of substitutes and rivalries among forms of grace. Furthermore, a disanalogy developed between the idea of Christian-Augustinian grace and the Romantics' sense of finding the voice of nature within. For various forms of Christianity as well as for Platonists, the love of God or the love of the good is the center of the good life. In contrast, the Romantics' expressivist conviction is not about the love of some transcendent object, "but rather a certain way of experiencing our lives, our ordinary desires and fulfillments, and the larger natural order in which we are set."[65] The imperative for the artist and the poet is to create expressions for this new experience of depth within the self, which is somehow connected to external nature.

The Romantic poets felt the need to articulate an original vision of the cosmos—to create a "subtler language," as Shelley called it—that could express the new awareness of nature within the soul or spirit as a moral source. "The poems themselves are finding the words for us. . . . [S]omething is defined and created as well as manifested."[66] Aesthetic creation becomes a metaphor for the work of language and the expression of moral sources. If he is successful, Taylor's identification of the Romantic ethos of expressivism, even in its transfigurations, regeneration, and attempted negations in modernism, will prove to be a powerful rehabilitation of agency within the moral systems of secularization and modernity. The effectiveness of this strategy depends, in part, on the plausibility of Taylor's identification of the morally transformative capacity of expressivism with the foundation of a significant convention in modern life. This is evident, for example, in various espoused commitments to self-fulfillment.[67] In addition, a great deal rides on the claim that expressivism is a crucial strategy for regaining access to moral sources that provide meaning and significance to otherwise narrow, shallow, and disenchanted ways of being in the world. In other words, Taylor's solution for the moral and spiritual predicament of modernity is to look to expressive forms, such as art, and in particular poetry, to render a reconnection with moral sources or constitutive goods.

Certainly, locating moral sources within the human is promising as well as potentially problematic for a reading of the religious dimensions of agency such as the one I am undertaking in this book. It is promising in terms of validating the human element of agency. And yet there is a challenge here as well: the expressivist ethos, especially in advancing the idea of the voice of nature, also marks a slide from an "orthodox" worldview, in which it is God's grace that transforms the will, toward highly anthropocentric conceptions of moral sources. Before exploring these issues, it is necessary to elaborate on the relationship Taylor is attempting to establish between the aesthetic and the moral, that is, between expressivism and agency.

Love of the Good among the Ruins and the Logic of Epiphany

The world about us would be desolate except for the world within us.
The major poetic idea in the world is and always has been the idea of God.
After one has abandoned a belief in God,
poetry is the essence which takes its place as life's redemption.
                                    —Wallace Stevens, Opus Posthumous

To identify the complex relationships between the religious, the moral, the political, and the aesthetic as crucial for understanding the contemporary conditions that make agency possible in Taylor's account of modernity is to acknowledge the continuing significance of the battle between the Enlightenment and Romanticism. As Taylor argues in Hegel:

> [m]odern civilization has thus seen the proliferation of Romantic
> views of private life and fulfillment, along with a growing rationali-
> zation and bureaucratization of collective structures, and a frankly

exploitative stance towards nature. Modern society, we might say, is Romantic in its private and imaginative life and utilitarian or instrumentalist in its public, effective life.[68]

Thus, Romantic expressivism, on the one hand, is a historical proxy for Taylor's argument for situated, engaged agency. On the other hand, it also initiates a series of influential moral and political visions whose significance is evident in the continued predilection for self-realization and fulfillment, nationalism, and the persistence of the faith in the transformative power of the creative imagination.

In the concluding chapters of *Sources of the Self,* Taylor takes up what he sees as the persistent centrality of the idea of the creative imagination, especially as conceived in the Romantic era. This notion is still crucial for the view that morally significant art, in particular poetry and literature, is "a creation which reveals, or . . . a revelation which at the same time defines and completes what it makes manifest." The continuity Taylor sees with the Romantic tradition, even in putatively counter-Romantic movements such as modernism, is the notion that the work of art issues from or realizes "an epiphany." It is a term adopted from Joyce but given a broader definition. Accordingly, an epiphany in a work of art is "the locus of a manifestation which brings us into the presence of something which is otherwise inaccessible, and which is of the highest moral or spiritual significance; a manifestation, moreover, which also defines or completes something, even as it reveals."[69] Taylor recognizes that the Romantics' faith in the capacity to provide a convincing vision of a meaningful moral order to nature, or what he calls epiphanies of being, no longer holds sway, especially given the crisis of affirmation of the good that he sees as symptomatic of modernity. Nonetheless, the inauguration of the transformative power of art elaborates on the original Romantic sense that art can express something beyond itself. In other words, the Romantics pressed the possibility of an immanent transcendence, as well as the presumption that that which is beyond the world could be rendered present *within* the world. Emblematic of the Romantic epiphanies of being are moments such as Wordsworth's "spots of time" in *The Prelude* of 1799 or the following from his poem "The Excursion":

> How exquisitely the individual Mind
> . . . to the external World
> is fitted:—and how exquisitely too
>
> . . .
>
> The external World is fitted to the Mind;
> And the creation (by no lower name
> Can it be called) which they with blended might
> Accomplish[70]

Within the high moments of Romantic expressivism, these epiphanies of being realized an expression of something, which in itself was considered an
unambiguously good moral source.[71] According to Taylor, for the Romantics
an epiphany

> encompasses not only an aesthetic of the work of art but also a view
> about its spiritual significance and about the nature and situation of
> the artist. It is a view not only about art but about the place of art in
> life, and its relation to morality. It is in fact an exaltation of art; for
> this becomes the crucial locus of what I have been calling moral
> sources. *Realizing an epiphany is a paradigm case of what I called
> recovering contact with a moral source.* The epiphany is our achieving
> contact with something, where this contact either fosters and/or itself
> constitutes a spiritually significant fulfillment or wholeness.... [T]he
> general understanding of the place of art is very widespread and deep
> in our culture, and this corresponds to a widely shared sense that
> the creative imagination is an indispensable locus of moral sources.[72]

Before unpacking the very large claims Taylor makes in this passage, it is
important to complete his genealogy of expressivism and its moral implications. The abiding faith in art as having the capacity to convey epiphanies of
being began to fade rapidly with the post-Romantics, that is, with the new
moral and aesthetic visions of Feuerbach, Marx, Mallarmé, Friedrich, Flaubert,
Zolà, and, most devastatingly, with Schopenhauer and Baudelaire. The transformation of this underlying moral vision ushered by the post-Romantics
brings, on the one hand, an enhanced sense of the powers of the creative
imagination and, on the other hand, a new understanding of the modern
"moral predicament." Taylor identifies this, or, more pointedly, *our* moral
predicament, as a crisis of "self-affirmation." This crisis comes to its first
strong and enduring articulations with figures such as Schopenhauer and
Baudelaire, who reinforced the idea of the human *inability* to see the good.
Schopenhauer will affirm the power of the aesthetic, yet he insists that there is
no inherent good either in art or in the universe. To put it in the idiom of
Taylor's theory of agency, this is a crisis in which there is a loss of contact with
the moral sources that previously affirmed a sense of the good and subsequently a thick conception of the self. Therewith, direct lines of access to these
constitutive moral sources that empower disappear. Moral sources that can affirm the self in such a way that one can see the good and thereby make it manifest appear to vanish from the scene.

While there are continuities between the Romantics and the post-
Romantics, as I noted, the transformations rendered by the post-Romantics
that eventuate in modernism squelch the utopian ideals of the Romantics,
such as the unity of the self. Subsequently, these transformations severely put
into question the faith in the power of the fragment as poetic epiphany to

convey or represent the totality or the whole.[73] In other words, the turn away from Romanticism is marked by the ascension of the masters of suspicion, such as Schopenhauer, Nietzsche, and Freud, and the out-and-out denial of the Romantic aspirations to discover the spiritual goodness of nature. While he does not see any way that this course of development could have been avoided, Taylor's disappointment at this turn is palpable. In a profound sense, the Romantics represent for Taylor the last great generation that held the ambition to right the relationships between the self and the world, and the self and the good/God in a complete and synthetic fashion. In short, the Romantics represent a highwater mark in the human attempt to re-enchant the world *within* the terms and conditions of modernity; which is to say, the Romantics sought to express the realization of a hope in the goodness of nature through the reconciliation of radical autonomy and expressive fulfillment.

Clearly, Taylor does not think that re-enchantment through regaining contact with moral sources is impossible. Rather, he acknowledges the insight and pessimism of post-Romantics such as Schopenhauer and sees that the recovery of contact with the moral is only available through newly configured, interior routes of the creative imagination. Baudelaire and Schopenhauer—as well as Nietzsche and Freud, afterward—help shape a new moral climate that affirms human expressive and creative powers, while at the same time denying any intrinsic connection between these powers and possible epiphanies about the good. The rise in the naturalist scientific worldview and the increasing disenchantment of industrial civilization, along with the decreasing belief in Christian theism as an unchallengeable moral framework in the modern west, deepened the sense of implausibility in regard to the belief that nature was a source of goodness. In sum, the crisis of affirmation is one in which the self is radically alienated from its moral sources. Consequently, under these conditions it is no longer clear how or whether nature, the world, being (what have you) can be affirmed as good. To put it in a Hegelian idiom, the crisis of affirmation is a state of unhappy consciousness. It is alienation all over again.

The pessimist challenge of Baudelaire and Schopenhauer enhanced the sense that new languages would be required for those who "stood in the tradition of affirming the goodness of nature." Note how Taylor perceives the centrality of this tradition in the modern West.

> [T]he position which affirms the goodness of nature isn't a marginal
> one. It has all the depth in our civilization of the combined weight of
> Christianity and Platonism. It is the basis of the most widespread
> secular ethics and political views, those which descend from the
> Enlightenment as well as those in full continuity with the original
> Romantics. And it is the necessary basis for a family of life goods
> which is widely recognized in our civilization, those related to

benevolence. The pessimists seemed to be undermining the grounds on which universal benevolence was seen as a good, the value of human life and happiness.[74]

This is all by way of saying that Taylor takes the climate of nihilism very seriously. He acknowledges that in modernity—that is, in the disenchanted world of moral pluralism, where visions of the good compete—there is no simple recognition of an order of goodness. Taylor is also quite aware that for "those committed to the goodness of being and benevolence—and plainly that still means the vast majority of us in this civilization"—there are alternatives. Among them is a return to older creeds such as Christian faith or a secularist Enlightenment embrace of reason and freedom or even the Romantics' belief in nature as a source of goodness.[75] Nonetheless, despite his own Christian (Catholic) commitments, Taylor pursues a different route that follows from his retrieval of elements within Romantic expressivism, and which entails a turn to works of post-Romantic and modernist literature. Taylor makes this move, in part, because of his belief that art maintains a privileged standing in modern culture due to its putatively revelatory capacities. Focusing on the aesthetic also allows him to establish a link to Romantic expressivism and to the ideal of the power of the creative imagination to transfigure ordinary reality through a recovery of the capacity to affirm goodness. In addition, turning to modernist literature helps Taylor reinforce the point that even those most deeply invested in a modern moral culture of alienation and negativity can still regain access to moral sources. To do otherwise would be to prescind from the affirmation of human freedom and creativity that, amidst the kind of crisis that Taylor identifies in modernity, would be devastating to his argument about agency.

Nonetheless, it is necessary to ask: if epiphanies of being are no longer presumed as realizable in and through the aesthetic, what kind of revelation does modernist art and poetry provide? After all, poets such as Eliot, Rilke, and Pound were not looking to discover the goodness of nature. As with the Romantics, the recovery that they sought was inward. However, in the case of the modernists they did not expect to find an order of being or a more authentic self waiting for articulation and unification. Instead, the turn inward toward experience and subjectivity that the modernists attempted to convey in their work would reveal "a fragmentation of experience which calls our ordinary notions of identity into question."[76] The epiphanies of modernism conjoin a decentering of the self, occasioned on multiple levels of consciousness of space and time. This is conveyed in modernist uses of juxtaposition and other techniques that avoid forms of description and transparent expression. The intention and effect is a disclosure or epiphany that disrupts and thereby breaks with ordinary discourse. In a manner of speaking, the modernists tend toward *the sublime*, which Taylor wants to infuse with the

Romantic expressivist belief in goodness. I analyze this connection between the sublime and agency in the next chapter. For now, let it suffice to say that the modernist epiphany is typically indirect and oblique. It does not offer clear visions of order but rather presents frames and spaces in which affirmation of the good *might* emerge. It is with this possibility in mind that Taylor argues that modernist poetry and art convey a nonexpressive relation between interiority and that which lies beyond the subject, as in the case of a poet who offers an experience of the presence of an ultimate reality. The juxtaposition of images (material presence versus ultimate reality, for example) suggests an indirect mode of communication that speaks both to the personal nature of the encounter and to the sense that it is possible to bring the remote closer and within reach.[77] The modernist sensibility is not an attempt to escape from reality but rather an insistence on reordering it. The modernist sublime is meant to issue shudders and shivers and not the consolations suggested by Romantic ambitions of elevation. As a result, modernism contends that the aesthetic encounter is capable of producing experiences that can transfigure one's vision, which means a transformation of how one sees the world. The modernist aesthetic offers the possibility of experiencing what Taylor calls "framing epiphanies," the presentation of spaces in which the inaccessible might be made available.[78] In writing about Eliot and Pound, Taylor imputes an oblique yet disclosive power to the work of these masters of modernism, such that he contends that "[t]he aim of epiphany is not so much to bring us close to an unrecoverable past or to hasten a more integrated future, but rather to realize a transhistorical unity, connecting us to the highest spiritual articulations of different ages.... The epiphany opens us to something perennial, and allows it to radiate again in our time."[79]

These epiphanies are indirect, so Taylor argues, and are refracted through the personal vision of the poet. The mediation of the poet is unavoidable and arguably even necessary in a secularized age. In the Romantic and post-Romantic forms, an epiphany puts the self into contact with that which is otherwise inaccessible. In other words, it is a medium for transcendence. The suggestion Taylor makes is that some form of the sublime—one that is capable of affecting moral orientations—is once again available through the aesthetic.

It is perhaps now necessary to modify the reading I offered earlier of Taylor's thesis on agency as a response to secularization and the disenchantment of the world. Taylor is not arguing, even in his historical account of modern subjectivity, that secularization is a unilinear, efficiently supersessionist process. Taylor's historical reading of the supercession of one vision of the good over another is not that the former is completely obliterated. Instead, Taylor takes the Nietzschean view of the transvaluation of values—the historical equivalent and expression of his version of practical reasoning—in which values and beliefs are retained even as they are replaced, which is one way of describing Hegel's dialectic of *Aufhebung* or sublation: a negation and a gathering up and integration of the negated into new forms. This notion of retaining while also negating is crucial for Taylor, since he wants to argue that expressivism, while losing its fight for presenting a plausible cosmology of the meaningful order of nature, persists in different forms, even in moral and aesthetic stances such as modernism, which are putatively negations of Romanticism. The difficult position that Taylor wants to inhabit is one that acknowledges the advances of modernity (the achievements and insights into human freedom, justice, the dignity of the human) as epistemic gains despite the persistent ways these advances are used in diminishing the legitimacy of religious belief or belief in the goodness of nature. Again, in Taylor's view, the affirmation of the ordinary life is an epistemic gain that has its roots in a religious movement (the Reformation and later with the Puritans), but it also initiates the breach with the religious tradition from which it came.

It seems, then, that Taylor is still left to answer questions about the goodness of nature, despite the shift he attempts to make to and *through* modernism. For example, if nature has this status as norm and moral source, then why subscribe to the notion of the disenchantment of the world? It is important to note that Taylor goes to this notion of nature as norm fully aware that, on the one hand, it renders a sanctification of the everyday, while, on the other hand, it is a sanctioning of moral, constitutive sources that no longer require a dependence upon God. In other words, the affirmation of ordinary life also means that humanity can find nontheistic moral sources that empower. The most dominant of these is the value that promotes the dignity of the free human being who has the capacity to control nature through reason.[80]

Despite the elegance of Taylor's reading of the power of modernist poetry, in particular, and the suggestion that these poems can serve as conduits for epiphanies, it is necessary to step cautiously here, especially given the apparent subjectivism involved. The problem derives from the reliance on epiphanies to function in a mode analogous to religious revelations. More specifically, there is a tension and paradox (perhaps even a contradiction) in the claim that framing epiphanies are, on the one hand, mysterious and, on the other hand, able to contain or convey crucial insights into what it means to be human, as well as provide information about the divine and other metaphysical concerns. No doubt, Taylor's argument that the modernists were able to convey epiphanies in their art is not about a self who can ground the significance of a source or standard—in other words, there is no Cartesianism here. Instead, Taylor's point is that the aesthetic can indicate the reality of a moral source or the transcendent through the grounding vision of the poet or the artist, who helps give a sense of meaning and significance to the source itself. The issue becomes less about the self and more about that which orients the self. Nonetheless, the meaningfulness of this source is available only through the self, which, for the poet, means a manifestation through her/his faculty of the creative imagination. And here the trail leads back to Taylor's hermeneutical self who is striving to articulate her/his moral horizon. The subjective and the transcendent are interwoven; and this connection is found in the expression issued by the self (as poet, writer, agent).

> We know that the poet, if he [sic] is serious, is pointing to some-
> thing—God, the tradition—which he [sic] believes to be there for all of
> us. But we also know that he [sic] can only give it to us re-
> fracted through his [sic.] own sensibility. We cannot just detach the
> nugget of transcendent truth; it is inseparably imbedded in the
> work—this is the continuing relevance of the Romantic doctrine of
> the symbol.[81]

Thus, the sense of how the vision of the poet contributes to Taylor's over-all project of rehabilitating and regenerating agency becomes apparent. The poetic epiphany provides insight by (re)opening connections to moral sources hitherto occluded and obscured by the secularized worldviews of mechanis-tic order and overly rationalized forms of discourse. Epiphanic art should, on Taylor's argument, open up the possibility of grace and its analogues, thereby providing recourse for meeting the crisis of affirmation in late modernity. Epiphanic art reveals the fundamental reliance that each of us has on back-grounds of meaning. In other words, the epiphanies found in art are a possible means to re-enchant the conditions of agency. This entails a hermeneutical challenge of keeping in mind Taylor's dictum that one must see the good in order to show and express the good. Furthermore, it also requires upholding the expressivist corollary to this dictum that the imagination helps complete what it reveals and that an epiphany prepares the self to receive grace, which is to say that the self must be open to the influence of an other which is beyond the self.[82] To regenerate agency on *these* terms reawakens the self to possi-bilities made available through the religious imagination.

> What we have in this new issue of affirming the goodness of things is
> the development of a human analogue to God's seeing things as
> good: a seeing which also helps effect what it sees. This can mean, of
> course, that the self-attribution of this power is a resolutely atheist
> doctrine, the arrogation to man of powers formerly confined to God.
> This will be so with Nietzsche.... But this doesn't have to be so. One
> of the most insightful thinkers to explore this power is Dostoyevsky,
> who sees it in a Christian perspective.
>   In fact the notion of a transformation of our stance towards the
> world whereby our vision of it is changed has been traditionally con-
> nected with the notion of grace. Augustine holds that in relation
> to God, love has to precede knowledge. With the right direction of
> love, things become evident which are hidden otherwise. What is new

is the modern sense of the place and power of the creative imagination. This is now an integral part of the goodness of things, and
hence the transformation of our stance and thus our outlook helps to
bring about the truth it reveals.[83]

This is a rich and evocative passage. And as with most rich and evocative texts,
there is much to affirm and dispute. In the next chapter, I will take up what it
is that Taylor seems to suggest by way of "grace" and the epiphanic, and how
the appeal to both affects efforts to address the problem of regenerating agency.

3

Through a Self Darkly

Projects of Regenerating Agency

Amazing Grace?

> My purpose is to indicate what happens when religious experience
> is already set aside as something *sui generis*. The actual religious
> quality in the experience... is the effect produced, the better adjust-
> ment in life and its conditions, not the manner and cause of its
> production. The way in which the experience operated, its function,
> determines its religious value... [as] attitudes that lend deep and
> enduring support to the processes of living.
> —John Dewey, *A Common Faith*

In this chapter, I want to focus on what I am calling projects of regenerating agency in late modernity and postmodernity. These are projects that reflect the late modern and postmodern condition of agency
as melancholic freedom: which is to say an understanding of the
quest for agency under conditions in which political ideologies, particularly in progressive politics, are unstable, at minimum, and vague
and lackluster, at best, and in which moral ideals and norms are
constrained by "principled" commitments to pluralism. As such,
I begin this chapter by recapping Taylor's diagnosis of the problem
of agency in modernity: a diagnosis that turns out to be a revised
version of the secularization thesis. I then move to Taylor's suggested
therapy for the problem of agency, namely, his invocation of the
aesthetic and poetic as epiphanic, that is, as a revelation of held moral
orientations, ideals, values, and ends. As a key feature of his project of
regenerating agency, I critique Taylor's treatment of the epiphanic

through a discussion of the relationship between the sublime and agency. I argue that Taylor's invocation of the epiphanic as sublime remains a gesture, that is, a promising movement and hope for a glimpse of transcendence. As such, it requires further development. More specifically, I contend that the promise of the epiphanic and the sublime for projects of regenerating agency becomes clearer when interpreted as part of the ends and aims of the disciplines of self-cultivation and self-transformation. This interpretation requires, I argue, a more sustained meditation on Romantic tropes and ideas than Taylor is willing to countenance. I want to give more credence to the dispositions and attitudes of Romanticism, such as the quality of aspiration, than Taylor does. This notwithstanding, I see the re/turn to Romanticism as an immanent and organic critique of Taylor. As I have already shown, while Taylor is deeply appreciative of the widespread influence of Romanticism, he seems to have given up on the promise of the Romantic tradition that remains.[1] I agree with Taylor's claim that the retrieval of aspects of Romanticism hinges on the viability of expressivism, Taylor's term of art to describe the movement that began with Rousseau's claims about authenticity and culminates with the Romantics, especially the German Romantics, and their response to the radical Enlightenment. Expressivism was, and in many ways remains, an effort to "situate freedom," that is, an attempt to establish a mutually constitutive relationship between freedom and self-identity.[2] Notably, Taylor goes on to reject expressivism because he discerns a corruption in contemporary moral and ethical culture of the ideals associated with expressivism: ideals of self-realization, authenticity, and autonomy or self-determination. In other words, Taylor abandons expressivism for the same reasons that he embraced it in the first place, namely, for its promise of situating freedom, for enabling self-realization and transformation, and for forging mediums—such as the creative expression of identity itself—that can suitably relate inwardness and interiority into forms of public expression.[3]

My aim is to reclaim expressivist and Romantic elements for projects of regenerating agency, particularly, through a reconsideration of forms and thinkers that Taylor rejects, especially in the postmodern claims for the legitimacy of difference. The re/turn to expressivism and Romanticism is not intended as a form of regress or some other reactionary response to the frustrations over contemporary moral life. Instead, drawing on the Romantic tradition and the ethos of expressivism serves three aims. First, it brings into relief a response to many of the shortcomings of the moral, political, psychological, and spiritual conundrums of modernity, especially the deracination of agency. The Romantic inheritance points to the aspects of agency and freedom that rely on the imagination, particularly in regard to questions about the genesis, formation, and sustaining of values. Second, for projects of regenerating agency and the religious dimensions associated with these projects, Romanticism offers significant lessons in synthesizing philosophy with aesthetics, morality with the affective, and the political with the spiritual. The Romantics' attempts at synthesis are provocative and deeply suggestive in a time in which philosophers and other theorists are increasingly turning toward the aesthetic and the sublime as resources.[4] Finally, this post-Romantic reading of agency—an interpretation that regards the relationship between agency, identity, and transcendent aspirations evidenced by the sublime as a subject of critical attention and affirmation—brings out a fundamental religious dimension to the contemporary discourse on agency: namely, *vocation*—a theme I take up in the final chapter.

Despite his capacious mindfulness about the history of ancient, modern, and even postmodern western thought, Taylor's project of regenerating agency is not an attempt to render a philosophical reversal of fortune, in which, if successful, the destabilizations sundered by reason, rationality, rationalization, and the like would be overturned. Taylor is no traditional traditionalist, in the sense of advocating a return to the premodern (his oft-paired peer MacIntyre more appropriately falls in this category). Taylor's more immediate predecessor on this score is Max Weber. The analytical task I have set in this chapter is to determine whether or not it is plausible and persuasive to invest, as Taylor does, in the powers of the sublime, that is, in powers presumably availed through epiphanies found in the aesthetic, and which in turn present a means or at least a spur to the regeneration of agency for the moral self. According to Taylor, the therapeutic effect of sublime epiphanies is to renew a sense of a good that lies "beyond life." This involves a reorientation of agency away from the strictures of obligation, such as those demanded by deontological moral philosophies, by moving, or, rather, by being moved *toward* the conscious as well as the unconscious inspirations of a love of the good. In other words, Taylor is banking on the conjecture that experience of the epiphanic is sufficiently akin to the sublime, such that the disenchanted, disengaged self of modernity can recuperate her/his agency by regaining contact with the transcendent, such as higher-order values that constitute meaningful and morally articulate forms of life. The hope of cashing in on the sublime in this manner is consonant with Taylor's moral realism; in particular, it is an acknowledgment that there is a good and, more specific to his own beliefs, a God beyond life that sustains and affirms. An arresting feature of this reliance on the recuperative powers of the sublime is the alignment of projects of regenerating agency with the work of the religious imagination. More specifically, the belief that the sublime presents an index of some kind of transcendence is a hallmark of one of the primary sources of inspiration for the Romantics, namely, Kant's *Critique of Judgment*.[5] Taylor is fully aware and has consistently argued that Romanticism enjoys a continuing influence on contemporary conceptions of the self, society, and politics. Nonetheless, he dismisses this inheritance by backing away from embracing the Romantic legacy, primarily because he is reluctant to affirm the associations of Romantic tropes such as authenticity and self-determination with modes of subjectivism and self-fulfillment that have proven to be among the most prominent inheritors of this legacy.[6] As I have indicated, it is ironic and even perhaps self-contradictory on Taylor's part to disparage the appropriation of expressivism and its *modus operandi* of self-fulfillment by contemporary figures such as Foucault, or, for that matter, even by "self-help" movements, given Taylor's grander ambitions for legitimating self-realization as a cultural value. While Taylor acknowledges the sublimation of religious energies into the expressivism he identifies with Romanticism, one suspects that his resistance to reclaiming the Romantic legacy has to do with his commitment to moral realism itself *and* his communitarianism. This explains, in part, his subsequently guarded attitude to those who come too close to the vaunted ideals of his tradition. While Romanticism is certainly one of the precursors to communitarianism—this is true especially of German Romanticism and Herder's influence in shaping the discourse of nationalism and national cultures, and Humboldt's insistence on the significance of common languages for social and political solidarity as well as for subjective identity—for a philosopher of modernity such as Taylor who seeks to engage in the processes of retrieving lost heritages, values, and ideals— in a word "traditions"—Romanticism turns out to be a mixed bag. As one of the first efforts to stay the tide of both Enlightenment naturalism and value-neutral political liberalism, Romanticism seems, on the face of it, to be a tradition worth retrieving, especially given Taylor's moral and political philosophical commitments. In addition, as an approach that holds as a regulative ideal the synthesis of the critical reason of the Enlightenment with moral subjectivity and aesthetic freedom, Romanticism should be a natural resource for Taylor.

In framing the rehabilitative work of these Romantic ideas as constitutive for projects of regenerating agency, I am, on the one hand, foregrounding Taylor's underscoring of background pictures or moral frameworks and, on the other hand, attempting to renew the centrality of motivation for an understanding of agency as melancholic freedom. In distinction to a negative freedom that finds expression in overcoming or negating encumbrances and authority, projects of regenerating agency as the one Taylor offers is positive— in the sense of Isaiah Berlin's famous distinction between positive and negative liberty. To be an agent is not simply to say, "I am not this or that," but it is to stake a claim on an idea, a set of values, and a way of life. Certainly, one can circumscribe parameters for agency around the operation of individual choices. Nonetheless, in contrast to the debates in analytic philosophy that frame agency as problems of free will and intentionality, Taylor's approach has the virtue and advantage of taking into consideration a wide range of conditions that affect how action, autonomy, and moral choice take place, especially through the mutual constitution between moral or ethical identity, on the one hand, and culture, history, politics, society, and religion, on the other hand.[7] This is not to say that agency does not involve choices. Taylor is, after all, working from Frankfurt's notion of agency as strong evaluation: that is, the determination, assessment, and judgment of higher and lower goods, pursuits, and the like. This ultimately means that agency for Taylor (and for philosophers such as Frankfurt, for that matter) involves an engagement of the will through reason and love, that is, through the mind and the heart.[8] On this score, projects of regenerating agency are intimately tied to the psychological, social, political, cultural, and deeply spiritual factors that shape the self and identity, which is to say that agency has strong affinities with the idea of vocation or calling.[9] As such, projects of regenerating agency do not end simply with reconnecting and reorienting the self to the good, but they also require a cultivation of sensibilities and dispositions akin to vocation. As Taylor argues, the articulation of one's moral sources has the effect of reorienting the "quality of the will."[10] And, as with the Christian idea of vocation, this reorientation of the quality of the will requires a specific relationship to the good/God, namely, love.

Rekindling a Love of the Good, or Being Good in a Heartless World

Passion has often worn our wandering hearts.
                            —William Butler Yeats, "Ephemera"

As I noted in the last chapter, Taylor thinks that "we," in the late modern West, are experiencing a crisis of identity and agency. Dominant strands of modern moral and political theory, as well as larger social, cultural, and political forces of modernity, have narrowed what counts as legitimate agency—a narrowing characterized by the normalization and naturalization of features of political liberalism and pluralism that dissociate the self from the moral sources that animate and undergird meaningful agency. Similarly, the processes of secularization and the rational ordering of nature (rationalization) and society (differentiation) have diminished the legitimacy of passionate politics and other forms of engaged, situated morality. Questions of the good—especially that which inspires and motivates the self and provides a sense of worth and meaning—are considered secondary to obligations and duty, which is to say, that there has been diminishing attention given to the significance of moral motives for engendering agency, especially in contemporary political theory and moral philosophy. This is, in part, what the phrase "the priority of the right over the good" is meant to connote.[11]

Political liberalism, scientific empiricism and naturalism, moral pluralism, and deliberative democracy are, on the one hand, achievements of reason over the unruly and potentially destructive natural forces of human passions, inexplicable "metaphysical" illusions, and the divisive and violent effects of strong attachments such as religion. On the other hand, constraints on the motivations for ethical and moral purpose and action—that is, the conditions that enable moral psychology—have been severely compromised by the moderating work of the philosophical discourses of modernity. Thus, in establishing requirements of moderation, humility, mutual respect, and the like, the modern condition is, in turn, one in which there is a corresponding attempt to diminish public, legitimate, and viable expression for efforts to provide visions of the good that are mutually constitutive of the self. As Taylor says, "[s]elfhood and the good [as well as] . . . selfhood and morality, turn out to be inextricably intertwined themes."[12] In contrast, Taylor develops a theory of moral agency that is at once a phenomenology of the experience of agency, as well as a critique of the dominant form of modern western identity, namely, the "disengaged self."[13]

As I showed in the last chapter, Taylor argues that the disengaged self is the ideal of agency employed by a host of moral theories that fall within the broad category of naturalism. These theories include behaviorism, utilitarianism, and political liberalism, and the associated accounts they give of the self as unencumbered, radically individualistic, and atomistic. The fundamental flaw naturalism commits is limiting, and even obscuring, the resources available to the moral self by restricting agency to concerns of obligation, as in the case of prioritizing a moral subjectivity that acts on the basis of what one ought to do or what is the right thing to do, rather than providing any affirmative account for the affective dimensions of morality, such as love, desire, and the passions. The Kantian notion of the centrality of duty for moral identity and autonomy is perhaps the most influential example of this mode of moral reasoning. For Kant, ethical authority derives from the self-legislation and self-determination of the moral subject. Moral agency thereby requires acknowledging responsibility to a universal community, specifically through the regulation of the will that maintains a duty to follow principles of action that are universalizable and not limited by convention, kith, or kin. Taylor does not deny the importance of questions of obligation but argues that this represents only one side of moral agency.

Moral theories that rely on obligation as the impetus to agency tend to ignore the centrality of motivation for human agency by stressing forms of negative freedom, that is, freedom *from* external authority.[14] In other words, naturalism, in Taylor's broad application of this category, ignores or downplays the dynamics of moral psychology—especially questions of motivation and the need for positive aspirations—and thereby suppresses the affective elements of experience such as feelings, passions, and hope. The dominance of naturalism has produced a false and incomplete picture of what agency involves. Taylor does not explicitly use the phrase "moral psychology"; nonetheless, the category aligns sufficiently within his moral theory insofar as the positive articulation of moral ideals and values figure as necessary concerns, motivations, and aspirations for the agent.[15] In other words, by arguing that the interpretation and articulation of our deepest moral instincts and intuitions make each of us more fully human, Taylor is also bringing to light the centrality of moral psychological concerns for the motivation of action. Agency requires a vision of what it means to be good and to flourish, and not simply a negative example of what it means *not* to be good and to suffer.[16]

Naturalism is an inevitable consequence of the cultural, social, and moral transformations wrought by modernity. Subsequently, secularization arises as a complementary effect to naturalism. This analysis bolsters Taylor's concern for the undermining and delegitimation of religious belief as a central problematic of modernity. He certainly views the disenchantment of the world as a critical concern. Yet, the modern condition of secularism and the effects of secularization are complex phenomena, as are the ways in which the categories of the secular, secularism, and secularization are used. On the one hand, secularism and secularization indicate a diagnosis and a description of the processes that produce social, cultural, and even theological conditions in modernity that require the removal or neutralize the impact of religious practices and the expression of beliefs in public life. The move to make passionate attachments such as religious beliefs private typically involves the attempt to drive religious commitments inward (into the self or into some private sphere) and away from the public sphere. On the other hand, secularism and secularization are *metaphors* for the conditions that leave the self estranged and alienated from the moral sources that animate the self's moral agency. Thus, "the secular mind," as Robert Coles calls it, reflects an unfulfilled and unrealized mode of agency.[17] It is this latter sense—secularization and the secular as metaphors—that I want to highlight. To anticipate: I am arguing that interpreting the secular as a symptom and not merely as an effect of modernity (along with the attendant Weberian notions such as the rationalization of the life world) captures the problem of moral inarticulacy, political neutrality, and spiritual deflation that Taylor's project of regenerating agency critiques.

To clarify this interpretive strategy, let me recap briefly the problematic of agency as melancholic freedom identified by Taylor in his attempt to close the gaps that have emerged in modernity between articulation/expression and moral orientation, and, more specifically, between the creative, or what I am calling the religious imagination, and the demands of reason. Taylor argues that being clear and articulate about the higher-order goods that enable qualitative evaluations or judgments of higher and lower, better or worse, good and evil, and so on, is crucial for agency. To be an agent is to be a strong evaluator. It means being able to make judgments of value and worth that reflect two fundamental aspects of agency. First, strong evaluation involves identifying courses of action and possible parameters of choice. Second, agency as strong evaluation is an expression of identity. How I choose to proceed in a situation, what I judge to be a better or worse course of action, and how I choose to live my life are all reflections of the values and ideals I believe in and of who I am as a person. Language is fundamental to agency insofar as it serves as the constitutive medium of my identity. To articulate what is of worth to me is to speak of who I am; it is an expression of my identity and the deepest commitments and underlying concerns I maintain. This is not to say that Taylor does not account for illusion or error, in the sense of making judgments and evaluations of right or wrong. He maintains a mode of practical reason predicated on the reduction of error and the stabilization of frameworks that enable moral judgment. After all, the approach is a theory of responsible, moral agency. As Taylor notes:

> [O]ur descriptions of our motivations, and our attempts to formulate what we hold important, are not simple descriptions in that their objects are not fully independent. And yet they are not simply arbitrary either, such that anything goes. There are more or less adequate, more or less truthful, more self-clairvoyant or self-deluding interpretations. Because of this double fact, because an articulation can be *wrong*, and yet it shapes what it is wrong about, we sometimes see erroneous articulations as involving a distortion of the reality concerned. We do not just speak of error but frequently also of illusion or delusion.
>
> We could put the point this way. Our attempts to formulate what we hold important must, like descriptions, strive to be faithful to something. But what they strive to be faithful to is not an independent object with a fixed degree and manner of evidence, but rather a largely inarticulate sense of what is of decisive importance. An articulation of this "object" tends to make it something different from what it was before.[18]

The "object" that Taylor has in mind in the essay "What is human agency?" becomes the concepts of constitutive goods and hypergoods in *Sources of the Self*, meaning higher-order goods such as benevolence or justice that transcend lower-order material desires and wants (what he formerly referred to as "first-order desires"). By foregrounding the necessity of articulating fundamental, grounding, and animating goods, Taylor is demonstrating that these constitutive goods are not always in mind, or at least at hand until some kind of crisis or threat to one's sense of self, community, or tradition (such as naturalism or secularism) is underway. In other words, I can go on with my life without being fully clear and articulate about the fundamental values that provide me with my sense of who I am and what my moral orientation is, barring any threat to this orientation. I can ignore the lack of depth in my life until I am forced to identify my core beliefs in the face of some kind of delegitimating challenge to my way of life. In other words, until a challenge or crisis to my fundamental values arises, I can persist in a state of moral ambiguity or even indifference, which is to say that the self can be obscure to itself. Clarity and a sense of urgency come when threats appear. These challenges can serve as occasions for rearticulating my moral commitments, which is to say, gaining moral clarity by identifying that which is of greatest significance and importance to me.

There are numerous literary examples of crises that induce heightened moral consciousness, such as Antigone's defiance of political authority in her insistence on burying her dead brother Polyneices. In this example, despite the prohibition of the burial by Creon, the king, Antigone comes to realize that the principle of piety to her family—elaborated as the preservation of honor—is of such fundamental importance to her that she is willing to chance death to defend it.[19]

Or consider Huck Finn and the change of heart he undergoes in his "escape" and travels with the fugitive slave Jim. Huck's conscience pushes him to the point at which he has to decide whether or not to send a letter he has written to Jim's owner, informing her of their whereabouts. At the brink of choosing between one world and another, between one sense of himself and another, Huck comes to an existential crossroads where his agency brings into relief the self to whom he will fully commit.

> But somehow I couldn't seem to strike no places to harden me
> against him, but only the other kind. I'd see him standing my
> watch on top of his'n, 'stead of calling me, so I could go on sleep-
> ing; and see him how glad he was when I come back out of the fog;
> and when I come to him again in the swamp, up there where the
> feud was; and such-like times; and would always call me honey, and
> pet me and do everything he could think of for me, and how good he
> always was; and at last I struck the time I saved him by telling the
> men we had small-pox aboard, and he was so grateful, and said I
> was the best friend old Jim ever had in the world, and the ONLY
> one he's got now; and then I happened to look around and see
> that paper.
>
> It was a close place. I took it up, and held it in my hand. I was
> a-trembling, because I'd got to decide, forever, betwixt two things,
> and I knowed it. I studied a minute, sort of holding my breath, and
> then says to myself:
> "All right, then, I'll GO to hell"—and tore it up.
> It was awful thoughts and awful words, but they was said. And I
> let them stay said, and never thought no more about reforming.
> I shoved the whole thing out of my head, and said I would take up
> wickedness again, which was in my line, being brung up to it, and the

other warn't. And for a starter I would go to work and steal Jim out of
slavery again; and if I could think up anything worse, I would do that,
too; because as long as I was in, and in for good, I might as well
go the whole hog.[20]

There are several features of Huck's conversion—his shift from finding
himself in one moral world and then another—that show him to be an agent
who is capable of judgment (strong evaluation), expressivism, and responding
to a vocation or calling. The example of Huck shows how agency, especially
when it involves a change of heart, amounts to acting through the condition
of melancholic freedom. Huck feels overwhelmed with guilt. The call of his
former world—a world ruled by an absolutist ethic of right and wrong and a
commensurate "system" of punishment—instills a sense of obligation in him
to "return" Jim. In writing the letter, Huck is responding to the Kantian
notion of the subjection of the will to a sense of duty and obligation to follow
the moral law; or as Freud might put it, Huck's superego, the internalized
mechanism of enforcing authority and morality in his life, commands him
through guilt and a sense of sinfulness that he should return Jim. In either
case, Huck believes returning Jim to his "owner" would represent an act of
redemption.

Is Huck's conversion at his decision to tear up the letter an instance of
ethical enlightenment, in the way that Levinas means when he says the self
comes to realize the overwhelming force of the ethical in the face of the
other?[21] Is it Jim's alterity that brings home the sense of ethical significance
and transcendence to Huck? Or is the Kantian ideal of universal humanity the
obligation that calls out to Huck? Is it the feeling of obligation *and* elevation
Kant associates with the power of the moral law over the will? While there
may be elements of both in the experience of Huck and Jim, the conversion
of Huck is richer and more complex than either the Levinasian or Kantian
ethical procedures suggest.[22] Jim is *the* other to Huck, but that status is not
what awakens Huck's ethical conscience, as Levinas would have it. In fact, one
could argue that Huck is, as a member of the underclass, an "other" as well.
Huck does feel an obligation to do the right thing, but he wrestles with what
the right thing actually is. In the moral world in which he was raised, white
supremacy dictates that the right thing to do is to figure out a way to return
Jim to his owner. And yet it is not alterity that brings Huck's heart around and
that allows him to hear the call of the ethical. Instead, it is the long journey—
the metaphor of traveling on the shifting, mighty river—that makes the right
and the just present to Huck. Without witnessing Jim's love and kindness,
reciprocated through his own admiration and growing affection for Jim, it
seems likely that Huck would have returned to his original moral world,
chastened but snuggly fit within its folds. Without witnessing Jim's nightly
"moaning and mourning" over leaving his family behind, Huck might not

have let go of one moral world and turned to grasp onto the edges of another. The ethical sublime appears not as a moment outside of time and space but rather as a deeply experienced recognition and acknowledgement of Jim's humanity. In deciding *not* to send the letter, Huck effectively becomes a new person. It is an act of agency that shapes his sense of self. It is an act that moves Huck to an intentional cultivation of the self. While it sounds like an offhand, near casual decision, or even an act induced through fiat, Huck's declaration of "All right, then, I'll GO to hell. . . might as well go for the whole hog" is instead, I would argue, an exquisite affirmation of his agency. Huck is willing to embrace what his past ("civilization") sees as "evil"; by aiding and abetting Jim's escape, he becomes a brother to a slave. It is an existentially profound moment, a Jamesian "forced option."[23] By deciding not to send the letter and to embrace his bond with and love for his friend, Huck faces the sublime in the form of the unknown future that somehow measures over and against the past and, in the spirit of conversion and the piety required to be an agent, moves him to new life. It is an act of moral expressivism or, more specifically, an instance of expressive freedom that is simultaneously an act of self-cultivation. Huck transforms his moral identity. To use Taylor's language, Huck affirms and expresses the good by revealing what it is. Huck reveals and manifests the good and simultaneously creates it. Without the engaged and embodied experience with Jim, ethical agency would have remained an abstraction to Huck. Without the psychic struggle of agency, Huck would not have realized his identity; which is to say that he would not have aspired to be someone else. His "conversion" is a turning from one version of himself to another. The resistance he feels against doing the right thing, and acting in such a way that he would be cultivating a new identity and sense of self, was strong. The experience of loss and of leaving a world—of exile and estrangement from the familiar and the dissociation and dissimulation with the past— proved to be the conditions for the possibility of realizing the melancholic freedom of Huck's agency.

As Taylor suggests, being clear and articulate about the higher-order values and ideals that matter to one's moral identity is also to be "faithful" to them.[24] Articulation and expression of these values and ideals bring into relief what one believes, what one is willing to fight for, perhaps even die for. Taylor's diagnosis of modernity as an age of secularization and disenchantment is consonant with the crisis of agency and its associated moral confusion and ambiguity. As such, secularization not only stands for the legitimation of disengaged, value-neutral subjectivity, but it also sanctions moral ambiguity through perpetuating a climate of opinion that views the moral and political judgment of strong evaluations with suspicion, that is, as potential forms of political, religious, and cultural extremism. This is, of course, part of the legacy of the Enlightenment: the moderating measures of cosmopolitanism and mutuality reflect the concern for order over the potential chaos of religious and ideological divisiveness. To believe too strongly or to live too passionately in public life is a formula for catastrophes such as religious wars and political extremism.

And yet there is a price paid for order and calm. There are many famous versions of describing this price, most of which fall within the rubric of *the discontents of modernity* or what Robert Pippin calls "the melancholy of modernity."[25] In fact, one can label many of the great critiques of modernity as depictions of the discontents or melancholy of modernity by identifying "the costs" of modern life, that is, what one feels obliged to *give up* or relinquish in exchange for the "advances" of modernity. For example, with the move toward scientific naturalism that began with Bacon and was eventually transformed into a cultural ethos in the Enlightenment, it is fair to ask what is the price paid for human freedom. The authority of purportedly divinely sanctioned institutions, such as the Church, diminishes, as does belief in the metaphysical. This is, after all, the myth (not necessarily in the pejorative sense of this term) of the disenchantment of the world. Gaining knowledge of how the natural world works, so the story goes, simultaneously creates the ability to learn how to control and predict nature. Subsequently there is a loss of faith in and need for supernatural forces—hence, the poignancy of Weber's term of art for this transvaluation of values: *Entzauberung*, "disenchantment," or literally "de-magification."[26] This condition is also part of the inheritance of the nihilism that one finds throughout modern western thought and culture.[27] Freedom and autonomy require independence, such as in the case of the moral agent who is able to self-legislate laws. As Kant says in his definition of "enlightenment," freedom and autonomy involve removing oneself from the tutelage of another and to go it alone or at least to rely on oneself.[28] The modern west gets this message from world historical "moments," such as the American and French revolutions, as well as from its best and most insightful prophets such as Luther, Kant, Sojourner Truth, Emerson, Douglass, Whitman, Nietzsche, and King. Insofar as the account Taylor offers in his genealogical works on the self and the *ethos* of modernity is concerned, he is not offering an "original story" but rather affirming what has become a common lament, a jeremiad of sorts. In this sense, Taylor's critique of naturalist and individualistic forms of agency is designed to buoy his moral realist faith in the independent existence of transcendent goods.

This is not to say that Taylor is antimodern or even countermodern either in his analysis of the spiritual conditions of modernity or in his normative suggestions for how to fix what he considers broken. It is possible, I am arguing, to turn to sources and the expressions of moral value that one finds in premodern eras without abandoning one's commitment to improving modernity itself. Taylor's genealogical predilections speak to this desire to be *in* modernity but perhaps not fully *of* modernity. His consistent efforts to show how contemporary dispositions, attitudes, and conventions have roots not simply in current institutional and structural arrangements, but also with forces that run more deeply and reach farther back to basic human ideals such as benevolence, justice, courage, and kindness or charity. These are, after all, remarkably similar to the virtues and ideals of moral excellence identified by the ancient Greeks. Taylor's point is that, despite the variations and trans-positions by figures such as Aristotle, Augustine, Montaigne, Rousseau, and Kant, there is a remarkable persistence in the preoccupation with articulating what constitutes living a flourishing and meaningful life, as well as with how to establish and enrich a good society. Employing a genealogical method for the sake of moral articulation, on the one hand, helps clarify the relationship between morality and identity. On the other hand, Taylor's historicist gene-alogy uncovers suppressed narratives and events that may prove not only to be counterhegemonic but, perhaps more productively, also turn out to serve as the basis for a counterhermeneutic. These ideals and virtues—such as charity, moral courage, and benevolence—are so widely held that they have become diffuse. They have become naturalized to such an extent that they have be-come part of what he calls our deepest moral instincts and intuitions. As I noted in chapter 2, Taylor argues in *Sources of the Self* that it is imperative for projects of regenerating agency to strive to be articulate about the higher-order goods that hold forth in the modern west. The move from obscurity to articulation of moral sources clarifies and transforms these ideals from the murkiness of instinct and intuition to the daylight of public life, which is to say that articulation makes these moral values and ideals public, real, and identifiable.

The trouble with leaving moral identity and agency at the level of moral instincts, even in the case of one's most basic instincts, is the problem that always comes with relying on instinct: once instincts are proven wrong, mis-understood, or misleading, then it becomes difficult to trust them, to rely on them. One no longer feels confident enough to rely on one's instincts to serve as a guide to action. Subsequently, there is a loss of faith in the values and ideals that these instincts reflect. Moral ambiguity affects the ability to be an agent not simply because of incoherence, but also because it leaves one feeling uncertain as to how to manage conflicts with those who hold different values, worldviews, and ways of life. In other words, being morally inarticulate and incoherent intensifies incommensurability. On this score, Taylor writes,

> [A]rticulation may not only serve greater refinement, and the draw-ing of more subtle distinctions. That may be a good in some cases. . . . [A]rticulation may also serve another purpose, not where we want to unpack what is involved in a practice about which we feel unproblematically positive, but rather where we experience a pro-found conflict about our practices, or else they conflict with each other. Here what we are looking for is not refinement of our existing

way of being, but a way out of the impasse in which we find ourselves. We articulate in order to become clearer about our options, to
see what recourse is open to us.[29]

The subtext of Taylor's rendition of the moral and spiritual predicament
of the modern self is the familiar story of alienation. It is helpful, on this score,
to highlight how theological versions of the alienation story are operative in
Taylor's theory of agency. Of particular note is his use and allusion to the
theme in which humanity is cut off from the grace and mercy of God (as in the
Genesis story of "the Fall") due to "our" sinfulness (read as a metaphor for
human finitude and limitations). This is an interpretation of human finitude
that echoes Hegel's allegorization of Christianity in his *Lectures on the Philosophy of Religion*. On my reading of Taylor, he ascribes qualities of melancholy to
the modern condition because it reflects a moral ambiguity that results from
alienation from moral sources. In other words, being inarticulate about one's
moral sources can be read as the condition of the loss of contact with *and* the
inaccessibility of these moral sources. Furthermore, it speaks to a state related
to mourning: the loss of a loved object that had at one time defined the self,
but a loss that the self is not able to let go of. In short, it reflects what Freud
calls "melancholia"; hence, the melancholy of modernity.[30]

Perhaps it is because he ambivalently identifies the decentering of the self
with modernists as well as with postmoderns, Taylor still wants to retain a
sense that the encounter of epiphanies found in the aesthetic and the poetic
renders a reconciliation of sorts. As I have indicated, the affirmation of the
human and the good, as well as the inflections Taylor gives to horizons of significance and meaning, signify a philosophical orientation toward wholeness.
In my estimation, it is precisely his insistence about the condition of "lost
contact" with transcendent goods—objects of love that still persist in modern
moral life—that qualifies Taylor's account of modern agency as melancholic
freedom. Recall Freud's characterization of melancholy or "melancholia" as a
psychic state in which one is unable to mourn the loss of a loved one or an
object of one's love. The loss can be material, as in the case of physical death,
as well as symbolic, in the instances of the "death" or negation of an idea or
the passing of a stage in a relationship. The latter is classically marked, as
Freud points out, in the transitions away from infancy and the concomitant
changes in the relationship between mother and child. In either case, the melancholic has suffered a loss of the object cathexis—the psychic focus and
intensification toward the object of love—which, in turn, becomes the basis
for an identity formed around this lost love.

The main point I am stressing here is that melancholy deals in memory
and forgetting. Melancholy is "an experience" as much as it is a persistent
condition in which the loss that augurs the memory of a central figure, feature,
or love of one's life chastens as well as inspires in a necessarily vague manner.

Melancholy persists through the paradox of absence and presence: the absence of that which was once near and dear, as well as the continued presence and reminder of lost love. The death of a loved one is a clear example of this. In a potentially less painful yet certainly significant vein, experiences of exile, displacement, and migration can produce analogous melancholic effects.[31]

So, what does this have to do with agency, particularly agency as moral or even political judgment? A major implication of Taylor's genealogy of modern moral sources is an argument that philosophy may not be up for the task of reestablishing contact and connection to these moral sources. As I mentioned earlier, Taylor has been deeply critical of various forms of naturalism and other philosophical positions that argue from a value-neutral perspective ("the view from nowhere"). From the perspective of moral pluralism and practical reason, Taylor contends, it is possible to argue that an ethical position is superior without making a deontological move or some other procedure of decontextualizing moral subjectivity, as in the application of and appeal to general principles. Each of us always argues from a position within a form of life and in regard to one or more higher goods, values, and ideals.[32] The operative aspiration is to understand disclosures of truth that help explain experience *from* experiences, not in spite of them. Thus, experiences of the sublime, such as Joycean epiphanies, are cohering insofar as the encounter with them transforms the self, as well as one's relationship to the world and to others.

Nonetheless, even after making this argument, Taylor acknowledges that there is a circular relationship between constitutive goods and life goods, between moral sources, such as God or other notions of the good, and the self. To put it in more positive terms, one might say that the relationship between the self and its ends is organic and thereby necessary. And yet in arguing that forms of engaged and embodied agency—a mode of agency reliant on this symbiotic relationship with constitutive sources—is superior to disengaged rationality, the punctual self, and other "unrealistic" arguments, it looks as if the hermeneutical circle is inescapable. Indeed, Taylor does not seek to break out of it. The challenge here to Taylor—critic of secularism, naturalism, and disengaged individualism—is to make a convincing case that exposure to epiphanies and other instances of the sublime will help in the cause of regenerating agency in a manner that verifies the indispensability of motivations. The task I have set for the rest of this chapter is to draw out more fully—that is, more fully than Taylor has done himself—the implications of the move and appeal to epiphanies and the sublime. I will do this by shoring up Taylor's prescribed therapy for late modern agency by arguing for a renewed consideration of Romanticism and expressivism. Taylor has insisted that the Romantic tradition, especially through the legacy of expressivism, continues to be influential, but in rather unappealing and unconstructive ways. My hope is that a re-examination of the expressivist legacy will reveal that there is more to affirm in it than Taylor is willing to countenance.

When Not Seeing Is Believing

The Plain Sense of Things

After the leaves have fallen, we return
To a plain sense of things. It is as if
We had come to an end of the imagination,
Inanimate in an inert savoir.

It is difficult even to choose the adjective
For this blank cold, this sadness without cause.
The great structure has become a minor house.
No turban walks across the lessened floors.

The greenhouse never so badly needed paint.
The chimney is fifty years old and slants to one side.
A fantastic effort has failed, a repetition
In a repetitiousness of men and flies.

Yet the absence of the imagination had
Itself to be imagined. The great pond,
The plain sense of it, without reflections, leaves,
Mud, water like dirty glass, expressing silence

Of a sort, silence of a rat come out to see,
The great pond and its waste of lilies, all this
Had to be imagined as an inevitable knowledge,
Required, as a necessity requires.

                                                —Wallace Stevens

Taylor certainly is not alone in the conclusions he draws about the limits of
philosophical discourse and the need for philosophy to look to resources outside of modes of reason, utility, and logic, that is to say, resources such as the
aesthetic (fine and material arts, poetry, literature, music, and so on). For example, consider the following remarks by Habermas in his essay "Themes in
Postmetaphysical Thinking":

> In the wake of metaphysics, philosophy surrenders its extraordinary
> status. Explosive experiences of the extraordinary have migrated into
> an art that has become autonomous. Of course, even after this de-
> flation, ordinary life, now fully profane, by no means becomes im-
> mune to the shattering and subversive intrusion of extraordinary
> events. Viewed from without, religion, which has largely been deprived
> of its worldview functions, is still indispensable in ordinary
> life *for normalizing intercourse with the extraordinary.* For this reason,

postmetaphysical thinking continues to coexist with religious practice—and not merely in the sense of the contemporaneity of the noncontemporaneous. This ongoing coexistence even throws light on a curious dependence of a philosophy that has forfeited its contact with the extraordinary. Philosophy, even in its post-metaphysical form, will be able neither to replace nor to repress religion as long as religious language is the bearer of a seman-tic content that is inspiring and even indispensable, for this content eludes (for the time being?) the explanatory force of philosophi-cal language and continues to resist translation into reasoning discourses.[33]

This passage is a useful example of a philosopher struggling with the lim-its of philosophy, precisely when philosophy is circumscribed by the parame-ters of rational experience. It is an extraordinary passage for a few reasons, not the least of which is that it comes from the pen of one of the preeminent "post-metaphysical" rationalists of our day. Habermas is a philosopher of a strongly Kantian disposition who gives pride of place to the power of rational-ity to order life and the world. Note that Habermas is admitting to the limi-tations of philosophical discourse, which in itself amounts to acknowledgment that philosophy may not be the medium that can answer all questions about moral motivations adequately. Furthermore, this admission also points to the struggle that modern philosophy has in attempting to provide an acceptable picture of meaning in a post-metaphysical age. Habermas is also concerned that philosophy cannot reckon with the sense of contact with the extraordinary, uncanny, or unconditioned that is available through the "language" of art. Furthermore, he admits to the need for some thing to mediate between the ordinary and the extraordinary, that is, something to take up the role that religion had played in mediating metaphysics and the supernatural to the everyday. One might say that he is making an argument about how to recon-nect with moral sources.[34] This suggestion is made even as Habermas con-tinues in his efforts to sustain the "unfinished project" of the Enlightenment. The significance of the convergence in the thought of Taylor and Habermas on this point is not simply a nod toward the power of the aesthetic. Unlike Taylor, Habermas would rather turn to secularized displacements of the sacred.[35] Finally, Habermas, like Taylor, gestures toward the continuing indispensability of the religious. In other words, the argument made here in regard to the sig-nificance of art and aesthetics likens them to the power of the religious.

This example from Habermas represents an acknowledgment on the part of a growing number of major philosophers that philosophy requires resources other than logic, mathematics, and the faculties of critical reasoning to under-stand the nature and conditions of human life. Despite what would seem to be mere common sense to the layperson comes as a revelation, even revolution, within the parochial realms of philosophers, especially Anglo American philosophy. Of course, the question of the limits and limitations of philosophy has been there since its inception. One need only look to Plato's *Republic* and the concern shown over the "threat" the poets pose to the philosophers. In large part, the modern circumscription of ethical and moral agency to the operations of reason, and not other aspects of human experience such as the emotions and the passions, is certainly a hallmark of the long shadow cast by Kant and Kantian thought. Kant insists that moral identity should find its proper expression only in the faculty of practical reason and not in the emotions, such as the desire for happiness and other worldly pursuits of satisfaction. He believes that deviation and making oneself exempt from moral duty (most starkly identified with "radical evil" as well as the confusion the self experiences over the proper ends of moral reasoning) is not only likely but also a near inevitability. Philosophers who have resisted this view of moral and ethical agency (philosophers such as John Dewey, Richard Rorty, Stanley Cavell, Martha Nussbaum, Cornel West, and Taylor himself), and who have attempted to argue for the centrality and not the marginalization of emotions and passions for moral identity, have consistently turned to the aesthetic (to literature, poetry, drama, and film, though less often to music) to make their case. In part this has been an attempt at rendering a massive correction to the abstractions of analytic philosophy. More important, the move to the aesthetic and affect is, I am arguing, an attempt to frame philosophical problems such as agency as reflections of the entirety of what it means to be a human being and not simply as expressive of rationality. With this in mind, Taylor's appeal to the epiphanic resources of the poetic is neither unprecedented nor particularly noteworthy in the recourse it makes to aesthetics.[36]

What *does* distinguish Taylor, however, from other contemporary philosophers who appeal to the aesthetic is that he draws on the literary and the poetic to argue not simply that they pose as acceptable "arguments" in philosophical reasoning. More important for my purposes of uncovering the religious dimensions of the contemporary discourse on agency, Taylor's appeal to the aesthetic and the sublime works as a way of cultivating a moral and spiritual disposition and sensibility—a disposition and sensibility that is attuned to possible engagements with the transcendent not only as "external" to the self but also as potentially residing *within* the self. As Taylor maintains, in a post-Romantic age, the epiphanies of aesthetic expressions are necessarily indexed to a personal and individual vision.

It is not the case that Taylor goes as far as to say that he would like to sanctify or consecrate the world; however, he appears to be leaning heavily in that direction at times. If one considers Taylor's diagnosis of modern subjectivity and agency and the aesthetic solution that he offers as a quasi-phenomenology of the sacred, the next question is whether this accommodation does any work for his philosophy of agency. It certainly brings out the religious or at least the possibility for interpreting agency to have a religious dimension insofar as it involves a potential relegitimation of religious sources for the practices of agency as moral judgment and the cultivation of self-identity. Again, agency as strong evaluation, according to Taylor, requires grounding in a transcendent good. The heart of the connection between agency and the religious hinges on processes in which the self is able to "see" the good and be the medium through which it is revealed or made manifest. This is what the religious imagination does. Recall Taylor's mantra: we create the good as we reveal it. Following Habermas's "post-metaphysical" assessment, this manifesting and mediating role was traditionally played by the religions.

The epiphanic and the sublime function, then, as a means of reorienting the self, of changing worldviews, if you will, such that one's grounding in the good becomes more apparent. Therewith, God's or the good's presence is no longer completely beyond the self. The epiphany (re)acquaints the self with the transcendent by revealing the self's limitations and finitude, subsequently generating a potential openness to the possibilities of the transcendent. As moderns who apparently suffer from a loss of contact or a foreclosing of access to the good—due largely to the social, political, and cultural engagements with and commitments to secularization and moral pluralism—regaining contact with moral sources requires some thing, some experience that will inspire openness to new orientations and approaches to finding meaning in one's life. Taylor invests in the notion of the moral transformation that occurs with the encounter with the aesthetic. Of course, this is not an argument that all aesthetic forms have this transformative power. Rather, the aesthetic power here is with subjective experiences with the sublime and perhaps even of the uncanny (*Unheimlich*). In other words, Taylor is invoking transformative experiences that generate the paradoxical effects, on the one hand, of dislodging held beliefs about one's identity and the world and, on the other hand, of affirming hidden or embedded truths about the self. The kind of epiphany that Taylor is describing is genuinely revelatory insofar as it can contrive or induce this uncanny experience in which the familiar is made strange, or, to be more precise, the familiar is given a depth and meaning that was previously absent. Taylor's logic of epiphany seems to operate along Hegelian lines; one overcomes alienation through sublation, that is, through a negation of an estrangement from the good that will render the good available again. Taylor's contention is that the "framing epiphanies" that are available in the post-Romantic age—which is to say after the radically skeptical critiques of Schopenhauer, Feuerbach, Marx, Nietzsche, and Freud—will not take the form of visions of cosmic order, but rather will juxtapose this-worldly, naturalist sensibilities with unsettling moments, such as those found in the modernist poetry of Eliot's *Four Quartets* or Pound's "In a Station of the Metro" or the poem that serves as the epigraph for this section of this chapter,

Stevens's "The Plain Sense of Things." The epiphanies of modernism are, in this sense, distressing, especially insofar as they are not offering an "argument" or presenting some kind of clear, propositional truth. Instead they disclose, manifest, and realize a world that is not transparently good. Taylor banks on the hope that the disclosure—the epiphany—is consonant with our moral intuitions, such that a moral source *might* be revealed.

What's Love Got to Do with It?

The Everlasting Voices

O sweet everlasting Voices, be still;
Go to the guards of the heavenly fold
And bid them wander obeying your will,
Flame under flame, till Time be no more;
Have you not heard that our hearts are old,
That you call in birds, in wind on the hill,
In shaken boughs, in tide on the shore?
O sweet everlasting Voices, be still.
     —William Butler Yeats

Undoubtedly, this is certainly expecting a lot of such experiences, and more needs to be said or at least developed to see how this might work. As I have shown, Taylor implies that these epiphanies are reflective of encounters with the sublime. In fact, Taylor trades here on the power and implications of the sublime without invoking the category or explaining how an experience of the sublime reconciles the self to its moral sources. Nonetheless, there are clues and gestures in *Sources of the Self* and elsewhere in Taylor's corpus. One of Taylor's favorite examples of the relationship between the sublime and the moral is Kant's "Achtung!," that is, an example of how a moral source serves as a motive for action.[37] "Achtung!,"—literally "pay attention!" or "wake up!"—is one of the moments *outside* of the *Critique of Judgment* in which Kant identifies the connection between morality and the sublime. "Achtung!" symbolizes for Kant a call to respect the other—other people—as ends in themselves and not as mere means. The play of the sublime and agency manifests as the ethical call to be reverent and respectful of others ("Achtung!"), as well as to adhere to the principle of universalizability found in the moral law. Kant says that the "Achtung" relates "an obscure feeling" that comes with the respect that attends to one's duty and obligation to the moral law. Unsurprisingly, Kant immediately backs away after making this claim (albeit in a footnote) by saying that the feeling is the result of a "rational concept," namely, the moral law. The relevant point here is that even in his metaphysical claims about our moral lives, Kant requires a moment of awakening and attunement—"Achtung!"—that unsettles the moral subject from its habits of following "natural" inclinations. More specifically, even Kant recognizes that as finite beings we need to feel compelled in any commitment we maintain to a "rational concept" like the moral law, that is, in order for the idea to have binding, normative force on the moral imagination.[38] As Kant says in the third proposition from the *Groundwork*: "Duty is the necessity of an action from respect [reverence] for law."[39] In other words, obligations are born not only from acknowledging the force of reason but also from strong feelings, such as reverence and respect, or, as Taylor would have it, love.

The necessity of feeling or the affective for morality was a central doctrine of the Romantics. And yet, despite what appears as an argument in favor of the necessity of the sublime in ethical and moral agency (which in turn would be an endorsement of the continuing influence of traditions that argue as much), Taylor is evasive and ambivalent toward Romanticism. Which is to say, he is critical of Romantic features of modern life while also acknowledging their lasting influence. This ambivalence and evasion takes the form of a philosophical stance that favors allusions to Romantic elements (epiphany, the sublime, even the uncanny) rather than identifying with Romanticism itself.[40]

Taylor invests in the expressivist conviction that realizing the good is somehow contingent upon seeing the good. He argues that if this claim is right, then this process will involve an affirmation of the good and of the human. In turn, the affirmation that is most powerful, according to Taylor, is one that involves God. Not surprisingly, it is on this issue that Taylor has drawn a great deal of fire from secular critics such as Rorty and Skinner.[41] His critics charge that Taylor's "theism" has caused him to run perilously close to predetermining what one might confront in these epiphanies. The suspicion is that being a theist means that one must also be a dogmatist. And yet Taylor's argument about the power and affirmation one draws from higher-order goods, from moral sources, is not exclusive to theistic claims about divine grace and the like. To wit, Taylor is sufficiently cognizant of meeting the challenges of skepticisms of various kinds. This is why he argues that "[t]he most reliable moral view is not one that would be grounded quite outside our intuitions but one that is grounded on our strongest intuitions, where these have successfully met the challenge of proposed transitions away from them."[42] The issue at hand for Taylor the "theist" is withstanding the challenges that threaten transitions away from his strongest intuitions. More precisely, he is attempting to vitiate the effects of the disenchantment of modern life and is thereby trying to clarify a moral vision that allows for the possibility and enabling of influences that can work in a manner analogous to grace and *agape*.[43] Appealing to the epiphanies experienced through the linguistic art of poetry speaks to the hope Taylor has in the possibility of reorienting the relationship between the agent and her/his horizon of meaning. It is, as I have suggested, meant as a kind of therapy for a melancholic, late modern subject. The conjecture is that experiences with epiphanies, with revelatory aesthetic and affective expressions, will confirm for the self an existing participation in a synecdoche—which is to say a tacit piety to the disclosive powers of the Humboldtian web that is a common language.[44] As Taylor puts it, "[t]o speak is to touch a bit of the web, and this is to make the whole resonate. Because the words we use now only have sense through their place in the whole web, we can never in principle have a clear oversight of the implications of what we say at any moment."[45]

By suggesting that Taylor is trading on the power of the sublime, I am arguing that he is making several moves. He begins with an appeal to the epiphanic sublime as an affirmation of the qualities of transcendence in his moral psychology. This is clear in Taylor's deployment of the concept of the constitutive good as incomparably higher than ordinary desires. In other words, by unsettling and juxtaposing, the sublime alerts moral orientations to a structure of goods, where it becomes possible to recognize the differences between ordinary, material life goods and those ideals and values that resonate with one's deepest moral instincts and intuitions about identity and morality. In turn, this awareness helps answer the questions "Who am I, and what ought I to do?" Through the work of interpreting and articulating moral intuitions and reactions to moral demands and situations, it is possible to gain a clearer sense of the higher-order values that shape one's qualitative distinctions and judgments between higher and lower, good and evil, better and worse, and so on. It is the case, according to Taylor, that "linguistic articulacy . . . [is] part of the telos of human beings."[46] Finally, this teleology derives from the idea that constitutive goods such as justice, benevolence, the affirmation of ordinary life, and God are

> something the love of which empowers us to do and be good. The constitutive good does more than just define the content of the moral theory. Love of it is what empowers us to be good. And hence also loving it is part of what it is to be a good human being. This is now part of the content of the moral theory as well, which includes injunctions not only to act in certain ways and to exhibit certain moral qualities but also to love what is good.[47]

Appealing to epiphanies and the sublime as therapies for the morally and politically melancholic agent also serves to elevate the significance of the aesthetic and the affective in projects of regenerating agency in late modernity. It is certainly of a piece with Taylor's communitarian critique of liberalism and his philosophical and sociological critique of the culture of individualism and atomism to argue for the significance of the aesthetic and the affective. The critical question, though, is whether the inclusion of the aesthetic, the affective, and the appeal to the sublime will render the kind of reconciliation with moral sources Taylor desires. Are literary and poetic epiphanies—representations of the sublime—sufficient therapies for the moral and political melancholy of modernity?

What is of interest here is not the dispute over the incommensurability between intellectual disciplines, such as the differences in how philosophy and psychology understand motivation, or the charge that Taylor is being a normative dogmatist. Instead, my concern is for the priority Taylor places on questions of motivation—what moves and inspires—in agency. Nonetheless, I want to be careful here. In focusing as I have on projects of regenerating agency and the pride of place that Taylor has given to experience of the epiphanic and the sublime, I am appealing *not* to Taylor's theism but to the structural features of his theory of agency—the aspects that arise from his phenomenology of moral experience in modernity—that highlight the aspirations and longing for transcendence, the constitutive role of the imagination in rendering moral visions real, and the power and necessity of particular kinds of experiences that are identifiable with the sublime. These are features that reflect the conditions of what it means to be an agent in late modernity (Taylor's phenomenological point), as well as aspects of a philosophical anthropology that speak to the aspirations and needs of experiencing the world, others, and oneself in ways that reflect ideals, values, and a strongly held moral identity.

All of these features and characteristics of Taylor's approach to agency reflect what I am calling the religious imagination, which is to say that they are indicative of the religious dimensions to human agency itself. Taylor's moral psychology, as with all moral psychologies, emphasizes motivations; but more specifically, Taylor stresses that which affects the quality of the will. And the quality of the will that Taylor seeks to uncover and retrieve in this age of secularism and naturalism reflects the loss of contact with goods that command "awe, respect, or admiration."[48] Thus, Taylor's use of the sublime in his moral theory appears not only in relation to the epiphanies of the aesthetic but also as a fundamental feature for his moral psychology. In other words, as Kant, Burke, and other theorists of the sublime have suggested, sublime epiphanies serve to reinstill and reinforce an understanding of limits *and* possibilities. Sublime epiphanies fill the self with awe, ambiguity, and terror. They also remind each of us of our limitations and finitude. Taylor does not fully develop the place of the sublime and the aesthetic-affective dimension of agency, perhaps, again, due to his ambivalence about our Romantic-expressivist inheritance.[49]

By pointing toward the need for the experience of captivation by epiphanies and the sublime (modernist or otherwise), Taylor reveals a place and space for a religious disposition and imagination in what, for many, is a secularist affair, namely, the experience of agency itself. There are echoes of a Hegelian determinate reflection here, in which the immediacy of experience is dialectically rendered into symbolic representations that also reflect a higher-order value. This Hegelian gloss can help make more sense of the operation of the sublime as it functions within the moral psychology suggested by Taylor. Nonetheless, as I have already noted, it is not altogether clear from what Taylor describes as our estrangement from moral sources, how an experience of the sublime or of an epiphany can reconcile this breach. Taylor repeatedly argues that "[t]he understanding of the good as a moral source has ... been deeply suppressed in the mainstream of modern moral consciousness."[50] It is one thing to argue that framing epiphanies such as the ones found in modernism can unsettle, juxtapose, and subsequently reorient as a means of *preparing* one for the possibility of encounter with the transcendent; it is altogether a different matter to say conclusively that the "transcendent" experienced through aesthetic media is necessarily "the good." Let me now rephrase a question I posed earlier: how will encounters with the sublime renew a love of the good? If Taylor is not fully convincing in making the point that such encounters regenerate affective dimensions of agency (that is, the characteristics of inspiration and empowerment to do and be good), is the only remaining option a reversion to the naturalism and secularism that he so deplores? The standard that Taylor sets for moral sources is to inspire the self with love, awe, or, in the least, respect, such that the agent/self is moved to act on the basis of these feelings or passions. Can the sublime, as described *and* circumscribed by Taylor's appeal to modernism, help achieve this kind of standard?

As Taylor leaves the argument, probably not. As I noted earlier, Taylor does not connect the dots for us on this score. After reading *Sources of the Self* one is left with a sense of the importance of overcoming an alienation and estrangement from one's moral sources; which is to say, Taylor is effective in making the diagnosis that the melancholy of modernity emanates from the loss of contact with moral sources like the good, the love of which is deeply embedded in the moral and social imaginaries of secular philosophies such as liberalism and utilitarianism. He sustains the argument that coming to terms with the melancholy of the late modern moral subject indicates that the aesthetic will, through the epiphanies it renders, provide a sense of something like grace: that is, the experience of captivation, of receiving the gifts of wisdom, insight, and love. Once again, I want to be cautious to note that Taylor uses the language of epiphany not to convey something on the order of an ecstatic religious experience. Nonetheless it remains that Taylor does not give us much to work with as to how the encounter with epiphanic art (and by extension epiphanies as phenomena in modernity) works. In addition, toward the conclusion of *Sources*, Taylor ascribes a compromised and awkward position for readers and critics (the recipients of purported epiphanies of art) in their ("our"?) encounter with the literary as an adumbration of the transcendent. I quote Taylor here at length on this point in order to give the full, unsettling effects of this move:

It is not just the epiphanic art of the last two centuries which fails to get its due by [the dismissal of expressions refracted through the personal]. We are now in an age in which a publicly accessible cosmic order of meanings is an impossibility. The only way we can explore the order in which we are set with an aim to defining moral sources is through this part of personal resonance. This is true not only of epiphanic art but of other efforts in philosophy, in criticism, which attempt the same search. This work, though it obviously fails of any epiphanic quality, falls into the same category. I have throughout sought language to clarify the issues, and I have found this in images which enable me to see more clearly than I did before. They could, I believe, be the animating ideas of an epiphanic work, but that would require another kind of capacity. The great epiphanic work actually can put us in contact with the sources it taps. I can *realize* the contact. The philosopher or critic tinkers around and shapes images through which he or another *might* one day do so. The artist is like the race-car driver, and we are the mechanics in the pit; except that in this case, the mechanics usually have four thumbs, and they have only a hazy grasp of the wiring, much less than the drivers have. The point of this analogy is that we delude ourselves if we think that philosophical or critical language for these matters is somehow more hard-edged and more free from personal index than that of poets or novelists. The subject doesn't permit language which escapes personal resonance.

We either explore this area with such language or not at all.[51]

So can Taylor's account of the expressive-constitutive nature of language and of the possibilities of the epiphanic be open to all of us if such a strong distinction is made between the artist and the audience? Are the aesthetic virtuosi the only ones who can receive the grace Taylor envisions?

This is certainly a question that should be posed to all who invoke the sublime. Consider once again Wordsworth's "spots of time" from *The Prelude*, by consensus one of the paradigmatic moments of the sublime in English literature. Famously, Wordsworth provides an example of the sublime here as a suspension of our normal abilities to synthesize and absorb perceptions and our experiences of the natural world. Fair enough. But there is a difference between one who has an experience such as the one described by Wordsworth in *The Prelude* and one who has the experience of reading *about* the sublime moment itself. To put it simply: it is necessary to distinguish accounts of the sublime from what might count as a form or source of the sublime. Taylor is stuck on the former distinction; he sees an insurmountable expanse between artist and audience, between the creative genius and the ordinary person who seeks the extraordinary in an aesthetic medium. And yet what Taylor seems to want—as do others who invoke the power of the sublime—is the experience itself, that is, the aesthetic experience of the sublime that defies the ability to make (immediate) sense of it while simultaneously changing attitudes, perceptions, and visions of the world, the good, the self, and others. In the chapters that follow, I will argue that Taylor circumscribes the realm of the sublime too severely especially by limiting it to the spare pool of minimalist forms that he identifies in *Sources* (Joyce, Eliot, Stevens). Expanding the scope of the category of the epiphanic and the sublime beyond the literary/poetic and into realms such as the political and the cultural can, I will argue in the coming chapters, draw out the aspirations for transcendence that Taylor associates with projects of regenerating agency. Furthermore, extending the reach of categories such as the epiphanic and the sublime also reveals how the religious imagination operates and functions. The critical project here is to show that agency as melancholic freedom reflects what I am calling a religious sensibility in its disposition and openness or attunement to the regenerative possibilities of the sublime. This religious sensibility seeks possibility and hope even when the prospects of finding them appear slim to none. The sublime has the potential to awaken the self to the calling of such moral life possibilities. Subsequently, the hope is that the shock and shudder of the epiphanic sublime can help cultivate moral attunement.

Taylor's argument for articulation, read as the aspiration to reconnect with moral sources, poses, then, as a demand to accept the compromised moral positions rendered by secularization and the disenchantment of the world. For the secularist, this means identifying and acknowledging, on the one hand, what moral ideals and identity animate the values that one holds, and, on the other hand, the need to accommodate and realize these ideals, identity, and values. For the believer, theist, and even the religious skeptic, this requires maintaining a faith or piety in the face of the achievements and doubts of modern rationalism and science. Taylor's reconditioning of agency as melancholic freedom reflects the synthesis he seeks between liberalism and communitarianism, as well as a reinterpretation of the organic relationships between the quest for self-fulfillment, moral expression, and engaged communal life.[52] Both of these reconciliations demand that all of us become pluralists who act with moral conviction and not with tentativeness, that is, to become agents who act through a humility marked by forthrightness *and* moral courage. Each of us *should* try, in principle, to convince others of the superiority of our respective beliefs and positions not only based on the strength of the better, rational argument but also on the weight and worth of the form of life proposed. This involves asking what kind of life does one want to lead, as well as what ideals of human flourishing are viable once it is clear that the principles and values of modernity may in fact be responsible for ruining sacred truths.

The articulation of moral sources and constitutive goods represents a mediation between ordinary and extraordinary experience, which is to say, it plays the role that Habermas claimed religion once filled.[53] For Taylor, the nihilism of modernity is less about the death of God and more about the genuine difficulty of holding onto a sense that one's moral framework and the qualitative distinctions of worth and value defined by this framework are valid, legitimate, and meaningful. Similarly, the effects of secularization as diagnosis and metaphor do not result in a "simple" yet complete disenchantment or "demagification" of the world, but rather indicate a psychological and moral condition in which strong evaluation and commitments—our passionate attachments—are compromised. The climate of opinion called secularism, interpreted metaphorically as I have suggested, is what induces pluralistic, contemporary societies to cast agency as melancholic freedom. As a late modern subject, it is not that I can no longer hold beliefs such as the existence of God or some other higher-order good. Instead, the contention is that it has become difficult and tenuous to do so *if* I am committed to the principles of moral pluralism, practical reason, critical reflection, and even democracy. As Taylor notes, "frameworks today are problematic." Moral pluralism means that there is no agreed-upon sacred canopy. Of course, this is not to deny that such a canopy actually exists.[54] It is, rather, to argue that specific representations of how the canopy covers and what it covers may be more relative than any of us realizes or is willing to acknowledge. The anxiety over meaning is a paradoxical condition for the possibilities found in agency as melancholic freedom: a state in which the agent seeks to be a strong evaluator and a free self without the confidence accorded by the faith and piety that was (supposedly) available to the premodern. The melancholic freedom of modern agency reflects the loss of contact and identity with moral sources. And yet this is a condition in which one is not fully able to mourn the loss of these moral ideals, because it is not a loss of negation but of clarity. Moral sources are obscure to the vision of the moral self, and its grasp on them (in the Hegelian sense of *Begriff*, of conceptualizing as grasping) has been loosened. As moral pluralists, tentativeness attends the expression of moral orientations. And yet doubt, skepticism, and uncertainty have pressed the necessity of the quest to regain connection with the good.

It is noteworthy that there is the kernel for regress in Taylor's conclusions, in particular in his conjecture that modern moral values, such as justice and benevolence continue to have a fundamentally parasitic dependence on "Judaeo-Christian faith."[55] This is, perhaps, not surprising for a project of retrieval. I think this happens for philosophical as well as personal reasons. Or, more accurately, Taylor is exemplifying how genuinely difficult it is to dislodge an agent—a "strong evaluator"—from her/his most dearly held values and evaluations or judgments. For example, it is easy to *say* that as a pragmatist one is deeply committed to a principle of fallibilism. But at what point, and on what terms, would the pragmatist give up on this principle? How tough a fight would that be? And how would such a scenario come about? Because giving up the principle of fallibilism would be tantamount to giving up on the very identity of being a pragmatist, this sort of abandonment of a fundamentally held value would constitute a massive identity crisis. Huck's conversion is another intense example of how severe these changes in moral and existential orientation can feel. This is the order of magnitude on which Taylor's practical reason takes place, at least when it comes to hypergoods that signify self-fulfillment and meaning. The transition away from these principles of identity and moral evaluation is a movement away from that which is most basic and most worthy. In sum, *it is a movement away from oneself.* The *ad hominem* issue here, if you will, is that Taylor is a Catholic and a Christian. He disperses several confessional statements throughout *Sources* about his "theistic" beliefs. At times, the tone he takes in *Sources* is nearly Schmittian. It is not so much a matter of "friends and enemies" but rather "believers and unbelievers." The philosophical, or rather existential, wager that Taylor makes implicates what he says in his own theory of agency and moral deliberation, namely, changing one's mind, in particular about what and why one holds certain core beliefs does not happen or rather *should* not happen on the basis of disengaged deliberation or leaps of faith. Instead, such changes should take place only through the strenuous process of testing how an alternative belief fits within the overall sense of one's experience and life and what new form of life that this alternative offers. This is the significance of clarifying, articulating, and expressing our strongest moral intuitions. Engaging in Taylorian practical reason requires the hermeneutical contemplation and evaluation of alternatives. As I have suggested, the overtones with the notion of conversion are apt. Of course, it is not that this condition necessarily leads to a movement to "nowhere" (wherever that is). In other words, the possibility of such transitions does not necessarily entail traveling down the road to nihilism. Nonetheless, the difficulty of making such massive shifts in fundamental beliefs raises a pointed challenge to Taylor's claims about the necessity of epiphanies. If these transitions are so difficult to render, then is the crisis of meaning that Taylor laments as severe as he makes it out to be? This is, of course, a different way of asking Taylor whether secularization and disenchantment are as thorough or universal as he claims. Taylor does remark that he is not saying that all of us are suffering from the kind of moral crisis of identity that he believes is endemic to modernity. Adherents to certain forms of evangelicalism and fundamentalism probably would argue that they do not have such problems. Instead, the argument that Taylor presumes about disenchantment and secularization is a more moderate or at least more complex one than found in claims about theistic nihilism and the thorough secularization of the world.

In order to clarify this state of affairs—of agency as melancholic freedom, of the work of the sublime in agency—I will now bring Taylor's project of regenerating agency into conversation with one of the most influential theorists of the American academy: Judith Butler.

4

The Agency That Difference Makes

Judith Butler's Theory of Performativity and the Irony of the Political

Prelude: After Freedom?

> The American Sublime
>
> How does one stand
> To behold the sublime,
> To confront the mockers,
> The mickey mockers
> And plated pairs?
>
> When General Jackson
> Posed for his statue
> He knew how one feels.
> Shall a man go barefoot
> Blinking and blank?
>
> But how does one feel?
> One grows used to the weather,
> The landscape and that;
> And the sublime comes down
> To the spirit itself,
>
> The spirit and space,
> The empty spirit
> In vacant space.
> What wine does one drink?
> What bread does one eat?
>   —Wallace Stevens

Why talk about "agency" rather than "freedom," "autonomy," "liberation," or even "emancipation"? No doubt, there are family resemblances among these terms. Freedom was and still is one of the hallmarks and arguably *the* defining value of modernity, going back at least to the Enlightenment, and arguably even farther back to the Reformation, with Luther and the Protestant movement. In part, the choice of addressing the problem of agency, specifically, the problem of regenerating agency, is also an argument that agency is the counterpart and successor value, if you will, to freedom and emancipation. The move here is not to argue that freedom is no longer viable or desirable. That is hardly the case. Instead, agency, especially in the approaches I am addressing in this book, reflects the conditions of freedom, autonomy, and liberation that are shaped by and in late modernity and postmodernity. I contend that the expressions of freedom generated in modernity—liberation as revolution, autonomy as a moral and political right, and freedom of thought and choice—have in late modernity and postmodernity become co-opted and, in some cases, have lost the sense of urgency and crisis that inspired earlier generations to fight for freedom. To paraphrase Hannah Arendt's largely misunderstood concept, I maintain that late modernity and postmodernity is an epoch in which freedom has become banal. Arendt coined the phrase the "banality of evil" to indicate how acts and institutions of evil had become accepted and made ordinary in the perversions of National Socialism and the Third Reich. Aryan ideologies, the dehumanization of Jews, gypsies, and homosexuals (among others), and subsequent mass murder were made to seem ordinary; that is, Germans diminished the ethical and moral tenor of these acts and institutions of evil and subsequently made them banal.[1]

In considering the religious dimensions of the contemporary discourse on agency, I have come to conclude that something akin to the banality of evil—the desensitization of our moral sensibilities—has taken hold in the political and moral landscape of the late modern and postmodern west. The achievements of freedom (such as liberation, emancipatory movements, and autonomy) have become ordinary; which is to say that they are being taken for granted. This condition is due, in part, to the success of earlier generations of freedom fighters. The civil rights movement is one of the clearest examples we have. The expansion of the franchise and other political rights not only in the United States but also globally as well as the increasing use of democracy and democratization as a requirement for political legitimacy are two of the epoch-making results of the movement. And yet, as with any social movement and the cultures that embrace or reject them, there comes a sense that the quest for political, social, and cultural change comes to an end. For example, in the rancorous debates over affirmative action in the United States, there is an argument made by critics that affirmative action policies amount to special pleading on the part of minorities and women. Affirmative action is no longer needed, so these critics argue, since the political battles for equity and equality have been won.[2] Just as the collective effervescence of social movements wanes when the pragmatic reality of creating policy decisions and constructing institutions that seek to fulfill the ideals of these social movements take the stage of public life, there is an inevitable loss as well as diminishing enthusiasm and urgency in political and social causes. The promise and excitement of revolution turns to the drudgery of reconstruction. Whereas earlier generations of civil rights activists could, with just cause, muster the moral and political attention and energy of vast constituencies, the institutionalization of civil rights has led many to the conclusion that there is no more work to be done in the name of freedom, justice, and equality. The battles are smaller, less spectacular, and often hidden and even obscured from view. To the so-called mainstream of America, for example, talk of the need for emancipation sounds quaint, at best, and to many ears, most likely hysterical (in the sense of sounding both laughable *and* crazy).

The banality of freedom comes about through a paradox. On the one hand, the increase in the life chances, opportunities, and political rights of minorities and women in the United States, for example, have been broadened to a scale thought to be utopian even a few generations ago. On the other hand, there has been in both the critical discourse of American public life as well as in academic discourse a resounding warning that, though the good fight has been fought, work still needs to be done, especially given that political and moral will continues to be lacking.[3] This change in the ethos of freedom—that is, in the transformation in the commitments and sentiments of freedom from the extraordinary to the ordinary and banal—has shifted the critical attention of many theorists (political, social, moral, and religious) from considerations of liberation, emancipation, and even autonomy to work on the problem of regenerating agency. Arguably, the academic discourse most affected by this has been feminist theory.[4]

This is not to say that projects of regenerating agency are completely distinct from projects of freedom. For example, Taylor's philosophy of agency really turns out to be a series of enactments of freedom through different practices of judgment. Accordingly, Taylor's strong evaluation is the act of the moral will to freely judge the differences of worth between higher- and lower-order goods and values. Furthermore, the regeneration of agency through the articulation of the moral sources for identity requires a judgment about what is truly of worth and meaning in life. This in turn entails the expressivist conviction to create freely and express personal, political, and moral values and ideals of integrity.[5] All of these forms of agency as judgment share in the sentiment of freedom, albeit in terms that are distinct from either negative liberty or the minimalist freedom of political and philosophical liberalism. To be an agent, on Taylor's score, is to aspire and strive *for* something, some notion of the good, and not simply to settle for the negative liberty of freedom *from* authority and the like.[6] As I argued in chapter 3, for Taylor, secularism functions as a metaphor that represents the paradoxes of modernity; which is to say, it is a metaphor for what is admirable in modernity, such as the achievements of freedom, tolerance, equal respect, and regard and compassion for human dignity. It is also a metaphor and representation for what ails us in modernity—such as the detachment from the moral ideals that enable human flourishing, or the political and moral challenges posed by the subsequent attenuation and alienation from the sources of agency that would otherwise be more readily available in times of crisis. If the defining features of Taylor's project of regenerating agency are expressivism, moral articulation, and a hermeneutical relationship to tradition, it remains to be seen whether these strategies can fulfill the aspiration for agency for those who stand at the margins of the modern western horizon he knows so well. After all, Taylor's concern in a text such as *Sources of the Self* is to make an argument to political and philosophical liberals, as well as to utilitarians and atomists, that the respective forms of agency they propose (whether they realize it or not) rely on the kind of moral imaginary and sources (justice, benevolence, human dignity, and freedom) that have the status, in practice if not in mind, of higher-order ideals, akin even to virtues. If these partisans of modernity are the targets of Taylor's critique, and if the implied melancholy of modernity relates to the conditions rendered by liberalism, naturalism, and the like, then the possibility remains that those who fall outside of the social and moral conventions and norms (as well as the manners and mores) of the majority culture of the late modern and postmodern west may have a different set of motivations to become agents. For those who stand in society but are not fully *of* society, for those for whom *difference* is not an option of existence but the definitional fact of being—the projects of regenerating agency undertaken by these people may be substantially different from the one Taylor calls for.

While Taylor's project of regenerating agency is primarily a response to what I would call the *exhaustion* of modernity—that is, the depleting and depletion of possibilities rendered by a modern ethos that demands disengaged, value-neutral forms of critical reflection, public life, and self-understanding—for theorists of postmodernism and poststructuralism, projects of regenerating agency are really ways of realizing emancipatory possibilities in post-emancipatory times. To wit, postmodern projects of regenerating agency address the problem of the depleting enthusiasm for emancipatory practices in an age in which the urgency and concern for freedom has become banal. For theorist such as Michel Foucault, Jean-François Lyotard, Jacques Derrida, and Judith Butler, the quest is to find a space and place for agency under conditions in which emancipatory acts appear foreclosed. Toward this end, the melancholic freedom of postmodern agency evokes the overlapping aims of revitalizing political and moral possibilities.

Taylor's lamentations over postmodernism, or at least over postmoderns, is twofold. First, Taylor is critical of theorists such as Derrida and Foucault for rendering political and moral problems into aesthetic forms in which a life is seen as "a work" (of art, of literature). The knock here is related to Taylor's other primary criticism of postmoderns; namely, that the postmodern concern for identity has stretched the seams of the public sphere to such an extent that fragmentation has become the order of the day. In *The Ethics of Authenticity*, for example, Taylor makes the case that the ideal of authenticity, though a powerful and once-influential notion in the development of modern moral identity and culture, has become diminished in an age in which the culture of narcissism (borrowing Christopher Lasch's phrase) dominates through the popularization of forms of atomistic self-fulfillment and the corresponding social fragmentation of public life.[7] Though his communitarian commitments have led him to advocate for versions of difference (this is the crux of "The Politics of Recognition" essay), it remains that Taylor's ambivalence about modernity pushes him to look for order and wholeness in private/personal, social, and political/public life.

The focus of this chapter is a turn toward an alternative vision of agency found in what has come to be called the politics of difference. The discussion I take up is primarily a critical engagement with one of the most influential contemporary theorists of agency: Judith Butler. I begin with some background on the politics of difference, specifically in the context of how it developed within feminist theory. I then move to a sketch of Butler's work on agency, specifically her theory of performativity: from her early critiques of subjectivity and the (near) totalizing effects she grants to power, to her more recent work that nuances the claims about power and agency, specifically in light of her use and appropriation of the idea of melancholy/melancholia.[8] In chapter 5 ("A World *Not* Well Lost"), I interpret Butler's treatment of melancholy as priming a sensibility and attitude that engenders the spiritual, psychological, and political possibilities of agency as a vocation, the topic of the final chapter.

To anticipate: I argue that a comparison between Taylor and Butler shows how each of their projects begins with distinctive forms of melancholy that create the conditions for the possibility of agency. I argue that Butler's turn to the relationship between the social and the psyche/psychic life is a search for possibility and hope under conditions of subjection by power. This search also effectively marks Butler's work as a project of regenerating agency. By characterizing both Taylor's and Butler's approaches to the problem of agency as projects of regeneration, I am proposing a connection that links agency as melancholic freedom to a concern for self-cultivation and self-transformation. I will make the case in the last chapter that projects of regenerating agency qualify as enterprises of spiritual development or advancement, specifically as forms of self-cultivation. In effect, projects of regenerating agency work to cultivate the disposition of attunement to possibilities and hope that are brought to consciousness through the sublime and the religious imagination's response to the sublime. In the end, both Taylor's and Butler's projects of regenerating agency are responses to melancholic freedom, that is, a melancholy over loss that has chastened freedom to speak in hushed, *sotto voce* tones. Projects of regenerating agency are political in orientation and even in intent but are arguably most persuasive as forms of preparation for the political rather than as theories of political action. As preparation for the political (or, as Stephen H. White calls it, a "prefiguring" of the political), these projects of regenerating agency are strongly and deeply suggestive of a desire for cultivation and transformation that is responding to and is in dialogue with transcendence of one form (metaphysical in Taylor's case) or another (material and psychic or psychological in Butler's).[9] Whereas Taylor is sympathetic yet critical of the notion of authenticity in his expressivism, Butler assumes a more oblique and ironic stance toward the authentic. Both look for sources to unsettle conventions and the exhausted *ethos* of modernity, either through the sublime (Taylor) or that which escapes language, such as the body and the psyche (Butler). In other words, while Taylor's agent aspires to critical authenticity and seeks the sublime as an aid to engage and reengage the self with its moral horizons, Butler's agent adopts an attitude toward norms and conventions that uses the critical leverage of the performative as parody and irony. Both approaches to agency speak to the uses of the religious imagination in projects of regenerating agency, especially in the cultivation of the quality of the will, the attention to the aspirations of agency, and the motivations that make agency possible in the first place. I conclude that the conjunction of the quest for meaning, agency, and identity, albeit in different expressions and perhaps intentions, are suggestive as forms of religiosity.

Difference and the Remains of Equality

Inconstancy. Things have various qualities and the soul various tendencies, for nothing presented to the soul is simple, and the soul never applies itself simply to any subject. That is why the same thing makes us laugh and cry.

Diversity. Theology is a science, but at the same time how many sciences? A man is a substance, but if you dissect him, what is he? Head, heart, stomach, veins, each vein, each bit of vein, blood, each humour of blood?

A town or a landscape from afar off is a town and a landscape, but as one approaches it becomes houses, trees, tiles, leaves, grass, ants, ants' legs, and so on *ad infinitum.* All that is comprehended in the word "landscape."
—Blaise Pascal, "Wretchedness" from *Pensées*

In an age in which democracy, albeit in deep complicity with capitalism, is the coin of the global realm, and political liberalism continues to dominate political and moral theoretical discourses despite more than a decade of attempts by communitarians to argue otherwise, it is reasonable to ask why should we persist with the advocacy of "difference." Should the claims of racial minorities, women, gays, and lesbians, and the underclass hold sway in deliberations over the quality of public life or continue to come into consideration in contemplating the ends and aims of human flourishing? How does the commitment to difference fit into projects of regenerating agency? Critics of the politics of difference accuse it of reducing the self to the provenance of the mantra of race, class, gender, and sexuality. In other words, the politics of difference and identity, so the criticism goes, employs these categories as if they are sufficient and complete articulations of what the parameters are for inquiring into, on the one hand, the contestations over political agency and legitimacy and, on the other, the content of cultural identity. Before taking up Butler's project of performativity and agency, it is helpful to first clarify the background discourse on difference and identity, particularly as it unfolded within feminist theory.

The contextual backdrop for this discussion is the contentious debate that took place in the late 1980s and early 1990s in feminist theory over "equality versus difference." As with the "moderate" positions that represent what many consider to be the resolution of the liberalism-communitarian debate— that is, positions sometimes characterized as "communitarian liberalism" or "liberal communitarianism"—a consensus seems to have developed within feminist theory circles that argues that pitting "difference" against "equality" is a false dichotomy.[10] After all, the ideal of equality has proven to be a standard that does not reflect women, minorities, and "the other," but was formulated in accordance with the experiences of white, European-descended, heterosexual, bourgeois men. And yet despite the conclusion that notions of equality as circumscribed in liberal theories of justice or, for that matter, in the "everyday" lives of American culture, have proven to set undesirable and even unattainable social norms for the underrepresented, marginalized, and other subjects of discrimination, feminists theorists and social critics working on race, gender, sexuality, and class insist that a reductionistic, essentializing identity politics still prevails.[11] In short, feminism requires the critical accountability of difference, at minimum, to attempt to recognize and acknowledge the diversity of experience among women.

As I indicated in the prelude to this chapter, while real achievements have been made toward the goals of establishing gender equity in the workplace, widening access to public services and political representation, and expanding opportunities to improve on life chances, these achievements have also *masked* the persistence of discrimination, marginalization, and other forms of oppression. The banality of freedom has taken away the sense of urgency that the civil rights, feminist, workers, and gay rights movements possessed to sustain themselves through struggle: an urgency that sought to attend to the lives and experiences of those who fall under the broad category of difference. The creation of a public culture and laws that purport to ensure equality through educational initiatives, for example, have also served as convenient means of overlooking the endurance of white supremacy, homophobia, sexism, and class bias and degradation.

An example from contemporary rhetoric is instructive on this point. The colloquial use of the phrase "politically correct" has taken on pejorative connotations for many. The upshot of those who label proponents of difference as ascribing to the ideology of political correctness is that attention to racist, sexist, class derogatory, xenophobic, or homophobic attitudes is not really about rights but is simply kowtowing to overly sensitive minorities and women. The charge of being politically correct often comes from those who consider themselves "liberals" and even progressives. These liberals and progressives believe they have in mind a genuine idea and ideal of equality based on a vague notion of universal humanism ("We're all just people *underneath*"). Conversely, the partisans of difference are supposedly being simply that: partisans. Often overlooked by those who use "politically correct" as an epithet (as in the phrase "oh, you're not being critical, because you're just being politically correct") is a failure to recognize that the rhetorical deployment of the term serves to diminish and even dismiss the reality that racism, sexism, homophobia, xenophobia, and class bias are still with us. Public civility, for example, can hide many dark thoughts of racism, discrimination, homophobia, and sexism. The irony, though, of political liberalism is that while it purports to preserve public order through the establishment of moderating principles such as toleration and mutual respect (that is, through principles that require a measure of detachment), these public performances leave potentially harmful "values," such as racism, "private." The point is not that the political should pervade into all realms of the private, but rather that even with moderating principles in play, private hatreds can have harmful effects that are hidden from view through the cover of principles such as toleration. It often takes public crises—the murder of a gay teenager, the beating of Arab Americans, the systematic refusal to allow women and minorities to climb corporate and academic ranks—to reveal hidden harms. But why wait for crises and martyrs? Is physical harm and death simply the price of civil and political liberalism? Or can a more vigorous account of difference do more?

The effort to safeguard equality among all human beings (a claim made, for example, in the discourse on human rights) requires the accountability provided by the politics of difference. The plight of women in times of war and the differential programs and effects of vaccination and aid distribution in the west versus Africa and Asia are two obvious examples of how attention to difference and diversity can be matters of life and death. The politics of difference begins with the critique of essentializing tendencies in which generalizations made about the past—as well as prescriptions for what should be the normative experience of "women," "minorities," "blacks," "queers," and "the poor"—continue to shape collective life and the dynamics of the public sphere and public policy, as well as how we understand agency itself. For many, it remains that the postmodern appeal to difference articulates a powerful and necessary antiessentialist critique. This is the case, for example, for the countervailing approaches found within feminist theory and race theory that attempt to conceptualize moral character on the basis of *experience*.[12]

Thus, a problematic arises within the rationale and logic of the politics of difference: is it possible to sustain experience as a viable category of identity while simultaneously maintaining a critique of essentialism? Whose experience counts in these analyses? Intellectual elites? The hoi polloi? I want to argue that the critique of essentialism *and* the work of agency go hand in hand. The appeal to "experience" will always provide some inflection and deviation from a posited generalization, which is to say that experience is by its nature a critical and crucial pivot for realizing agency.[13] Consider the discourse on race. How does the opposition between "blackness" and "whiteness" define most if not all discourses about race? There is a way in which, without historical, cultural, social, and political analyses of experience, "race" as a category is sifted and reduced to "a black issue," rather than a discourse about a multivalent, multiracial reality. Furthermore, deviation is an inevitable consequence in any broad, generalizable marker of identity. This is why normative claims about the moral character of women or "the black experience" should be open to revision. Thus, proponents of the politics of difference, often branded with the blanket term "postmoderns," appear to be left with a stark and problematic choice: either adopting capacious categories of identity and subjectivity that overlook more than they represent, or going with fragmented and decentered conceptions of subjectivity that abjure any attempts to describe and define identity as essentialist and therefore unacceptable.

Critics of difference and so-called postmodern politics, such as Taylor, argue that positing "fractured" or "fragmented" identities militates against any form of viable politics.[14] If we follow the reasoning of postmodernism fully, so the critics of difference argue, we must abandon any conception of the self altogether and therefore give up on the project of engaged political agency.[15] Given such possibilities, the concern is that postmodernism serves the factionalizing and fracturing purposes of oppression and dominance by white, masculinist, heterosexist culture and society. In other words, the postmodern advocacy of difference reinforces the cultural and social norms that it purportedly is attempting to resist.[16]

This is surely a powerful critique of the politics of difference. Nonetheless, the critique seems to function on the basis of two questionable assumptions about desires. The first assumption is that a claim of difference (of gender, sexuality, race, class, and so on) represents a desire to remain "separate," as in the idea of living and being apart from the rest of society and culture. The second assumption of the critique presumes that identifying with "fractured" identities or to adopt a notion of decentered subjectivity means that this is a desirable mode of being. I will take up the second concern about fragmented and decentered subjectivity more fully in the discussion of Butler's work that follows. Let me here address the first assumption about difference as a desire for separation from dominant culture and society.

The separatist tendencies of the politics of difference ring true insofar as they reflect the social and political realities of many societies, American and otherwise. As such, there are correlations between racism, class discrimination, and homophobia, on the one hand, and the creation, for example, of racial/ethnic and same-sex enclaves and ghettoes in class-stratified cities and suburbs, on the other hand. Theorists and critics of difference argue that forms of separatism are inevitable insofar as the United States remains a chronically racist, class-stratified, homophobic, and sexist state.[17] This notwithstanding, the charge that women who advocate for the politics of difference are separatists by design often come from white, "mainstream" feminists who argue on the basis of a reformed and refined political liberalism. Feminists who also consider themselves political liberals, such as Seyla Benhabib, argue for the necessity of assuming a pragmatic approach that ensures that women/feminists present some kind of united front in public sphere encounters, that is, engagement in the realms of the political, the cultural, and the social. Nonetheless, the political pragmatism of creating voting blocks or overarching policy initiatives can prove counterproductive. There is an ironic undercutting of feminist principles in reformed, feminist liberalism. For example, in the construction of categories such as "women's rights," the potential is great for an antiliberal bias to take hold through the deployment of the metacategory of "women." Generic identity categories can minimize rather than account for the different experiences of racial minorities, women, lesbians and bisexuals, and the underclass. In other words, feminists have engaged and continue to struggle with multiple public spheres: the public of majority/majoritarian society; the public of diverse feminist communities; and the public of constituencies that are neither part of the mainstream of society nor of conventional feminist groups, such as communities of color and gay, lesbian, and bisexual communities and so on. The demands of feminists who are also political liberals have often framed the discussion of difference in the simplistic terms that charge that claims for difference are politically irrelevant and/or detract from arguments about equality, which are presumably based on the principles of liberal humanism.[18]

Just as Taylor's project focuses largely on a critique of the costs of freedom and subjectivity in modernity, the core of the debate over difference versus equality for feminists was, and perhaps still is, the question of the costs of postmodernism insofar as postmodernism represents a call to account for the specificity and diversity of experience. Postmodernism and difference often raise unsettling questions for feminists about the politicization of life. As I suggested earlier, feminists who are also political liberals, such as Benhabib, argue that the politics of difference does more harm than good. The politics of difference, or what Benhabib labels "the cultural studies approach", diminishes political efficacy through the relativism that underlies claims to difference and through the destabilization of the political subject as fragmented and decentered. Along similar lines to Taylor's constructive project in *Sources of the Self*, Benhabib argues that the ends and aims of feminism are better served by narrative and coherentist conceptualizations of the self. In other words, feminists such as Benhabib prioritize *political* agency over other forms of agency and subsequently dismiss as politically unviable and psychologically unmanageable approaches to agency, subjectivity, and identity that are not narrative and coherentist in form.[19] The rhetoric of "the personal is political" takes on existential freight when difference is seen as a series of litmus tests over the legitimacy of representation (who can speak for "us," for example). A further concern arises as to whether or not the political claims for difference and those made on behalf of equality amount to a standoff between incommensurable positions. In short, it is imperative to ask the following: does a cultural (and by implication political) identity need to be a complete articulation of a specific identity in order to achieve salient political goals? If not, then must we persist with attempts to represent and account for the increasing specificity of the ever-growing and changing group of participants in the politics of difference?[20] Does the aspiration for greater correspondence between cultural identity and the self, even as a dynamic product of construction, increase the life chances of the oppressed and marginalized?

The Arts of Resistance and the Agency That Difference Makes

[W]e can read ourselves against another people's pattern, but since it is not ours ... we emerge as its effects, its errata, its counternarratives. Whenever we try to narrate ourselves, we appear as dislocations in their discourse.
            —Edward Said, *After the Last Sky: Palestinian Lives*

> Scraps of heard, of seen things, in
> Ward a thousand and one,
>
> day-nightly
> the Bear-Polka:
>
> you're being re-educated,
>
> they'll turn you back into
> he.
>   —Paul Celan, from *Lichtzwang*

And yet: what if attempts to establish a narrative and coherence to identity—political, cultural, and psychic identity—amount to a pipe dream? What if choosing a coherent self over supposedly incommensurable identity markers—of sexuality, gender, class, and race—is *not* a genuine option? That is, what if the imperative to construct and identify a coherent and narrative self proves to annihilate that which has shaped you or is most dear to you, such as a heritage and history of racialized existence, class bias, or same-sex desire? What if projects of regenerating agency are oriented not toward establishing wholeness and harmony but rather toward the cultivation of strategies of survival, if not full-blown flourishing, in the face of uncertainty? What if projects of regenerating agency that seek out an enabling moral psychology, measured by the invocation of ends that motivate and inspire the agent, are not predicated on conventional forms of meaning(fulness), legitimacy, and coherence but rather seek modes of agency that begin with and refuse to let go of the experience of loss, deprivation, and discrimination? What kind of agency and subjectivity might come from these experiences? Is it possible to move the discourse on difference away from the problem of divided loyalties and toward a focus on the unavoidability of pain and loss that sits at the heart of the claims of difference? Furthermore, what if loss is not only the beginning but also the middle and the end of theorizing about agency?

It is with these questions and the background of the difference versus equality debate in mind that I turn to Judith Butler's work on agency, difference, and performativity. Butler's writing has been enormously influential in gender studies and in the creation of the field of queer studies. It has also served as a resource for theorists who deal with the problems of difference, identity, and agency in social theory, political theory, literary theory, and the study of religion. Through the development of her theory of performativity and the increasing attention she has shown to the relationship between the political, the social, and the psychic, Butler has been at the forefront of the advancement of a school of poststructuralist thought that has been trying to move beyond earlier preoccupations with the totalizing effects of power. In light of this, she is, I would argue, the intellectual successor to Michel Foucault. In works such as *Discipline and Punish*, Foucault powerfully and dramatically presented the early poststructuralist claims that seemed to reduce all forms of life and identity as products of social construction. Butler has consistently examined and engaged the persistent effects of power, while simultaneously seeking to uncover the possibilities of agency within cultural, social, and political regimes. For some critics, like Martha Nussbaum, the kind of theory Butler engages in marks the beginning of the end of the usefulness of theory as a form of practice.[21] And yet for others, the theory of performativity has been an engrossing and productive resource to interrogate the constant shifts in individual and collective identity, especially given the way it highlights the relationship between cultural production and political life, as

well as helps to uncover the continuities and discontinuities between the social, the cultural, and the psychic.

With the publication in 1990 of *Gender Trouble*, Butler gained notoriety, as
well as infamy, for the highly provocative claim that "woman" is no longer
a legitimate or viable category of identity. She devised the claim as a critique of
foundationalist and essentialist accounts of gender, thereby laying the groundwork for an ambitious critique of the ethical subject. I will say more about the
latter in the next chapter in my discussion of Butler's treatment of melancholy.
In the meantime, consider the rejection of the identity categories of "woman"
and "sex" in the following passage from *Gender Trouble*:

> At stake is not whether it still makes sense, strategically or tran-
> sitionally, to refer to women in order to make representational claims
> on their behalf. The feminist "we" is always and only a phantasma-
> tic construction, one that has its purposes, but which denies the
> internal complexity and indeterminacy of the term and constitutes
> itself only through the exclusion of some part of the constituency that
> it simultaneously seeks to represent.[22]

In this passage, Butler raises what have become common criticisms of
essentialist treatments of identity. The feminist "we" is descriptive of "women"
for some pragmatic purposes but not for all contexts. As I described earlier, the
criticism of the lack of accountability of the "large" identity categories inevitably excludes many who are meant to be constituents of the categories: in
this case, *all* women. Who falls outside of these identity categories? Generally
speaking, it is those who are considered abject, deviant, and aberrant (such as
lesbian women, transsexuals, or bisexuals, or nonwhites, and so on) who tend
to fall outside the purview of meta-identities such as "women." Certainly, a
counterargument comes quickly to mind in the form of a caveat: the deployment of these identity categories (mostly) occurs in rhetorical situations in
which there is some *common* understanding of the parameters of the meaning
of a category such as "women;" that is, the speaker and the audience share
some mutual agreement as to who does and does not fall under the category.
Nonetheless, in the political rally, in the classroom, and even within families,
assumptions about "sameness" or identity can force difference into hiding.

While there is some merit in this counterargument, it also serves to demonstrate Butler's point: when it comes to claims about identity, exclusion is
inevitable. And since not all exclusions are alike in how they shape and constitute lives, the point about mutual understanding in the inclusiveness and
exclusion of identity is more problematic than it might at first appear. No doubt,
it is a truism to say that a category of identity will not fully describe or depict
the experience of all who purportedly fall under the category. In short, there
are always exceptions to any rule, and categories of identity often serve rule-
based functions, for example, in regard to membership and even citizenship.

Nonetheless, the claims to difference, as well as the critiques of essentialist identity politics, are not meant as salves for the white, male, mainstream soul. Instead, they serve as the critical responses of those whose experiences fall, paradoxically, within, yet outside of, conventions and norms that have potentially harmful social, political, and psychic effects. There are, subsequently, qualities of symbolic death that are identifiable with the experiences of the constituents of difference.[23] If difference is accepted and made innocuous, then a significant political impetus is lost. This is evident in a historical moment that has seen significant cultural sea changes marked by the ascension of women as heads of corporations and universities as well as the popularity of openly gay characters on television. And yet when difference is seen as a threat (whether or not the acceptance of difference is actual), or the occasion for crisis, the perception remains that the need for social change has diminished.[24] *This* is the problem of the banality of freedom.

With this background of the parochialism found in identity politics and the subsequent neglect of difference in mind, Butler introduces in *Gender Trouble* her theory of performativity: an approach and critique that focuses on the play of language and discourse on how we understand the self/subjectivity and agency. In *Gender Trouble* and subsequent texts, Butler generates her theory of performativity through a creative appropriation of two different versions of speech act theory: one by J. L. Austin in his lectures published as *How to Do Things with Words*; and the other by Jacques Derrida in his landmark essay "Signature, Event, Context," which is itself a commentary on Austin.[25] In performativity, language is not always a vessel of meaning; it is often a mode of action. Thus, Austin argues that language is not simply descriptive of the real; that is, it is not always reflective of statements of fact as found in claims about truth or falsity. Such statements of description are "constative utterances." Instead, a great deal of language is made up of "performative utterances." Performative utterances are simultaneously statements *and* actions; that is, saying or making a statement/utterance is also the performance of an action. "I challenge you [to a duel]," "I forgive you for lying," or "You are hereby authorized to pay" are all examples Austin gives of performatives.[26] Performative utterances assume their status as actions through a rhetorical situation in which there is some basis of agreement between the intention of the speaker and the reception of the utterance/performative by an audience who hears the utterance. Austin does not equate words with acts; nor does he argue that acts are reducible to words. Instead, he maintains that context and circumstances (the mutuality of understanding and the tacit agreement on the meaning of a word or convention) is the required setting and background for a performative to serve as an action. Austin's concern is to establish that performatives can have a kind of power—what he calls the "force of utterances" as "perlocutionary" statements—in contrast with illocutionary statements that produce effects. While I would argue that the distinction that Austin makes

between the perlocutionary and the illocutionary is less marked than he suggests, the larger significance of the approach for Butler's purposes is the
notion that language has a reach beyond statements and judgments of fact,
truth, or falsity. In other words, Austin provides Butler with an anti-realist
theory of language that is in line with the core of her own theoretical formulations: namely, her anti-foundationalism and anti-essentialism.[27] Furthermore, an additional and perhaps more significant appeal for Butler is Austin's
insistence that there is no self prior to language; that is, there is no performer
independent of or prior to the performance/performative itself. Before elaborating on this point, a word on Derrida's treatment of performatives as a resource for Butler is in order.

Austin goes to great pains to demonstrate that the accountability and
avoidance of misunderstandings and miscues are contingencies and conditions of language functioning with the force of the performative. Nonetheless,
in terms of the political aims Butler has in mind, which include subversion of
the claims of gender ontology and universalist assertions about moral subjectivity, Austin's cautionary moves on misunderstanding, though fruitful, do not
go far enough. For Butler, Derrida's deconstructionist techniques of destabilization prove to be a necessary mediation of Austin's idea of the performative.[28] Recall that Butler seeks to interrogate the limits of claims of gendered
subjectivity and the moral and political implications that follow from such
claims. Her critique in regard to difference is against the essentializing tendencies found in identity politics, in which monolithic categories such as
"women" or "blacks" suppress difference while intending to account for it. She
is able to synthesize Austin's notion of the performative with explicitly political
concerns by way of the method of parody she borrows from Derrida, as well as
through a vigilance about the demands and effects of power she gets from
Foucault. In fact, the possibility of agency for Butler arises from reading performativity as a "practice of parody" as well as a "constitutive constraint" that
constructs the conditions "to be able to think, to live, to make sense at all."[29] In
other words, on the one hand, Butler's theory of agency requires performing
the constructs and constitutive effects of discourse and language as the repertoire and stage for "life" to take place, while, on the other hand, the performativity of existence occurs through unpredictable repetitions, citations, and
reiterations of social norms. The unreliability of the "accurate" performance
opens up for Butler the possibility for agency as resistance and subversion.
Given Austin's cautions about misunderstanding, parody and the parodic fall
outside of his account of the performative. Conversely, the unintended and
unanticipated consequences and reception of language and discourse fall
squarely in the wheelhouse of deconstruction and poststructuralism. According to Butler, the practice of parody is able to produce "subversive repetitions"
of the compulsory norms of identity categories. In other words, the fact that it
is possible to repeat a compulsory norm of heterosexual, gendered, or other

forms of social identity in a manner that proves to be not only "inauthentic" but also subversive is simultaneously an act of resistance and of parody.

In *Bodies That Matter*, Butler expands on the agency possibilities of language and discourse she introduced in her deconstruction of the category of "sex" and "woman" in *Gender Trouble*. While parody works as a form of irony that seeks to reveal the fallacy of identity categories such as "sex" by working within and against the authoritative codes and regulations of particular cultural regimes, it does not necessarily reveal, as social theorists like to say, a way out of the dynamics and binds of structure versus agency. In order to probe deeper into how it is possible to be within a system but not completely subject to its mandates, Butler turns to the question of the source of the force of performatives, that is, determining how and why performative norms have the power that they do. Thus, in *Bodies that Matter*, Butler looks at Derrida's reading of Austin, specifically Derrida's rendering of the performative as a practice of reiteration and citation that a discourse produces. In "Signature, Event, Context," Derrida asks:

> Could a performative utterance succeed if its formulation did not repeat a "coded" or iterable utterance, or in other words, if the formulae that I pronounce in order to open a meeting, launch a ship or a marriage [all examples from Austin] were not identifiable as *conforming* with an iterable model, if it were not thus identifiable in some way as "citation"?...[I]n such typology, the category of intention will not disappear, but from that place it will no longer be able to govern the entire scene and system of utterance [*l'énonciation*].[30]

The force of the performative derives from the prior legitimation of the speaker as an authority to repeat or cite a formula. For example, the judge or the priest has and is perceived to have the authority to repeat or cite a formula such as "I declare you man and wife" with the force of law behind her/his pronouncement. Significantly, the discursive power of the performative does not mean that there is a prediscursive "I" or subject prior to the enunciation/citation/ iteration of the performative. Analogously, this reflects the constructivism that Butler reads into gendered subjectivity. The judge or priest does not have the force of law and authority "outside" the performative discourse, that is, the "acts" of speaking in a particular context, historical moment, and rhetorical situation.

Butler's theory of performativity seeks to establish the possibility of both political efficacy and agency, as well as generate new terms of legitimacy for gender and sexuality in cultures and societies. Butler's use of performativity, repetition, and citation develops an understanding of the subject/self who is constantly negotiating the social, cultural, political, and even psychic sources for identity that emerge from the distinctions and inflections established by power. Performativity deals with a self that is always already *in media res*. There is no conjecture about the reality or possibility of a prediscursive subject. And yet, the self is not a passive recipient in this process. Instead, for Butler, there is a "there there," that is, a person who is receiving, enacting, and responding to power. In other words, Butler is advancing a theory of the subject that stands in contradistinction to an interpretation of poststructuralism that posits the self as a thorough social construction, whereby power is absolute.

As I indicated earlier, Butler gained notoriety in *Gender Trouble* through her critique of the adequacy of the category of "woman" and the usefulness of categories such as "sex." At first blush, this kind of claim would appear to put a discussion of agency entirely off the map, insofar as it frames identity and subjectivity outside of the rhetorical repertoire of political and cultural legitimacy. The criticism Butler faced was similar to the charge often made against the work of the early Foucault (that is, after the publication of *Discipline and Punish*), namely, that the account of power, language, and discourse is too totalizing and deterministic. Discourse and language may shape the subject, but they do not fully create and construct the self, so critics argued.[31] In her writings since the publication of *Gender Trouble*, especially in *Bodies That Matter*, *Excitable Speech*, and *The Psychic Life of Power*, Butler has responded to these critiques and subsequently nuanced her theories of ethical and gendered subjectivity as responsive to the effects and responses to power; which is to say, she has developed a more nuanced analysis of the relationship between the forces of the social imaginary and the dynamics of the psyche.

Butler now admits that the position she took in *Gender Trouble* on the impossibility of subjectivity was hyperbolic.[32] Rather than grant the social play of power and culture with the ability to construct the self (her feminist version of the Foucauldian social construction of the subject), she now stresses the language of "constituting" and the "constitution" of the subject over terms such as constructivism. In short, she has shifted and granted the individual subject more play and flexibility in responding to the forces of power by arguing that power enables as well as oppresses through the enactments and citations of discourse and language. In other words, through speech acts, discourse *constitutes the subject* rather than constructs it. To critics of poststructuralism and the postmodern, the distinction may look like hairsplitting. Nonetheless, the distinction between constructing the self/subject and constituting the self/subject is significant. Arguing for the notion of the construction of the subject leaves the theorist vulnerable to the interpretation that power is total and complete. This is precisely the kind of reading that left Butler's theory of performativity open to the criticism of being self-contradictory. How can one engage in the practices of parody or subversive repetition, for example, if power is absolute in shaping the subject? If it is absolute, as Foucault's description of the effects (the shaping, really) of the penal system on prisoners suggests, then the poststructuralist critique of the impossibility of agency persists. In tempering her position in regard to the subject—that is, in arguing that the subject is constituted rather than constructed—Butler has made a shift not only from what had seemed like a preoccupation with the seamlessness of social power but also to a more complex account of power and agency that focuses on the materiality of the body as well as on the constitution of the moral subjectivity of the psyche. For the latter, she has turned not only to Freud to supplement the resources she finds in Foucault, but also to Althusser and an interpretation of the problematic of the subjection of moral consciousness and the psyche by social conventions.

Butler has also responded to critics who read her as arguing that the subject is constituted *only* by discourse. She still has to determine, so her critics argue, how the constitution of the subject takes place, that is, through which mechanisms, institutions, and media. As I have already mentioned, she has backed off from what now looks like a hyperbolic position that the subject is constructed entirely by discourse. In her work subsequent to *Gender Trouble* Butler has done this by arguing that other factors, not the least of which are the materiality of the body and the unpredictable dynamics of the psyche, come into play in the constitution of the subject. Though a certain logic dictates that a consideration of Lacan's psychoanalytical approach is warranted in an exploration of this relationship between discourse (as language and languages that arise from the political, the cultural, the social, and the psychic) and subjectivity, Butler turns instead to early (Freud) and to more recent psychoanalytical sources (Althusser, Kristeva) to supplement her theory of performativity with theories of subjection.[33] It is significant that though she does not reject Foucault's poststructuralism altogether in making this move, she has come to acknowledge the limitations of a discourse on power that does not account for the psyche, as well as for "the vulnerability and the unpredictability of subject constitution."[34]

On the one hand, Butler's theory of performativity reveals the "untruth" of identity norms and the ways these norms erase and/or mask particularity. On the other hand, the theory also suggests how agency is possible despite the social construction of these norms. Performativity works with a picture of the self that is *in media res*, and thus always already involved in the process of constituting the subject. As I noted earlier, Butler's move away from a "power is absolute" perspective required an argument that the subject is not a passive recipient in the process of constitution. There is a "there there": one that is subject to structurally imposed norms of identity and yet *complicit* in the performance of speech acts, especially in the perpetuation of these norms. Thus, the character of agency and subject constitution that performativity suggests is not devoid of a self-conscious self. On the other hand, the performativity of the speech act—that is, the enactment of identity as gendered, racialized, and so on—means that there are inherent constraints to the performance of identity that occur within and against the repertoire of available cultural categories.

Therefore, the conditions of performativity do not subscribe to the notion of freedom as complete liberation or emancipation from extant oppressive structures of meaning and the organization of the lifeworld. According to Butler, the subject performs social norms through a complicity in the appropriation, internalization, and citation or repetition of identity categories. The critical paradox of Butler's theory of agency is that she argues that implicit within the performance of these oppressive and exclusionary categories is the possibility of the subversion and transformation (perhaps even replacement or displacement) of these modes of identity, and thus the *possibility* of engendering agency. Butler's main point about agency is that it takes place in and through the moments of the performative, that is, in the gaps and ironic repetitions that are made possible through the very contingency of discourse and language. Performativity and the repetition/citation of identity norms provide insight into the politically contested and yet cooperatively constructed character of identity categories. In short, the very conditions that power shapes and oppresses are also the limits and conditions that enable the agency work of resistance and subversion in the first place.

To clarify this picture of agency as complicit yet subversive, as performative yet resisting, consider Butler's discussion of the changes in the use of the term "queer." The transformation of "queer" from an epithet to a symbol of empowerment is an illuminating example of what Butler calls the "catachrestic performance" of performativity. "Catachresis" is an incorrect yet purposeful use of words, through irony, parody, and mixed metaphors. In the case of a social norm and signifier such as "queer," the transformation of its idiomatic use took place through the catachresis of a stereotype and identity norm that eventually created a new field of discourse around the term. Prior to its subversive turn, "queer" had carried the freight of hatred, marginalization, and abjection. Through performative inversions, "queer" has gained the cachet of a marker of empowerment, subversion, and coalition for gays and lesbians. This co-optation of a pejorative identity category is an instructive example of how performativity, citationality, and negotiation work as subversive and ironic discourse. For Butler, the subversion occurs within an extant discourse; hence we can witness how agency emerges from a situation of marginalization and oppression. She writes: "We no more create from nothing the political terms that come to represent our 'freedom' than we are responsible for the terms that carry the pain of social injury. And yet, neither of those terms are as a result any less necessary to work and rework within political discourse."[35] Butler identifies this as the logic or reasoning behind laying claim to identity categories such as "women," "queer," "gay," and "lesbian." These are terms that have subjected, respectively, women, gays, and lesbians in the past without their consent. However, in the performative parody of these terms arises the potential for political and cultural subversion. How? Recognizable though negative categories of identity, terms such as "queer" indicate the abject and marginalized status of the subjects they name; at the same time, these terms provide rallying points for political representation and coalition.

There is a similar move made in racialized political and cultural discourse. For example, "brown" has been transposed from a pejorative term into a signifier of affirmation for Chicana/os. Calling a Chicana/o "brown" requires a speaker to employ the term knowingly *and* ironically. This affirms that the speaker (and presumably the audience) acknowledges a history of derogation and racism while also recognizing the ongoing work of resistance to the effects of that history. Irony and parody, subversive repetition and citation all require some kind of "inside" knowledge. As Butler says, "the necessity to mobilize the necessary error identity (Spivak's term) will always be in tension with the democratic contestation of the term which works against its deployments in racist and misogynist discursive regimes."[36] In other words, despite the "inaccuracy" of markers or signifiers such as "queer" or "brown," these terms have become shibboleths to cultural and political participation. After all, it is safe to declare that universal consensus or agreement on how to apply a term such as "queer" or "brown" to gays and lesbians and Chicana/os will most likely never come about. The point is that the democratic disputes within an identity "group" are necessary for the expanded use of these terms and to contribute to their deconstruction.

As with all rule-governed activity, there is always variation in any attempt to adhere to a rule. We find this in music, for example. Regardless of the degree of specificity, a composer may impose or designate in a piece of music (meter and tempi settings, dynamic markings, and so on), it is left to the musician's performance to give the music life, that is to say, *to make it an experience*. No two performances, even by the same set of musicians, are alike. Moods and temperaments, the chemistry of an ensemble, audience size and expectations, and even concentration levels and mental lapses affect how closely (if at all) the composer's intentions will be matched (repeated, enunciated, cited) in performance. On the one hand, it is through these deviations from a standard that new forms of style are set, as in the case of the early music movement. On the other hand, the possibility of deviation is what gives the individual performer freedom of expression and interpretation.

The Religious Imagination and the Performative Agent

Certainly, there will always be a gap or cultural lag between broad, normative identity categories and individual experience. This has been a critical issue in sociology of culture and anthropological methodology for decades. Feminist theorists such as Butler and postcolonial theorists such as Homi Bhabha are stressing that we should begin with the assumption that there will always be a gap associated with theorizing about identity, and *then* move from there. As Butler argues:

> Insofar as heterosexual gender norms produce inapproximable ideals, heterosexuality can be said to operate through the regulated production of hyperbolic versions of "man" and "woman." These are for the most part compulsory performances, ones which none of us choose, but which each of us is forced to negotiate. I write "forced to negotiate" because the compulsory character of these norms does not always make them efficacious. Such norms are continually haunted by their own inefficacy; hence, the anxiously repeated effort to install and augment their jurisdiction.
>
> The resignification of norms is thus a function of their *inefficacy*, and so the question of subversion, of *working the weakness in the norm*, becomes a matter of inhabiting the practices of rearticulation.[37]

"Working the weakness of the norm"—Butler's aphoristic formulation of performativity—allows the subject to become an agent. By working the weakness of a norm, the speaker or actor is able to salvage a surplus of meaning from the social norms associated with categories such as "queer" or "brown." In other words, an identity that sustains conventions, manners, and mores can simultaneously generate subversive consciousness. The subversive act of enunciation is disruptive yet oddly faithful to language and discourse. It implies being in and of language and discourse yet somehow being outside of it at the same time. This doubleness brings to mind Stanley Cavell's Emersonian perfectionism that posits the idea of the "next self," in which "next" implies a temporal sequence (as in the notion of a self that is to come and that is, hopefully, attainable), as well as proximity (as in the idea of standing *next* to another person).[38] I will press Cavell's reading of Emersonian perfectionism into fuller service in the final chapter in my discussion of agency, cultivation, and vocation.

The main point I am making here is that Butler's use of performativity as a resource for subversion and resistance to power qualifies her work as a project of regenerating agency. While it is perhaps more obvious in Taylor's case, I maintain that Butler's project of regenerating agency is also a call for the cultivation and the transformation of the self. No doubt, I have some work ahead of me in the remaining chapters to argue that the aspiration and desire for cultivation and agency constitute expressions of the religious imagination. Nonetheless, to anticipate a bit: the features of a desire not merely for social change but, more fundamentally, for a change *within* and *for* the self are evident in Butler's project of regenerating agency. This is the power of the performative. Furthermore, her project of regenerating agency also focuses, despite denials to the contrary, on a longing to cultivate meaningful subjectivity. Analogous to the reading I offered of Taylor, the religious and spiritual significance of Butler's project of regenerating agency is not found in the specific ends and aims of the project, but rather in the *qualities of aspiration and striving*. These qualities signify a desire for transcendence, though not in the metaphysical sense of Taylor's moral sources (those sources that are "beyond life") but rather in the immanent experience of yearning to move beyond the conditions of life as they currently affect and constitute us. This yearning and aspiration are tied to what I have been calling the religious imagination: the faculty and ability to envision and, in Butler's case, to enact a new life, the "next self." As with Taylor's expressivism, the agency of performativity—of subversive parody, repetition, and citation—requires the religious imagination to spur catachresis, that is, to express a "truer" self in the risks that are taken by *not* adhering to the normative force of power. After all, is it not the imagination that brings together disjunctive, seemingly disparate elements? David Hume meant as much when he wrote: "The imagination of man [*sic*] is naturally sublime, delighted with whatever is remote and extraordinary, and running, without control, into the most distant parts of space and time in order to avoid the objects, which custom has rendered too familiar to it."[39] This effort to bring together disjunctive elements is also evocative of the dialectic that the Romantics sought to sustain between authenticity and irony. The dialectic is a play of the imagination that emerges from efforts to maintain and strive for a sense of integrity and authenticity through a disciplined and paradoxical movement between risking idealizing hubris and the tempering influence of critical irony. As such, it is the imagination that renders the authentic real while also applying the judgments of reason through the critical reflection and detachment of irony.[40]

Though irony is more clearly represented in Butler's approach than it is in Taylor's, it is possible to discern ironic elements in Taylor's expressivism, albeit in mostly oblique ways, and primarily through his understanding of practical reasoning as giving the best account possible for how moral judgment works. In other words, if there is irony in Taylor, it is evident primarily in the critical attitude he maintains in order to uncover the false-necessities held by the social imaginaries of modernity, that is, the cultural norms that stress secularism as the best means of maintaining social order. Butler, as I have already said, is more squarely within the parameters of the ironic, particularly in what I referred to as the doubleness inherent in maintaining performativity as a subversive medium for the realization of agency. Conversely, whereas Taylor's expressivism is more deeply aligned with the Romantic idea of authenticity and the self-reliant sense of being true to oneself, there appears to be an undercurrent of authenticity running throughout Butler's discussion of performativity and the possibility of agency. Why else, for example, would the subject of difference experience discontent with social norms, conventions, and mores? The doubleness of the self allows for the possibility of one self (the self of difference) to thwart the other self (the self constituted by social norms). This is not to say that irony implies a lack of commitment. On the contrary, in Romanticism as well as in Socratic discourse, irony only has force and persuasion if one has a conviction in and a piety to a position or belief that somehow lies "outside" of the conventions of common understanding. Charles Larmore describes irony this way:

> [I]ronic two-mindedness depends on commitment. And so it has a place for a sense of belonging and for the recognition that our moral substance stems not from reason as such but from the form of life within which alone we can reflect critically about what to believe and do. Irony amounts to the awareness that such belonging can never be total and all-absorbing. In some cases, ironic distance may involve imagining how commitments, which we have so far no reason to question, might nonetheless be replaced by something different or better. But irony is not fundamentally an "epistemological" attitude, in which we entertain how beliefs might be revised. It expresses, instead, the essential nonidentity between the commitments we have and our ability to commit ourselves.[41]

The consonance of Larmore's description of ironic commitment with Butler's understanding of performative agency as "working the weakness of the norm" is clear. Romantic irony and performative agency speak not only of embeddedness within a social world but also to the struggles of maintaining moral commitments that escape the compass of a given form of life. Furthermore, Butler's performative agency is also suggestive of the Romantic value of striving and aspiring to breach the constraints of the conventional. Nonetheless, this raises the following question: given the inherent play of the ironic for Butler's performative agent, are irony and parody genuinely sufficient means of escaping the forces that compel the self/subject to inhabit social norms? Why and how does a self/agent advance the risk of subversive performativity in the first place? Under the political, social, and cultural conditions marked by the banality of freedom, what spurs agency? One answer might be the undercurrent of authenticity I alluded to earlier. But more likely it has to do with the fundamental disposition of *ambivalence* that Butler identifies as a central feature of the moral psyche: an ambivalence born of a life shaped by the paradox of foreclosure and the desire for a robust social and psychic identity. This hard-won identity seeks to gain clarity for a self that has become obscure to itself. So it is that authenticity and irony, when engrossed by ambivalence, dwells in the challenges of identifying and identifying with self-discoveries as well as the attendant losses of and for the self. This brings me to the enormously important place of melancholia in the psychic life of difference.

5

A World *Not* Well Lost

Melancholy, Foreclosure, and Agency

Recollection's love is the only happy love, says an author who, as far
as I know him, is at times somewhat deceitful, not in the sense
that he says one thing and means another but in the sense that he
pushes the thought to extremes, so that if it is not grasped with
the same energy, it reveals itself the next instant as something else.
He advances this thesis in such a way that one is easily tempted
to agree with him and then forgets that the thesis itself expresses the
most profound melancholy, so that a deep depression concentrated
in one single line could scarcely express it better.
—Søren Kierkegaard, *Repetition*

What compels us to follow one set of practices over another, to take
one set of conventions and codes of conduct as compulsory, or to
accept certain norms as legitimate and others as illegitimate? In a
manner of speaking, agency and the self or identity find common
purpose through the identification of sources of normativity. The self
as moral *and* political agent asks: What is it I feel compelled to do?
What induces this feeling of obligation in me, such that what I do is
also a reflection of who I am? There is, of course, the Kantian answer
to these questions that puts forward the test of universalizability—the
categorical imperative—and uses humanizing ends as regulative
ideals to establish principles of action.[1] Our duty and obligation to
a universalizable moral law—our ability to legislate such a law *to
ourselves*—is the basis of our autonomy, according to Kant. Our obligation and conformity to the moral law is, as Cavell says about
Kant, how we express our moral selves.[2] For Kant, morality is set in

opposition to our natural inclinations, such that duty "infringes [thwarts] all my inclinations."[3] Kant regards inclinations and feelings as uncontrollable and hence as unreliable resources for morality. As finite, fallen human beings, we need the compulsion of duty to keep our inclinations and desires in line in order for the will to act and choose on the basis of moral principles. Without the "ought" of the law, we would merely follow conventions and external sources of authority (what Kant calls "heteronomy"). As Kant says in the *Groundwork of the Metaphysics of Morals*:

> Since I have deprived the will of every impulse that could arise for it from obeying some law, nothing is left but the conformity of actions as such with universal law, which alone is to serve the will as its principle, that is, *I ought never to act except in such a way that I could also will that my maxim should become a universal law*. Here mere conformity to law as such, without having as its basis some law determined for certain actions, is what serves the will as its principle, and must so serve it, if duty is not to be everywhere an empty delusion and a chimerical concept.[4]

The compulsory force of Kant's morality derives from the *form* of the law, which is to say that our sense of obligation and duty, our morality and responsibility follow from how we act *before and under* a law we consider to be universally binding. We feel compelled to bend our wills to the moral law, according to Kant, because we believe that it is binding, in principle, for everyone.

Contrast this Kantian binding of the subject by the force of law to Taylor's depiction of the self's commitment to higher-order, moral goods. Recall that a central reason that Taylor gives for why the self has and holds a commitment to the authority of the good is that the self experiences (and, by experiencing, values) the good as incomparably "higher" than any other ordinary life good that shapes its agency and will. As I discussed in chapter 3, the sublime of the moral law is a central example for Taylor. According to Taylor, we feel awe before the moral law ("Achtung!"). Furthermore, the self acknowledges the power of these moral sources in its agency by becoming articulate about what these sources are, that is, by expressing the value placed on these higher-order goods through the language and everyday practices of leading a life. Agency, according to Taylor, is a faithful response to these moral sources. This means that as agents, Taylor argues, we are bound by our love of the good. Moral identity is constituted by the moral obligations one feels and by the aspirations that serve as the go-cart of hope. Thus, according to Taylor, the self needs the good for a sense of meaningful identity, as much as it does for the capacity to be an agent. We are bound to the good just as we are bound to a particular vision of ourselves.

For Butler, the moral may in fact be the problem. In other words, the very fact that we *feel* bound, obligated, and compelled is not a sign of an affirming connection with a transcendent good but is rather an indication of the oppressive conditions that make subjectivity and agency possible. Whereas Kant's moral autonomy requires a detachment from our phenomenal selves as beings bound by natural forces and laws; and whereas Taylor views obligation to a higher moral value as innately good and enabling, Butler maintains a less sanguine perspective on agency and moral boundedness. Butler follows Foucault as well as Austin, Derrida, and Althusser in arguing that we are bound not by our free wills but by power, which is dispensed through myriad sources that are public as well as private, intimate, and even intrapsychic. Power finds one of its clearest expressions in the coincidence of the force of the law and the force of authority. The coincidence and continuity between the forces of law and authority are manifest, in particular, in the modes of compulsory behavior and acceptability they require. This is made poignantly clear in the example of the compulsory heterosexuality that Butler analyzes. Butler's treatment of this relationship between social norms and the psyche is a nuanced and complex portrait of agency under conditions of subjection and power that is reducible neither to a pat poststructuralist view of totalizing power nor to a post-Marxist conception of the internalization of external norms. Although Butler treats the subject as complicit with her/his own subjection, she also acknowledges the relationship is a complex play of desires that conventional accounts of power do not address. It is, in other words, a condition of ambivalence.[5]

Butler's critique of the life of power and the concomitant ambivalence it generates revolves around two main questions. First, how do regulatory codes and laws of conduct shape conventions and structure desire? Second, how is it possible to break—in the sense of violating and transgressing but also of escaping (breaking from)—these codes, conventions, and social norms that exercise the force of (regulatory) law? In other words, Butler is asking why oppressive norms of identity persist, even after they have been shown to be oppressive. Why do the subjects of oppression continue to desire these norms even when resisting them? The question of resistance to oppressive norms can be broken down even further into the categories of difference, and done in such a way that makes it clear that the theories of performativity and subjection are also critiques of the conventions of identity politics. For racialized subjects who recognize the harmful effects of white supremacy and its attendant racial stratifications and hierarchies, the question remains why they ("we"!) still cling to race. For gendered subjects who acknowledge the harmful effects of sexism and patriarchy, an analogous ambivalence occurs in regard to the recurring return of conventional gender norms. The question facing Butler as a theorist of performativity is how is it possible, under conditions in which the forces of power shape and confine subjectivity, that the constitution of the subject and the instantiation of agency work simultaneously. To answer: "This is simply how power works—it forces us to do these things" is in effect a non-answer. This response neither explains the mechanisms for internalizing what power dictates (such as the norms that power insists bear the truth), nor does it explain how resistance to these mechanisms of power takes place at all. Butler identifies a fundamental ambivalence evident in these paradoxical performative enactments of identity. Consider the following: I need to have a social existence. And yet if I am in fact "different," then it is more likely than not that the "materials" and resources for this existence will give me a means to social recognition while also negating who it is I believe myself to be. In short, my desire to live a life and to gain recognition in the networks of society pressure me to assume obligatory social roles and practices that induce me to lose a sense of my self. According to Butler, the ambivalence that follows from the feeling that one *must* assume social norms of identity is a primary indicator of melancholia/melancholy as a central feature of the psychic life of power and agency.

Butler's turn to melancholy—to the enforcements of morality and moralizing through the psyche, and to the inquiry of the deep, passionate attachments that structure desires—place her in a heritage that stretches back from Foucault to Althusser, from Lacan to Freud, and from Adorno to Nietzsche. As with Nietzsche's and Freud's conjectures about the ways that guilt becomes the primary mechanism for internalizing and naturalizing the force of the law (moral or otherwise) in the form of conscience, Butler identifies how the external authorities of compulsory heterosexuality *constitute* the subject. The subject/self performs the roles, norms, and conventions that have been set and are perpetuated by the law-giving and law-like structures that make up the social and moral imaginaries that dominate society. Just as Taylor's preoccupation is with why and how it is that modernity—specifically, the modern west—became secular and still retains secularism as a defining feature, Butler seeks to determine why and how it is that the social imaginary persists in foreclosing the legitimation of same-sex love and desire. Both secularism and homophobia entail constitutive losses: for Taylor, it is the loss of constitutive moral goods; for Butler, it is a loss of a constitutive love found within the structure of desire.

Following my earlier discussion of Butler's appropriation of Austin and Derrida on speech acts and the performative, it is necessary at this point to turn to her incorporation of Althusser's and Freud's theories of "subjection" and "subjectivation" to clarify the political aspects of performativity. Put simply: subjection and subjectivation are processes that make an individual a self under conditions in which ideologies and their institutions have the power to shape our sense of who we are and how we should act. Butler finds in Althusser's theory of subjection a sustained investigation of ideology and ideological apparatuses (institutions, conventions of law, governmental organization and enforcement, social and family structures). Similarly, Freud's theory of the subconscious provides Butler with resources, on the one hand, to understand how the psyche comes to desire some things and not others, and, on the other hand, to uncover why it is we obey some sources of authority and

normativity and not others. Thus, Butler turns to Althusser to supplement
her account of how and why we respond to the normative demands of social
power. Similarly, she looks to Freud's definition of melancholia, as the inability to mourn the loss of an object of love, as a strategy to investigate the possibility
of agency in light of the interplay between the scalar effects of power and
the psyche's responses to power. This perspective on the constitution of the
subject is evident in Butler's contention that Austin's theory of the performative is interesting less for what it has to say about language use, and more
for how Austin "charts, without knowing it, a fantasy of sovereign power in
speech."[6] In other words, performativity presupposes that we invest language
and discourse with an authority, sovereignty, and normativity that occurs only
through the speech act itself, that is, only in the enactment of language and
discourse as a field of symbols that constitute life. This argument affirms, in
effect, the denial of the reality of a prediscursive self.

Butler's criticism of the assumption of the existence of a prediscursive
self is thus a critique of the attempt to locate agency not with the subject that
presides over "some stable existence prior to the cultural field that it negotiates." Instead, she argues that we have been thoroughly colonized by an epistemological perspective on the self that posits binary oppositions—of subject
and object, us and them, male and female, white and nonwhite, rich and poor,
heterosexual and homosexual, and so on—as "natural" truths. What has become obscure to the self is that these binary oppositions effectively sustain
systems of exclusion and oppression. The metaphor of *negotiation* is useful,
albeit in a limited way, to understand how the self/subject, through performativity, resists becoming irrevocably stuck within the hermeneutical circle of
existing cultural constructs and political configurations. As Butler argues "the
culturally enmired subject *negotiates* its constructions, even when those constructions are the very predicates of its own identity."[7] A brief sketch of
Althusser's concept of interpellation can help clarify what Butler means here
by the subject negotiating its constructions.

In "Ideology and Ideological State Apparatuses," Althusser asks how it
is that ideology comes into existence and how does it permeate society as well
as the individual consciousness and conscience. Althusser posits that in the
process of subjection there is a complicity between what is conventionally understood in Marxist discourse as "state apparatuses" (repressive regimes, especially the ruling classes) and the "private" institutions of family, religion, arts,
education, and so on. In other words, the process of inculcating and bringing
a subject/self into being (subjection) occurs through the inculcation of pre-
established categories and values imposed by the laws of religion, family, ethics, politics, and the like, in creating and reproducing life practices. These
private sectors instill disciplines of behavior that regulate morality, such as our
sense of right and wrong, into a set of skills that come to determine how the
conscience works. According to Althusser, this form of ethical reproduction

parallels the modes of production of labor, that is, the system in which each of us is a part of an apparatus that produces material reality (objects of consumption, especially) under conditions in which workers neither own nor control the means of production. In other words, in neither the reproduction of social values nor the production of labor is any given subject "in control." The effect of this condition is subjection and interpellation. The individual only becomes a subject by subjecting herself/himself to the existing values of any given institution.[8]

Althusser elaborates on the processes of subjection and interpellation through his famous allegory of "the hail." From behind, I hear a police officer calling "Stop!" She is hailing someone on the street. If I stop, I am subjecting myself to the authority and law represented in the figure and the hail of the police officer. I would therefore be acting on the assumption that I am the one being hailed. If I stop as a response to the hail, it is because my conscience calls me to do as much. I am called—interpellated—into the subject position of someone who obeys the authority of the law. The hail works as an interpellation through a call that forms and constitutes me as a subject. In responding to the hail, I am reproducing the skills of the moral order that I have internalized both through the private spheres of my life and from the more remote though no less powerful structural influences of "official" ideologies and law.[9] Yet, there is the possibility that I might not stop, either because I believe that the officer is addressing someone else, or, more provocatively, I might be engaging in an act of defiance. It is the contingency, ambiguity, and unpredictability of the hail and interpellation that draws Butler's attention to Althusser on subjection. As a theory of subjection it provides both an account of how the subject comes into being through discourse (I am hailed; I am thus a subject of the state; in responding to the hail, I enact and recognize myself as a subject of the state), as well as an indication of the possibility of *not* following the law and obligation (I keep walking and, at least implicitly, defy the authority represented by the police officer and the hail). This chance of *not* following, of *not* responding to the interpellation of the hail is the possibility to resist a subject position and thereby to manifest or express my agency. As Butler says, "the real task is to figure out how a subject who is constituted in and by discourse then recites that very same discourse but perhaps to another purpose. For me that's always been the question of how to find agency, the moment of that recitation or that replay of discourse that is the condition of one's own emergence."[10] Subjection through interpellation implies: ambivalence over what it is I desire; who or what is the object of my passionate attachments; and how the ambivalence over complicity with oppressive social norms and the foreclosed loves of my psychic life induces melancholy.

In Freud, Butler finds a corollary to Althusser's theory of subjection and the disciplining of consciousness and conscience, especially in the comparison Freud identifies between mourning and melancholia/melancholy. The melancholy of difference emanates from a loss that cannot be mourned. As Butler contends, melancholy reflects how loss constitutes subjects of difference. Difference—as the subjective experience of alienation, estrangement, and loss—is also a sorrow and inability to grieve and mourn; which is to say, it reflects a psychic condition in which it is not always clear or meaningful why one desires one form of social existence over another. The melancholy of difference concerns the strange ungrievability found in a condition in which the self/subject is uncertain why it believes that a good life will unfold through submission to norms it knows will not only dehumanize but also annihilate that which is considered most dear. Butler's melancholic freedom is an agency that is not fulsome in its aspirations; instead, it lends itself to skepticism. The subtlety of the theory of performativity is that it insists not on an ideologically formulated process of internalizing social norms, but instead ponders how the desires we have are simultaneously ours and not ours, that is, the sources of oppression as well as of our freedom and agency.

The main point is that, for Butler, performativity represents the aspiration for agency, and that this aspiration is really about possibility or what I would call hope. It is a desire to seek and find possibility where none was thought to exist, specifically possibilities for social existence. It is "the condition of one's own emergence." The paradox of subjection—a paradox in which the very conditions for subjection are the conditions for freedom—is a melancholic affair. That is to say, it is a condition in which one is not able to grieve and mourn that which is lost, because it remains too dear, too close to one's heart. If marginalization, oppression, and alienation are the marks of difference, then it follows that these features of melancholy aptly hold for those who live and claim difference.

According to Butler, the subjection of desire constitutes a melancholic subject through the foreclosure and prohibition of grieving forbidden love and desire. In other words, the delegitimation of particular forms and modes of social existence (what I have been referring to as "difference") represents the subjective experience of loss. It is a legitimation crisis that covers the span of experiences ranging from the lack of social recognition all the way to the fallout from defying laws, customs, and conventions that proscribe one's passionate attachments as unlawful, sinful, and even evil. It is important to underscore that the melancholy Butler describes (the ungrievable loss of love produced by the denial of the legitimacy of forbidden love in the first place) is not the loss of an individual love but rather a *symbolic* melancholia.[11] In this sense, the melancholy she ascribes to the process of subjection is analogous to the idea of secularization as a metaphor I identified with Taylor. The experience of loss is present in both accounts, but neither appears to subscribe to an orthodox version of their respective melancholies. Taylor laments the secularization and secularism of modernity, but his concern is not for the actual loss of religion (death-of-God-style nihilism); it is not about the actual disenchantment of the world.[12] Instead, the secular is a metaphor for the self's detachment from moral values and norms, represented by philosophical and political liberalism, moral pluralism, and epistemological naturalism. Similarly, Butler's lamentation and melancholy is not over the loss of specific individuals (objects of love), but is rather an attempt to describe the psychic condition(s) of difference itself. Melancholy is the psychological counterpart to subjection and performativity; both reside with ideas, ideals, values, and forms of love and desire that, paradoxically, form the conditions for the denial of one's existence as well as the possibility for new life. For Butler, identity contains sorrow and affirmation, despair and hope, denial and possibility.

The form of melancholy shared by Taylor's and Butler's accounts is the feature of symbolic loss in the constitution of the self and the central role that symbolic loss has in creating the conditions for the possibility of new modes of agency. The convention in appropriating melancholy is to follow the comparative example Freud established between mourning and melancholia (melancholy), in which the character of loss and the reluctance to give up on an object of love in the latter (melancholia/melancholy) takes its lead and form from the former (mourning).[13] Although Freud pathologizes melancholia as a kind of overbearing narcissism, it is clear that theorists such as Butler and others are appealing to melancholy/melancholia for more constructive and critical purposes. Recent commentators on Freud and melancholy/melancholia—such as Julia Kristeva, Wendy Brown, and Peter Homans, as well as Freud's immediate followers (in particular Melanie Klein and D. W. Winnicott)—remind us that in "Mourning and Melancholia," Freud suggests that melancholia presents itself through a certain irony: the attachment to the object of one's sorrowful loss supersedes the desire and effort to recover from the loss. In other words, melancholy *is* the resistance to moving on from the loss; it is a condition in which one is unwilling or unable to relinquish the burden of loss.[14] As such, the melancholic comes into being and is strongly identified with the personality that has arisen in light of the loss of an object of love. Living with yet not overcoming loss is the mark of a melancholic's identity. Subsequently, the attachment to the lost love object turns into an attachment to being sorrowful itself. The melancholic personality is one who believes something like the following: "I want to grieve the loss of my love/passionate attachment, yet I cannot grieve or mourn, because grieving would mean letting go, which in turn would mean no longer loving the one I lost. Therefore, I have become this person who is unwilling to let go of this love and subsequently I am unable to grieve." As Brown argues, "This is what renders melancholia a persistent condition, a state, indeed a structure of desire, rather than a transient response to death or loss."[15] This idea of the structure of desire helps clarify and foreground both the operation of melancholy in the processes of subjection and the relationship between social norms and the desires that make these norms part of the psyche. As a structure of desire, melancholy involves a longing, or what I prefer to call an *aspiration* to hold onto a lost love by resisting mourning, insofar as mourning means a further loss: a final departure, a resolution that marks an end to love and desire itself. To persist with melancholy is to hold on dearly to the loss and to insist on a passionate attachment despite the strong ambivalences that may endure.

Butler's interpretation of melancholy expresses the delegitimation of desires and loves such as same-sex love. It is a powerful account of what it is to love despite the denial of recognition or acknowledgment. This unrecognized and unacknowledged love requires defiance through the work of the imagination, in a manner suggestive of Wallace Stevens's remarks in "Imagination as Value":

> Nietzsche walked in the Alps in the caresses of reality. We ourselves crawl out of our offices and classrooms and become alert at the opera. Or we sit listening to music as in an imagination in which we believe. If the imagination is the faculty by which we import the unreal into what is real, its value is of the way of thinking by which we project the idea of God into the idea of man. It creates images that are independent of their originals since nothing is more certain than that the imagination is agreeable to the imagination.[16]

Stevens's suggestion that the imagination transforms us by importing "the unreal into what is real" echoes Butler's convictions about the melancholy of the subject. If melancholy is a condition in which my identity is "unreal," and if performativity as agency (rendered through enactments that allow me to work the weakness of social and cultural norms) hinges on sustaining the possibility of the unreal becoming real, then the imagination appears to have a central though largely unacknowledged role in the work of the resistance and subversion that Butler is advocating. Performativity and melancholy reflect the doubleness of the self I described earlier, in which one aspect of the self/subject seeks public acknowledgment, while another insists on the integrity of a denied love. This dynamic mirrors the interplay of the Romantic dialectic between authenticity and irony. The resistance that constitutes the agency of performativity entails an aspiration to overcome the denial that marks the loss of love; it is to transgress against the denial of one's social existence. Just as Taylor requires the sublime to unsettle the modern secular mind in a way that reopens and reawakens the possibility of transcendence, Butler invests the gaps and losses of the performative with the sublime possibility of unsettling held beliefs and conventions. One might say that performativity employs the aspirations of the (religious) imagination to defy the social imaginary of norms and conventions.

A largely unacknowledged aspect of Freud's essay is the point he makes that melancholy entails "a loss of a more ideal kind [than mourning]. The object has not perhaps actually died but has been lost as an object of love."[17]

There is, Freud suggests, an ambiguity to melancholy, in which the melancholic often does not know what features of the object have been either loved or lost. Freud argues that: "This would suggest that melancholia [melancholy] is in some way related to an object-loss which is withdrawn from consciousness, in contradistinction to mourning, in which there is nothing about the loss that is unconscious."[18] Butler maintains that this ambiguity figures in the foreclosure of same-sex love and desire, as well as the foreclosure of grieving the lost love and prohibition of this love *within* heterosexual culture. At the heart of Freud's conception of melancholia is the loss of an original passionate attachment. The psyche copes with the loss by transfiguring the self into a melancholic subject: a self who forms a life through a process of despair, even suicide (*thanatos*/the death drive). Butler expands on this by arguing that passionate attachments such as sexual identity or the "idea" of one's race become forms of idealization. The gendered, racialized, "classed," and "sexualized" subject suffers the indignities of the denials of social existence as melancholic loss. Subsequently, the sublimated self as a lost object of love (sexual identity, race, and the like) survives through the idealization of what has been lost and denied. The melancholic self here is revealed with the aspects of the self that are obscured and/or denied legitimacy. The strategy of self-identity for the melancholic can take a form of mania, but more often it finds expression through the mechanism of guilt associated with the pain of letting go. This strategy produces a strange masochism, or what Butler calls the "ambivalence" of psychic desire. This brings me back to the questions I raised at the beginning of this chapter about norms, compulsion, and identity. For example, if it is revealed to me that a norm is oppressive or subjects me to a regime of truth that is harmful, then the question arises why I would repeat and cite the norm in the future. Are the mechanisms of subjection so intransigent? And if they are, then how are social change and political action, let alone mental health, at all possible? After all, isn't the idea of framing performativity as a form of agency predicated on a tacit assumption of change if not transcendence? For Butler, melancholy reflects the ambivalence of guilt: why do I return to the repertoire of social norms that I know denies and refuses to acknowledge my social existence? The denial of same-sex love also reflects, so she argues, the guilt of heterosexual desire that seeks to hide the fact that heterosexuality is predicated on the existence and subsequent repression of same-sex love; that is, same-sex love is something we all experience, but it is a remnant of childhood and is rationalized away as a suppressed attachment to a parent, for example. There is also the guilt associated with holding onto a passionate attachment that the dominant social culture considers abject. In all of these cases, the inflection of guilt reveals how power has force *in* the psyche through the condition of melancholy. So it is that the significance of melancholy/melancholia for Butler's detection of agency in subjection and performativity derives from the interpretation of melancholy as symbolic loss.[19]

As Peter Homans argues, mourning as symbolic loss is "the reaction to the loss of a loved person, or to the loss of some abstraction . . . such as liberty, an ideal, and so on."[20] This suggests a much sharper set of associations than Robert Burton's classic definition of melancholy as "sorrow without cause." As Butler argues, gender melancholy is not a global and diffuse depression but a stickier and perhaps darker psychic condition.[21] As symbolic loss, melancholy mimics nihilism, in the sense that one's deepest beliefs and loves have been shaken and lost. The eye rolls of critics who consider such talk as breast-beating about social marginalization do not appreciate how deeply the wounds and losses of difference can cut. In fact, I would say that the language of marginalization is not strong enough to capture the feelings of estrangement and alienation Butler identifies with melancholy.[22]

Indeed, one of the central lessons drawn from Butler is that language inevitably fails the needs and desires of subjectivity. The melancholic subject seeks a language that can express pain, suffering, and anguish. And yet it remains that words falter in attempts to capture those experiences. It is important to reemphasize the significance of language in this consideration of difference and melancholy. Kristeva is especially helpful on this point. She links melancholy to experiences of symbolic breakdown, which she defines as a condition in which language loses its capacity to express linguistic, existential, and psychic meaning for the self. Language becomes empty and yet, paradoxically, the only resource for conveying and articulating the state of one's psyche. This is the conundrum of identity and agency that Butler's theory of performativity conveys. Consider Krisetva's account of symbolic breakdown:

> The spectacular collapse of meaning with depressive persons—and, at the limit, the meaning of life—allows us to assume that they experience difficulty integrating the universal signifying sequence, that is, language. In the best cases, speaking beings and their language are like one: is not speech our "second nature"? In contrast, the speech of the depressed is to them like an alien skin; melancholy persons are foreigners in their maternal tongue. They have lost the meaning—the value—of their mother tongue for want of losing the mother. The dead language they speak, which foreshadows their suicide, conceals a Thing buried alive.[23]

It is critical to underscore that Butler views melancholy not in terms of the incapacitating despair Kristeva describes but rather, like discourse and language, as a condition that enables the possibility of agency even as it oppresses. Gender melancholy, as well as what I am calling the melancholy of difference, involves not only the laments of nihilism but also a condition that indicates new possibilities of being in the world. This is, of course, the affirmation that Nietzsche comes to after the death of God. We have lost God and think that the horizon has been wiped away, but in fact we are now free from the guilt-inducing encumbrances of slave morality. After all, Nietzsche's "gay science" is also a series of meditations about the folly of freedom if not its happiness (*fröliche*).[24] The melancholy of difference, exemplified in Butler's work, reflects the inability and even the refusal to sustain what Frederic Jameson calls the organizational fiction of utopian narratives that attempt to structure and "make sense of" the estrangement of difference.[25] This refusal to take on an organizational fiction, to deny a unifying coherence to the disparate elements of experience and life, is also what allows melancholy to constitute the possibility of agency. Butler calls this the possibility that derives from the constitutive loss of the subject.[26] This is the possibility and hope that arises from the impossibility and foreclosure that Butler identifies with agency and melancholy. The performative, then, marks the possibility of the breakdown of symbolic worlds, which, in turn, represents death and life, loss and hope.

As I proposed earlier, Butler's melancholy of difference is the psychic analogy to nihilism—a metaphoric death of God—that is suggestive of emancipatory possibilities. The spirit of exile that animates Butler's idea of melancholy is the means by which she is able to theorize agency. It is an ironic stance through which the subject of difference simultaneously engages and disengages with the material contexts of new languages and discourses for the body, identity, and moral judgment. As such, Butler is essentially asking Foucauldian questions about the relationship between subjectivity/the self and the ethical. Consider these questions posed by Foucault: "How have certain kinds of interdictions become the price required for attaining certain kinds of knowledge [*savoir*] about oneself? What must one know [*connaître*] about oneself in order to be willing to accept such renunciation?"[27] The psychic strain of difference that results in melancholy reflects the ambiguity, ambivalence, and uncertainty about self-possession. Are the things I know and believe about myself true and authentic, or are they the effects of power? In the case of history, this raises the question: how am I to forgive past wrongs? I am the product of this history, and I can never be fully free from it. In regard to the history of racial injustices, of gender discrimination, of homophobia, of class degradation, the melancholic of difference asks: is there any redemption and forgiveness? For example, among the tortuous lessons of the South African Truth and Reconciliation Commission is the sense in which learning the details of a horrific history may become one of the conditions for the possibility for social reconciliation. Nonetheless, this does not necessarily mean that what Walter Benjamin calls "[the] revolutionary chance in the fight for the oppressed past" truly goes away.[28] The melancholy of difference calls into question whether wholeness is truly redemptive. Furthermore, it asks if relenting to what Cioran calls "the temptation to exist" amounts to assenting to a totalizing historical memory that occludes oppressions, violence, and suffering.[29]

Melancholy persists precisely because it is not always possible to be assured that this will be the case. The past cannot be fully mourned for fear that it will be lost. Again, mourning requires letting go of an object of love. None-theless, Butler is fully aware that it is more likely than not that much will remain unchanged even after piercing the veil of the truth. The melancholic freedom of Butler's performative agency enacts an agonistic struggle with what Wole Soyinka calls "the burden of memory and the muse of forgiveness."[30] The suffering of memory is painful and yet defines who you are. The past as memory and forgetting, as history (minor or oppressed), constitutes the self even when one is unaware of it.

And so it becomes apparent how subjection takes place not only on the level of the social but also at the level of the psychic. As such, the regulation of desires, the will, and action requires an account of the subject that "must be traced in the peculiar turning of the subject against itself that eventuates in acts of self-reproach, conscience, and melancholia that work in tandem with processes of social regulation."[31] As Butler concludes, this self-thwarting requires a refusal of "the ontological dualism that posits the separation of the political and the psychic, [and subsequently requires] a critical account of psy-chic subjection in terms of the regulatory and productive effects of power."[32] My main point here is that this resistance, defiance, and refusal—all of which entail envisioning a different way of being in the world—are products of the work of the religious imagination: the faculty that seeks to render the "unreal into what is real," that is, to realize aspirations for transcendence. By enabling the self to chance on hope, the religious imagination marks what Derrida calls the ability to "anticipate the unanticipatable."[33] It is, as such, the engine of hope and aspiration.

In contrast to earlier critical theorists, such as members of the early Frankfurt School who had sought to synthesize the critical aims of Marx and Freud by attempting to identify how social norms become internalized, Butler's attention to the psyche is an effort to understand how a desire for social ex-istence can be read as an effort to refuse social and symbolic death. Butler is quite powerful on this point:

> [O]ne might consider that certain forms of love entail the loss of the object not only because of an innate desire to triumph, but be-cause such objects fail to qualify as objects of love: as objects of love they assume a mark of destruction. Indeed, they may threaten one's own destruction as well: "I will be destroyed if I love in that way." Marked for "death," the object is, as it were, already lost, and the desire to vanquish the object is precisely the desire to vanquish an object which, if loved, would spell destruction for the one who loves.
>
> Can we read the workings of social power precisely in the deli-mitation of the field of such objects, objects marked for death? And is this part of the irreality, the melancholic aggression and the desire to vanquish, that characterizes the public response to the death of many

of those considered "socially dead," who die from AIDS? Gay people, prostitutes, drug users, among others? If they are dying or already dead, let us vanquish them again. And can the sense of "triumph" be won precisely through a practice of social differentiation in which one achieves and maintains "social existence" only by the production and maintenance of those socially dead? Might one not also read the paranoia that structures public discourse on such issues as the inversion of that aggression: the desire to vanquish the dead other than through a reversal comes to mark that other as the threat of death, casting the other as the (unlikely) persecutor of the socially normal and normalized?[34]

Just as performativity is an argument about forces that compel the self/ subject to assume norms and stereotypes even as they provide the tools to become agents, it is under the dolorous conditions of melancholy that difference finds its purpose and meaning. The melancholic freedom of agency arises out of the constitutive losses that mark the subjectivity of the exiles of a symbolic order—whether the symbolic order is oriented around heterosexual culture, the priority given to male desires, the regimes of white supremacy, or the materialist empires of capitalism. As Butler writes, "[p]erformativity describes this relation of being implicated in that which one opposes, this turning of power against itself to produce alternative modalities of power, to establish a kind of political contestation that is not a 'pure' opposition, a 'transcendence' of contemporary relations of power, but a difficult labor of forging a future from resources inevitably impure."[35]

The constant that has remained through the changes in Butler's work— that is, from parody to citationality, from repetition to interpellation, and her interrogation of the productive effects of melancholy—is the drive to defy and yet inhabit conventions and norms in a political emancipatory project.[36] This drive has animated and energized the theory of performativity and is one of the greatest appeals of the approach, especially for political progressives who lament the banality of freedom. In other words, the melancholic freedom of performative agency is an apt expression for an age in which the exhaustion and depleted vitality of progressive movements and intellectuals have led many to ask whether there is any viable rationale for action for the post-Marxist, political left that is not merely "academic," in the most pejorative sense of that term.[37]

While Butler is hardly the first to describe resistance to power as the site of agency, her reading of subjection and the shaping of the subject and moral consciousness is a highly sophisticated critique of those who would want simply to identify agency as any instance of resistance, large or small. More to the point, the connections that Butler seeks to establish between the constitution of the psyche and the possibilities of agency in political, social, and cultural conditions that actively deny these possibilities place the project on a higher order of sophistication than most attempts to depict a progressive and emancipatory politics.[38] To wit, Butler's project of regenerating agency stands squarely with the traditions that have valorized the arts of resistance.[39] The ends and aims of performative agency seek to open up possibilities out of conditions of foreclosure; and by identifying possibility, like Taylor, Butler is, as I argue in the final chapter, auguring a cultivation of political sensibilities and moral dispositions that attune the self to hope, despite the persistence and possible inescapability of melancholy. Subsequently, the religious imagination at work in the cultivation of performative yet melancholic freedom is a bulwark against a conception of agency that seeks to strictly identify resistance as a form of transcendence, as found in invocations of utopias or other hyperbolic and romanticized pictures of what resistance involves.

Oppression can occur in tandem along lines circumscribed by race, gender, sexuality, and class. These forms of oppression affect each of us in different ways, although often in concurrence with one another. As such, they represent not so much the chaos of multiple selves but the obstruction of the self from realizing itself in a way that keeps these different aspects of identity from coalescing. This idea of the self that is obscure to itself is a crucial insight for projects of regenerating agency and for the work of the religious imagination. It is reminiscent of the Socratic quest for self-knowledge as well as Augustine's self-inquiry in which he ponders how it is that "a question have I become for myself" (*quaestio mihi factus sum*).[40] One can find meaning, albeit a negative meaningfulness, in the experience of oppression. As bell hooks has incisively argued, advocating for difference cultivates the potential for coalition, not dis-aggregation and chaos. The politics of difference has the potential to do this because of the increasingly widespread experience of "a sense of deep alienation, despair, uncertainty, loss of a sense of grounding even if it is not informed by shared circumstance." That is to say that "[r]adical postmodernism calls attention to those shared sensibilities which cross the boundaries of class, gender, race, etc., that could be fertile ground for the construction of empathy—ties that would promote recognition of common commitments, and serve as a base for solidarity and coalition."[41] Hooks calls this common psychological state that allows for the crossing of boundaries "yearning": a yearning for critical voices against "master narratives." Yearning is akin to the feature of aspiration that I have identified with Butler's and Taylor's projects of regenerating agency. And it is to these features of aspiration and yearning, as well the role of the religious imagination in projects of regenerating agency and self-cultivation, that I turn in the next and final chapter.

6

Agency as a Vocation

Calling All Agents

What shall I do, and how shall I live?

—Leo Tolstoy

Here I stand. I can do no other.

—Martin Luther

Agency as melancholic freedom is a deeply ambivalent affair. It speaks to the uncanny experience of feeling indebted to yet alienated from the glorious legacies of modernity: the legacies of liberation, of emancipation, and of autonomy. Late modern and postmodern agency share a concern for the banality of freedom, which is to say, the loss of urgency that had once attended the great struggles for freedom and emancipation from the forces of oppressive authority and dehumanizing domination. Given the banality of freedom—that is, the ways in which we speak about freedom either through hollow words or in hushed, *sotto voce* tones—it would seem that it is impossible to avoid talking about ambivalence when raising the subject of agency in our times. For these reasons I begin this final chapter on agency as melancholic freedom by bringing Taylor and Butler, both of whom express a fair degree of ambivalence, into conversation with another theorist of ambivalence, Max Weber.

I have chosen the two epigraphs for this chapter because they each represent points of climax in Weber's famous essays "Science as a Vocation" and "Politics as a Vocation."[1] In addition to the drama that each of these quotations elicits, they are especially evocative for the theme of this final chapter: agency as a vocation. Weber uses the quotes to stress the theme of loss that pervades all of his writings, especially the loss and delegitimation of the resources for meaning in modernity. According to Weber, this loss is evident, for example, in the German university system's abandonment of the ideals of *Bildung* or cultivation in its attempt to develop a highly rationalistic and instrumental ethos shaped by scientific culture, as well as in the pragmatic and utilitarian politics that were dominant in his day. The vocation essays are not, of course, the first time Weber invokes the idea of vocation or "calling" (*Beruf*).[2] The secularization of the Reformation notion of vocation/calling/*Beruf* is a central feature of Weber's *The Protestant Ethic and the Spirit of Capitalism*, in which he defines a calling as "a religious conception, a task set by God," and which the Puritans interpreted as "a life task." According to Weber, seeing one's work as vocation had been the means through which

> the fulfillment of duty in worldly affairs [became] the highest form that the moral activity of the individual could assume. [It] inevitably gave every-day worldly activity a religious significance.... The only way of living acceptably to God was not to surpass worldly morality in monastic asceticism, but solely through the fulfillment of the obligations imposed upon the individual by his position in the world. That was his calling.[3]

By the time Weber gives the vocation lectures, he has shifted from the explicitly Christian *née* Reformation conception of the term to a critique of the colloquial and idiomatic understanding of vocation as a "job" or profession (a term that has its own Christian connotations of witness and prophecy). Significantly, the critique of the instrumental and utilitarian culture of modern science and society—cultures that lacked "wisdom" and "imaginative insight"—is also the context in which Weber declares "the world is *disenchanted*."[4]

The vocation essays are meditations on whether there is any possibility of finding a replacement for religion in modernity, which is to ask, whether worldly activities such as science or politics could provide meaning in a disenchanted and demystified world. Weber is typically withering in the conclusions he draws on this score in regard to both science and politics. Modern science cannot fill the spiritual hunger of the human spirit; more specifically, it cannot answer the questions once considered central to the human condition: questions about the existence of God, the immortality of the soul, and the meaning of life. Furthermore, science fails to qualify as a vocation, in Weber's estimation, because it cannot answer the question Tolstoy considered the most basic to human existence: "What shall we do and how shall we live?"[5] Similarly, modern politics comes up short because it cannot reconcile "the ethic of ultimate values" (the concern for religion and the spirit) and "the ethic of responsibility" (the utilitarian and pragmatic concern for collective life). Weber notes how rare it is for a modern politician to exhibit the qualities of maturity and the singularity of conviction of a Martin Luther—which is to say, a figure who stood fast for his commitments in defiance of the most powerful authorities of his day to declare: "Here I stand; I can do no other." Notably, Weber concludes that the ethic of ultimate values and the ethic of responsibility are not "absolute contrasts but rather supplements," which, if found in accord in a person's actions, would constitute the person as "a genuine man."[6] In short, the political can only be a vocation if it serves as a medium for *integrity*.[7] I will take up the relationship between vocation and integrity presently, but first it falls on me to answer the following: *If science and politics fail and falter as vocations, then why turn to agency?*

As Weber makes abundantly clear, it is difficult to find a way of life in modernity that can fulfill the spiritual demands of vocation or calling. Nonetheless, the examples that Weber chooses (the secularized and sublimated asceticism of the Puritans; the utilitarian cultures of science and politics) are examples of historical transformations and, arguably, deviations from the ideal type of Christian vocation. By framing the problematic of our times in terms of "the banality of freedom" and "agency as a vocation," I am certainly playing on the ambivalence and ambiguity that attaches to the trope of vocation/calling, as well as working with a Weberian sensibility that is preoccupied by the persistence of religious categories and idioms in a secular age. In effect, my characterization of agency as a vocation serves the ends of clarifying the religious dimensions of the contemporary discourse on agency that I have been discussing throughout this book, especially, I hope, by helping refresh a religious category that has gone a bit stale.

It also stands to reason that I turn to the religious potential of the trope of vocation and its most famous modern interpreter since, as I suggested at the beginning of this chapter, Weber shares the quality of ambivalence that is so prominent in Taylor's and Butler's theories of agency. With all three thinkers, there is a fundamental ambivalence toward what they perceive and diagnose as the conditions that hinder as well as enable agency. For his part, Taylor inherits a great deal from Weber, both in the common ethos that defines their thinking, as well as the deep ambivalence they share over the price paid for the achievements of modernity: the rationalization of life practices; the increasing control over natural forces reflected in the disenchantment or "demagification" (*"Entzauberung"*) of the world; the increasing dominance of instrumental rationality; and the diminishing resources for public action and life.[8] Consider this passage from "Science as a Vocation"; it could easily serve as an abstract for Taylor's *Sources of the Self*:

> The fate of our times is characterized by rationalization and intellectualization and, above all, by the "disenchantment of the world."

> Precisely the ultimate and most sublime values have retreated from
> public life either into the transcendental realm of mystic life or into
> the brotherliness of direct and personal human relations. It is not
> accidental that our greatest art is intimate and not monumental, nor
> is it accidental that today only within the smallest and intimate cir-
> cles, in personal human situations, in *pianissimo*, that something
> is pulsating that corresponds to the prophetic *pneuma*, which in for-
> mer times swept through the great communities like a firebrand,
> welding them together.[9]

It is my contention that the *sotto voce* of the banality of freedom "sings" in
concert with the *pianissimo* of the modern prophetic spirit/soul described by
Weber.

Butler, though perhaps not a direct successor to the Weberian tradition,
does call to mind qualities and conclusions that are familiar to most readers
of Weber: the idea of being overwhelmed by the structures and systems of
modern life; also, the dread of being trapped within the mechanisms and
institutions of modernity, in which Weber's "iron cage" connotes not only an
unabiding rationalism but also the processes that make each of us objects
rather than subjects or selves.[10]

So it would seem that I have three melancholics on my hands, that is,
three figures whose ambivalences about modernity, late modernity, and postmodernity begin with assumptions and preoccupations with loss, and who
each feel ambivalent about how their respective "epochs" reflect that which
has been lost and gained in the conditions for the possibility of agency and
freedom.

And yet: the reason that vocation is suggestive in bringing out the religious dimensions of the work on agency by philosophers and theorists such as
Taylor and Butler has less to do with the affinities they share with Weber
himself and more to do with the Weberian qualities that are found in their
theories of agency. These are qualities evident in the evolution of the notion
of vocation, that is, qualities that mourn the suppression and obscuring of
conditions that, given full expression, would otherwise enable freedom and
meaning for the self. As I noted, Weber uses the occasion of the vocation lectures as a diatribe against the German university system for abandoning the
educational tradition of *Bildung*. It is this connection that Weber makes between the demands of vocation and *Bildung* (what I am calling cultivation)
that I want to pursue in this final chapter. It is a connection that speaks to a
religious heritage that links vocation to duty, commitment, and piety, as well
as to a determination to cultivate aspirations for intellectual and spiritual integrity along with moral purpose. I am therefore engaging the idea of vocation for largely Weberian reasons, by which I mean that I am interrogating
a religious category that has become dissociated from its spiritual heritage

(the Reformation notion of *Beruf* or calling) and yet continues to have currency precisely because of its paradoxical dissonance and resonance with this heritage.

I am fully aware that the approach I have taken on the question of the religious qualities found in nonreligious thinkers will appear oblique to many and thus overly expansive in my ambitions for what I identify as modes and forms of religiosity and spirituality. After all, I have chosen two figures who are, by most lights, concerned with "secular" matters (although Taylor does wear his "theism" on his sleeve). I am sure to face critics who will argue that disembedding terms such as "the religious" or even "the spiritual" from more traditional uses will result in losing the meaning of religion altogether. Just as Sheldon Wolin argues that the expanded use of the category of "the political" (as in the phrase "everything is political") would mean that nothing is political, my future (im)perfect critics might argue that if everything is religious, then nothing is religious.[11] Nonetheless, it is not the case that I am arguing that everything is political or religious. I aim to make a subtler argument that seeks to connect the common purposes of so-called secular categories such as agency, expressivism, the sublime, difference, and melancholy to forms of religiosity. In other words, I am attempting to establish a connection between the poles of the secular and the religious—which is to say that by way of bridging and mediating concepts such as aspiration, possibility, vocation, and cultivation I am challenging the conventions that attempt to distinguish sharply "the religious" from "the secular." The desire to maintain exacting separations and distinctions between the religious and the secular, as well as the sacred/spiritual and the profane/worldly, is a reflection of strategies that seek to create artificial and potentially false constructs. It also constitutes a failure of the imagination, in my view, by refusing to acknowledge the expansive power and complexity of these terms. In this sense, I am following the lead of figures such as Josiah Royce (in his *The Sources of Religious Insight*) and John Dewey (in his *A Common Faith*), that is, philosophers who recognize the persistent possibilities of religious categories such as "salvation" (Royce) or "faith" (Dewey), even when they travel beyond the bounds of "the traditions." This is what one hears when Royce implores his readers to "[b]e willing, then, to generalize our term and to dissociate the idea of salvation from some of the settings in which you usually have conceived it."[12] Or when Dewey insists that *there is* a distinction one can make between "religion versus the religious."[13] If we no longer narrowly define and associate terms such as "Zeitgeist" or "paradigm" with German social theory or Kuhnian philosophy and history of science, then we should at least entertain the possibility of more expansive applications of the contested categories of the religious.

As I indicated earlier, I believe that even after terms such as "vocation," "conversion," and "grace" have taken on secular meanings it remains that the rhetorical power and effect of these tropes persist, in part, because they continue to bank on the religious overtones and associations they evoke. This is certainly the case with Weber's use of the category of "vocation" in the late lectures. While for Weber it may fall to the initiated to fully understand the significance of the intellectual genealogy of the idea of vocation (from the thesis he develops in *The Protestant Ethic* about the sublimation of godly vocation into worldly and materialistic concerns to his eventual dissociation of vocation from its Reformation heritage), there remains a continuity even in the stated discontinuities between the sacred understanding of vocation and its secular variations. This continuity has to do with *form*. That is to say that Weber can only recognize and acknowledge science or politics as "a vocation" insofar as *the form* and not the content is the same as the Reformers' understanding of *Beruf*. The question is not necessarily, for example, "Am I called to be a child of God" or whatever specific content one believes should attend the message of the call. Instead, vocation is a response to questions such as: "What am I called to do?" "What am I willing to die for?" and "What gives my life meaning and value?" There is, therefore, an explicit connection between the idea of vocation and agency.

Cultivation of the Self, or Agency as a Way of Life

Liberta va cercando ch'e si cara
(He goes seeking freedom which is so dear)
—Dante, Canto I, *Purgatorio*

As I alluded earlier, a striking feature of Taylor's and Butler's approaches to the problematic of agency is the commitment they share in promoting projects of regenerating agency that are coincidental with the cultivation of the self. By "cultivation of the self" I have two related features in mind.

First, *moral identity*. A deep and engaging moral identity requires continuous critical reflection on the conditions for the possibility of human flourishing. This involves, on the one hand, an assessment of the conditions that constrain and limit meaningful subjectivity, and, on the other, discerning and determining that which enables well-being. Cultivating the self entails a form of self-understanding that is intimately tied to a sense of moral, political, and psychic *integrity*. Toward this end, melancholy, loss, lack, void, absence, discontent, and dissatisfaction are the necessary concerns that inspire the cultivation of the self. The critical self-examination of self-cultivation also involves the acknowledgement and articulation of the aspirations for well-being that the agent has in mind, such as the legitimation of social existence (Butler), envisioning and articulating the possibility of authenticity and transcendence (Taylor), and finding a sense of purpose in one's moral and spiritual commitments and duty (Weber).

Second, *spiritual exercise*. Cultivation of the self serves as a form of spiritual exercise for projects of regenerating agency, by which I mean disciplines—broadly defined as political, moral/ethical, and spiritual/religious practices. On the one hand, these disciplines and practices keep the self mindful of the limits of agency and subjectivity. In this way, the quest for self-understanding is crucial to self-cultivation. On the other hand, the discipline of critical self-reflection helps sustain and even inspire the aspiration to transcend and transgress moral, social, political, and spiritual limits, especially through the identification of the necessary concerns that call the self (vocation) and enable the process of becoming an agent as well as a self.[14] Self-cultivation thus entails a transformation of the self in a manner that is organic with a worldview that takes agency not as an epiphenomenal and episodic occasion but rather as *a way of life*.

This concern for self-cultivation and agency as transformative is evident in Taylor's reconstruction of expressivism, in which a regulative ideal of authenticity takes hold of the religious imagination through the articulation of the moral sources that ground moral identity. This is the impetus, I believe, behind Taylor's critique of deconstruction and of postmodern culture, both of which he takes to task for an obsession with one side of the ideal of authenticity, namely, self-determining freedom. This amounts, so Taylor argues, to seeing choice and resistance as values in and of themselves. The problem with this perspective, according to Taylor, is that it ignores the other side of the ideal of the authenticity of the self. This is the side of authenticity that sees the self not in the mode of a narcissistic Romanticism that seeks absolute freedom but rather as a being who comes into her/his own through introspection, as well as in dialogical engagement with horizons of meaning and "significant others," such as family, community, and even tradition. Taylor argues in *The Ethics of Authenticity* that the postmodern culture of self-determining freedom (he also refers to advocates of this culture as "neo-Nietzschean") degrades the ideal of authenticity by turning it into a "soft relativism" that holds forth a narcissistic conception of identity that is based on personal choice rather than on the deeper and more complicated context he covets (think conscientious and deep-souled communitarians).[15] As I discussed in chapter 3, Taylor presses the sublime (in the form of the framing epiphany) into the service of disciplining moral agency and identity. In other words, the sublime framing epiphany disciplines the self by making it aware of the moral frameworks, horizons of meaning, and other sources that lie beyond the individual self. As epiphanic, the sublime is meant to awaken the agent to the "reality" and possibility of transcendent moral sources that are already operative in ordinary life, that is, through the moral intuitions for freedom, justice, benevolence, and the affirmation of the ordinary life. Be that as it may, an experience with the sublime spurs the imagination of the not yet realized self to engage in the activity of articulating what these sources and potential identities are and elaborating on how they can become manifest in one's consciousness and in the life one wishes to lead. Taylor argues that the act of articulating what one's moral sources are involves creative expression and manifestation. It is, I am proposing, a discipline of self-cultivation. Furthermore, the characterization of agency as the capacity for moral judgment (Taylor's strong evaluation) is itself suggestive of the aesthetic and the imagination.

In Butler's theory of performativity, a regulative ideal of irony and parody fixes the imagination on the possibility of change in the service of agency. As a response of resistance to dominant/normative discursive practices that discipline the self, performativity is also an alternative mode of self-discipline that reveals conditions that limit possibility. Though she prefers the discourse of parody and melancholia, I have argued that performativity also involves a deep use of irony. I will say more about Butler's use of irony and counterregulatory practices in a moment.

By employing Romantic tropes such as authenticity, irony, and the imagination, it is not my intent to argue that Taylor and Butler are in fact Romantics, although Taylor often flirts with the label by tentatively embracing the Romantic ethos of expressivism and authenticity while also distancing himself from it. Nor am I attempting to recuperate Romanticism itself—a tradition whose cuffs and hems have become long-since frayed. Like Taylor, as well as other philosophers such as Charles Larmore, Richard Eldridge, and Stanley Cavell, I look to Romanticism as providing a set of resources and concepts for understanding the engagements of critical agency with rational self-reflection. As Taylor, Larmore, and Eldridge have each argued, we should pay attention to the persistence of Romanticism not because more of us should identify ourselves as "Romantics" (Cavell is probably the exception in this crowd), but rather because the late modern west still maintains an inheritance from the Romantic legacy, specifically in the widely held ideals of self-fulfillment, authenticity, and, more obliquely, in the uses and expressions of the creative imagination and irony.[16]

I have retrieved the ideas of authenticity, irony, and the imagination from the Romantic tradition as a way of clarifying the work required by projects of regenerating agency and their attendant dimensions of religiosity. I have turned to these Romantic tropes, in part, because I believe they are still quite "alive" in contemporary discourse. Furthermore, I maintain that the spirit of Romanticism, as Schleiermacher pointed out in his Second Speech on religion, is largely an attempt to live and practice religion without the religions. The Second Speech is a devastatingly incisive and powerful rhetorical display in which Schleiermacher argues for the centrality of subjective experience, while also pointing out to his fellow Romantics that their attempts to establish a necessary relationship between interiority or inwardness and nature were identical to the religious and theological ideals of relating the self to the world or universe. Schleiermacher focuses on the centrality of feeling (*Gefühl*) and intuition to make this point; which is to say, he hits at the heart of the Romantic critique of the Enlightenment's dismissal of the affective dimensions of human experience.[17]

This brief sidebar on Schleiermacher's critique of the Romantics is not an effort on my part to say that "the Romantics were really talking about religion, and thus my use of concepts from Romanticism in my interpretation of agency proves that what I'm talking about is also about religion." My method, I hope, is subtler than such remarks would suggest. My use of Romantic tropes is an appeal to *the spirit* of Romanticism that sought to fill what was perceived as a void left by the Enlightenment's critique of religion and the affects. And so I am arguing that there is an elective affinity between Romanticism and a critique such as the one I have been making of projects of regenerating agency, which is to say, a critique that is seeking to uncover dimensions of religiosity that have gone undetected or undeveloped in the largely secular discourses of contemporary theory.

My point here is that the aspects of self-cultivation that envision agency as a way of life and as a vocation also involve the use of what I have been calling the religious imagination. The religious imagination requires a willingness to risk conceiving of life otherwise than it is now. It is, so to speak, the exercise and discipline of the religious imagination that connects identity with agency, the political with the moral, and memory with culture. The passionate commitments, aspirations for life chances and possibilities, and attempts to envision impact in the world and for the self are all reflections of the religious imagination. I refer to this imagination and corresponding set of dispositions as "religious" (just as one might refer to works of art as products of "the creative imagination") not because the imagination and dispositions in question are reducible to any particular religious tradition or to a broad account of the moral. Instead, I call them religious because of the overlapping concerns between what I have been identifying as the religious/spiritual work of agency and the features associated with philosophical (read "secular") accounts of the relationship between agency and moral identity. I have been seeking new ways of interpreting the work of agency that pushes the bounds of conventional accounts and theories of agency into what I believe are fruitful and underexplored modes of religiosity.

In this vein, Cavell's work on Emerson is enormously helpful and illuminating in establishing the connections between the cultivation of the self to the role that language, discourse, and finding a voice plays in engendering agency. In his reflections on the ordinary life, Cavell describes Emerson's inheritance of the Kantian and Romantic traditions as indicative of a "doubleness of the self." For Kant, the doubleness is the split he identifies between the phenomenal and the noumenal; for Emerson, the division is between the self that is encumbered by and within the ordinary world and the "unattained yet attainable self," or what Cavell calls "the next self" or "the further self." Emerson serves as a mediating figure for Cavell in this regard, insofar as he (Emerson) is a thinker who effectively depicts the philosophical skeptic's perspective on herself/himself and the world. This is also to say that Emerson speaks to the concerns of a philosophical and cultural skepticism that is preoccupied with the potential for *non*identity between the self and the world, the self and others, and how one experiences both.

It is fruitful to read Taylor's and Butler's projects of regenerating agency as examples of what Cavell describes as the process of "becoming intelligible to oneself": a critical feature of moral perfectionism.[18] The individual agent experiences the call of moral perfectionism, according to Cavell, by adhering to an imperative to search for apt forms of self-expression and to move from "self-obscurity" to the discovery and discernment of "which among the voices contending to express your nature are ones for you to own here, now."[19] This depiction of the call of and for the self jives with what Taylor refers to as the Romantic valorization of the "inner voice," that is, the notion that interiority will allow us to express our authentic nature. It is also consonant with Butler's concern for how the self responds to calls of subjection to particular norms of identity that come to constitute gender, sexuality, class, and race. The idea that one's sense of self is obscure, and that one needs to work to become intelligible to oneself, is also reminiscent of the Socratic ideal of self-knowledge, as well as Augustine's "anthropological" notion of becoming a question to oneself. To use the idiom of the ancient Greeks, my distinct identity is not (always) clear or transparent to me. Furthermore, my distinct or unique identity (my *daimôn*) "appears and is visible only to others."[20] Being obscure to oneself speaks to Taylor's injunction to transform the self from a condition of moral obscurity to becoming morally articulate, which is to say, to recuperate authenticity through new and modern forms of cultivation. It also applies to Butler's interrogation of the conditions of agency that arise from the interplay between the forces of power and the psychic life. In other words, both the alienation from the good that creates the need for regenerating agency for Taylor and the subjection of desires that constitutes the conditions that obscure yet enable the self for Butler represent forms of melancholy that require clarification and response from the self who seeks to realize her/his agency.

Again, Cavell is a helpful mediator here. Cavell's idea of becoming intelligible to oneself is the heart of what he calls "Emersonian perfectionism" or "moral perfectionism." By "perfectionism" Cavell is alluding to a vague yet compelling ideal that lures the self forward without a definite vision in mind. It is predicated on the ideal of moral perfection, though not in the sense that there is a teleology or a clear notion of "perfection" involved.[21] Instead, as Cavell notes, he holds onto the trope of "perfection" because of its resonance with Emerson, as well as Freud and Plato, who all argue

that *each* state of the self is, so to speak, final: each state constitutes a world (a circle, Emerson says) and it is one each one also
desires (barring inner or outer catastrophes). On such a picture of
the self one could say both that significance is always deferred and
equally that it is never deferred (there is no later circle until it is
drawn).[22]

Emersonian perfectionism relates "to the state of one's soul" or self, which is
to say, not to the content of morality but to the relationship of the soul/self to
that content. There is no "true" self. Instead, the self is always *imperfect* and
limited by a particular point of view; therefore the self is subject to transcendence, or to what Butler calls "self-thwarting." The "unattained but attainable self" that Cavell finds in Emerson is meant to convey this "imperfect"
perfectionism.[23] Through his perfectionism, particularly in essays such as
"Self-Reliance," Emerson is admonishing his contemporaries for their lack of
will. Emerson is especially hard on those who seek the affirmation of authority of
all kinds, whether it is the authority of family, convention, or popular opinion.
Significantly, Emerson and Kant share a profound faith in the human capacity
for free will. As a counterpart to Kant's invocation in his "What is Enlightenment?" essay of Horace's injunction "Sapere aude!" ("Dare to use your own
intelligence!"), Emerson inveighs in "Self-Reliance": "Trust thyself," that is,
"dare to be wrong." Trusting ourselves and daring to be wrong may be the only
ways of chancing on the right and the good. In pressing the case for self-trust
and self-reliance, Emerson is not making an argument for "great men" or extraordinary acts of genius, although at times it sounds that way. Instead,
Emerson is arguing for a kind of new world Socratic ethic, in which courage is
forged through an examination of the self.[24] This is what Cavell means by the
perfectionist injunction to become intelligible to oneself. It is an interpretation
of self-examination as a mode of self-cultivation and education.[25] By following the imperative to engage in self-examination and the pursuit of self-
understanding, Emerson argues that we should see our own lives as works of
art, in contrast to Taylor's protest that this kind of aestheticization of identity diminishes the self to the status of a mere "work." As Harold Bloom suggests, Emerson was a great dramatist of the self; he was someone who was able
to dive into the depths of inner experience and reveal a sense of pathos and
vitality *within*.[26]

Just as Kant has faith that each of us has the ability to be free, by which he
means the ability to give ourselves universal rules of action and duty, Emerson
argues that each individual has the capacity and possibility of genius. As with
Kant's use in "What is Enlightenment?" of oblique metaphors for the moral
self ("man of learning") and the universal community ("the entire reading
public"), Emerson employs his own code, as it were, for depicting the *resistance* associated with freedom. He casts self-reliance and self-trust as matters

of genius, though the appeal is not a claim for elitism, as in some kind of aristocracy of the soulful. Instead, Emerson seeks to awaken the genius of ordinary people.[27] In a similar vein to Kant's charge that immaturity derives from dependence on the influence of others, Emerson finds sources of inspiration in nonconformity, that is, the willingness to avert convention especially given the possibility of realizing one's own singularity. Genius is reflected in the capacity to face (Emerson calls it listening to and the "perception" of) death, disappointment, disenchantment, powerlessness, and failure, and to emerge from that encounter with one's own distinctive voice. In short, *genius involves listening for an inner calling or vocation.*[28] In Emerson's estimation, the sin of conformity is the sin of not listening to one's own instincts—a condition that subsequently prevents the self from being open to the truth of the world, especially to nature. The attunement to the call of nature is one of the features that situates Emerson comfortably within the Romantic tradition. It is also a mode that links the cultivation of self-knowledge and perfectionism with the sense of duty and necessary concern found in the idea of agency as a vocation.

Nonconformity is about transgression not for the sake of sabotage or even of revolution, though some of these connotations do hang tenuously on Butler's theory of performativity. Instead, the transgression and resistance of nonconformity relies on an individualistic communing with things of the soul. It speaks of the value of the poet and poetry, of the creative voice that is able to respond to the immediacy of feeling and perception. Emerson's notion of self-reliance is as much about faithfulness to an authentic self as it is a commitment to its subversion, that is, seeking singularity and finding one's uniqueness while knowing full well that a next self is waiting in the wings. It is, I am arguing, an expression of the religious imagination. As Emerson describes it, the religious imagination of self-reliance requires that one hear agency as a vocation not from an extant repertoire of external sources but rather as an attunement to the genuinely uncanny and new. "When good is near you, when you have life in yourself, it is not by any known or accustomed way; you shall not discern the foot-prints of any other; you shall not see the face of man; you shall not hear any name—the way, the thought, the good, shall be wholly strange and new. It shall exclude example and experience."[29] This is, I believe, why Cavell likens Emerson's notion of self-reliance and the corollary defiance of conformity to Kant's idea of duty to the moral law. Self-trust or self-reliance, in short, is the willingness to defy the opinions and affirmations of the present such that one takes the chance of achieving the acknowledgement that comes with the potential for greatness in the future. Casting the self-reliant and the self-trustworthy in terms of "greatness" and "genius" is Emerson's way of acknowledging how rare self-reliance is in practice.[30] Indeed, it is analogous to Weber's contentions about the rarity of integrity of character and personality in politics and science. While Emerson wants to broker the divide of the imperfect, conventional world to the realm of freedom, he is not confident that it will happen with frequency or with ease. Indeed, in "Self-Reliance," Emerson makes a Kantian move by positing a regulative and elusive ideal for self-reliance in the form of a self-sufficient and self-existing god: a supreme cause that enters all lower forms and thereby gives them—*us* the power to exist.[31] Emerson is effectively arguing that God is within each of us in our uniqueness and our singularity; and not as we are when we exist and act and think as a member of "a mob," which is to say, when we are being unreflective and kowtowing in order to garner the affirmation of others. Emerson is fully aware of how difficult and solitary self-reliance is. "We must go it alone," he writes. He is invoking Kant by suggesting that trusting oneself is a matter of rigorous virtue and duty. It requires the cultivation of a discipline that sees agency as a way of life and, as I have been arguing, as a vocation. "Inasmuch as the soul is present," Emerson writes, "there will be power not confident but agent."[32] As with Kant's criticism of immaturity or tutelage, Emerson recognizes that it is simply much easier to look to standards outside oneself. Self-reliance requires a nearly superhuman attitude that "insists on oneself" and holds to the discipline for the self that says "never imitate."[33]

Emerson, like Kant, posits that freedom occurs not as instances and forms that all of us would understand immediately, but rather in ways that will most likely be in defiance of the familiar. The risks are daunting and alienating; furthermore, the rewards are likely not to be seen in one's lifetime. Hence, Emerson's famous line on greatness: "Is it so bad... to be misunderstood?" He goes on to liken the risk of misunderstanding to the great achievements of Luther, Shakespeare, and even Jesus. "To be great is to be misunderstood." Even though it is a lonely endeavor, the hope is that all of us will at least take a shot at it.

A Revolution of the Spirit: Attunement to Discontent and Hope

It is easy to see that a greater self-reliance must work a revolution in all the offices and relations of men [*sic*]; in their religion; in their education; in their pursuits; their modes of living their association; in their property; in their speculative views.

—Ralph Waldo Emerson, "Self-Reliance"

What I think Emerson shows, at least in this all-too-brief comparison with Kant, is a way to sharpen and clarify an understanding of the role of melancholy in regenerating agency, particularly by revealing the possibility of seeing modernity, late modernity, and postmodernity not so much as epochs but as sets of attitudes and dispositions. Taylor, in effect, observes that the melancholy, or what he calls in *The Ethics of Authenticity*, the "malaise" of modernity, is the pervasiveness of the attitude and disposition of discontent. Butler identifies postmodernity also with discontent but through a deeper melancholy than Taylor manages to face. Despite these differences, I have been arguing that the attitudes and dispositions of the melancholy of modernity *and* of difference also bank on the possibility of hope and aspiration; which is to say, by seeking new ways of experiencing ourselves, the world, time, space, and history, these forms of melancholy imply a detachment from dominant and dominating habits of being. In other words, Butler and Taylor, in different but at times overlapping ways, are calling for a change in disposition and the cultivation of a radical attitude toward those things that have grounded experience in the past, that is, a dissent toward the dominant ideas of the age— ideas that range from the cultural ethos of secularism to more vexing world-views such as sexism, homophobia, and white supremacy. These constitute movements toward *a revolution of the spirit,* which means that they are as concerned for the internal convictions and commitments that are necessary for realizing freedom as they are for the practical reality of living the examined life. Both Butler and Taylor write at a time when the moral imperatives of the ethos of freedom have become banal and melancholic. In other words, the achievements and, more precisely, the achievability of freedom are taken for granted.[34]

In pressing the case for the urgency to attend to projects of regenerating agency, particularly as calls for the cultivation of the self and revolutions of the spirit, I want to underscore here that it is critical to keep in mind that the regeneration of agency requires a deep commitment to the enterprise of revealing false necessities. The discontents of modernity and postmodernity inspire change. As Emerson suggests toward the end of "Self-Reliance": "Discontent is the want of self-reliance: it is [an] infirmity of the will." Toward this end, some of the functions of religion begin to take shape in an interpretation of projects of regenerating agency as forms of cultivation—functions of religion such as: cultivating an abiding concern for the self (this holds even in Butler's poststructuralist decentering of subjectivity); the construction of visions of the world that affirm the passionate attachments that are born of the self, and; paradoxically, bringing to consciousness that which thwarts a sense of integrity in one's understanding the world and the nature of reality. In short, the perfectionist ethos brings into relief the continuous work of orienting the self *to itself* as well as to "the world" (universe, cosmos).[35]

On the one hand, certainly, it is more difficult to make the case that the cultivation of the self applies to Butler's project as much as it does to Taylor's, especially given the problematization of subjectivity that lies at the heart of her project. On the other hand, even with her insistence on contingency and the idea of living with the instability of the self, it still stands that a fundamental dissatisfaction resides in her political and cultural analysis that in itself is suggestive of a desire for change. The desire for change is not, as Butler makes clear, predicated on a utopian vision of transcendence that often operates in emancipatory projects. And yet Butler does characterize her explorations of the performative, as well as the relationship between the psychic and the political/social, as emancipatory in their ends and aims. Butler is upfront that the agency that performativity renders is not identical to, for example, the political agency of social action or political movements. Nonetheless, there is a basic change in self-understanding that comes through in her allusion to the idea that possibility can be a political good.[36]

The idea of agency as a vocation in Butler's work does not figure as a simple response to a calling "from beyond," as in Taylor's contentions about the reactions elicited by the sublime. Instead, my point is that agency as a vocation occurs in the performative moment in which we are hailed by institutions, practices, and figures of authority and are subjected to become what power calls us to be: straight, measured against masculinity, whiteness, wealth, and the like. Agency occurs in moments when a choice must be made to submit in either an orthodox or unorthodox way to the call (hail). Read as a process, the hailing of and by power calls the subject into being; this means being called into a mode of social existence, such as a subject who is beholden to the force of the law. The subject/self is *formed* by the calling/hailing of power. As with the Weberian retrieval, vocation calls us to do something that we *must* do. In other words, agency as a vocation compels us to respond. The critical task, which in turn is suggestive of a cultivation of subjectivity for Butler, is to determine if one's response to a hail or interpellation is genuine, or whether it is a result of the distillations of power in the psyche. Here is the correlation to Emerson's self-trust and self-reliance. In other words, the ambiguity of what constitutes integrity for the self under conditions of power instills a sense of urgency and necessity to practice critical self-examination and cultivation that lends the self to the transformative possibilities of regenerating agency. Furthermore, the decentered self in Butler's theory can only realize her/his agency through the ambiguity and ambivalence of melancholy. This means continually insisting on the vocation of perfectionism with the knowledge that an unfettered and unencumbered subjectivity is not only a pipe dream but also a potentially lethal distraction. Through his perfectionism, Emerson could entertain the ideal that self-reliance and the idea of trusting oneself only requires the gamble of being misunderstood. In making the case for the strenuous life of the melancholy of difference, Butler is effectively showing how the interpellated/subjected self is in a state of being in which the possibility of agency must measure and weigh the costs of becoming an agent beyond mere misunderstanding, that is, where the performative quickly turns from parody to the critical detachment of irony, and finally falls to a dire choice between conformity and the risks of social death. Performative agency is, in the end, melancholic freedom.

For Taylor, the idea of agency as moral vocation is less problematic, since he takes as axiomatic that a moral source is inherently good. In the scheme of the Althusserian interpellation that Butler adopts, the question of being called or hailed is, again, a highly ambiguous affair. In contrast, Taylor does not entertain "dark" possibilities, such as the idea of a Cartesian deceiving devil posing as a potential "caller." In other words, he does not seriously consider the possibility that a transcendent source that calls on the self may actually be evil. Allowing as much would mean entertaining the notion that a source that calls on the conscience to make judgments of value and worth may *not* in fact be good. In the end, this is an evasion on Taylor's part. There is evil in the world, and who is to say it does not exist even in the transcendence that lies "beyond life." Taylor admits to the ambiguity of framing epiphanies in as much as they issue features of the sublime. And yet the piety generated by a moral source that calls us to articulate it and to construct and lead a life according to its mandate, on Taylor's score, requires a belief in the goodness of the vocation. Ultimately, Taylor's account of agency as a vocation is persuasive not because of the claim that we are drawn to the good or that we cannot escape horizons of meaning and significance, but rather for the *formal* aspects of the theory that suggest that encounters with the epiphanic and the sublime discipline the self and the soul. By "discipline," I mean that the subjective experience of the sublime is necessarily ambiguous and unsettling, and it should not be taken as a transparent moment of revelation. Instead, the sublime's defiance of reason humbles our ability to make sense of it. This forced humility should be a spur to aspire to pierce the veil of the sublime (and presumably of the self) and to envision what stands, as it were, on the other side of that which turns us away. The sublime disciplines the self, as Kant argues, in the effective ways that it reveals the limits of what and *how* we know. The sublime also lures the religious imagination to seek out transcendence *despite* the fact that the subjective encounter with the sublime turns out to be a failure of the imagination.

Taylor's moral realism and his piety about the inherent goodness of moral sources would most likely come off as uncritical optimism from the perspective of an advanced poststructuralist such as Butler who is drawing not only from Foucault, Derrida, and Althusser, but also from Nietzsche and Freud: all of whom possessed deep suspicions about why we respond to moral vocations, especially when the response involves the force of guilt in the conscience. Nietzsche's slave morality, Freud's hyper-disciplining superego, Althusser's interpellation by authority, and Foucault's subjection to power all inflect a sense of necessity in the psyche through an obligation that feels paradoxically external *and* interior. Why do we turn in response to the hail of the police officer? Why do we cooperate with our own submission and potential negation? Butler's response is that we answer these calls even when we know that it means submitting ourselves to forces that will potentially deny that which is most dear to the self. Why? Because we desire to be. We also desire social existence. Subsequently, we find ourselves answering the call of authority and come to find that the hail of power is the ticket and the shibboleth to recognition as social beings.[37]

Nonetheless, the question raised by power's ability to call the subject into being through language and discourse is to ask how or even why it is possible to resist the call and respond to a different vocation. As a precondition for agency, Butler needs to give an account of why one voice, and not another, is more compelling. Or, as Cavell asks, "which among the voices contending to express your nature are ones for you to own here, now."[38] In other words, agency as a vocation, as I have formulated it, insists that there are some things we simply must do and some ways of life we simply must choose to live. The implication is that there are sources for resisting power that take the form of a calling. Certainly, this is what Kant implies by our obligation to the moral law, or Plato when he says we desire and are drawn to the good. Taylor's recourse to the sublime augurs the call to cultivate and enact our moral identities and agency. The question is whether there is an analogous calling for Butler's thoroughly discursive world. That is, is there a vocation for Butler that demands a response to the ethical and the political calls of justice, freedom, and agency that instill the possibility of resisting subjection and subjectivation on the terms dictated by power?

Butler clearly believes this to be case, otherwise her arguments about the agency revealed in the unpredictable and contingent performances of social norms would be unpersuasive. And yet while the points she makes about rethinking power and working the weakness of the norm are provocative in identifying power as imperfect and unstable in its ability to reproduce itself, Butler needs to provide more compelling alternatives than the ideas of unpredictability and contingency to transform her claim about agency into an assertion about the political and the ethical.[39] Framing the argument around the inevitable contingency of power's ability to reproduce itself would simply imply that Butler is making a phenomenological observation and subsequently is leaving the possibility of exploiting the imperfections of subjection and power to serendipity. Butler clearly sees agency as subversion and resistance to be a value as well as a potential political good; therefore, she recognizes the necessity of identifying a mechanism, as it were, for ethical-political vocation. In her use of theories of subjection, she reckons with this problem and identifies the potential for ethical-political vocation as opening up through the aspects of existence in which power affects deeply but not completely: namely, through the body and in the psyche.[40]

The body is a strangely elusive thing. As Butler argues in *Bodies That Matter*, the body has its own materiality that falls outside of language but only insofar as it calls language to respond to it. The body in its materiality—of life, illness, and even death—is not passive to language but rather poses

a demand in and for language, a "that which" which prompts and
occasions.... [W]ithin the cultural fabric of lived experience, [it calls
to be] fed, exercised, mobilized, put to sleep, a site of enactments
and passions of various kinds. To insist upon this demand, this site,
as the "that without which" no psychic operation can proceed, but
also as that on which and through which the psyche also operates, is
to begin to circumscribe that which is invariably and persistently
the psyche's site of operation; not the blank slate or passive medium
upon which the psyche acts, but, rather, the constitutive demand
that mobilizes psychic action from the start, that is that very mobili-
zation, and, in its transmuted and projected bodily form, remains
that psyche.[41]

Here, Butler identifies the materiality of the body as a referent that language
cannot capture. As Stephen K. White suggests, it correspondingly "takes its
place in language as 'an insistent call' to be attended to."[42] Following White's
reading here, it appears that Butler locates a source of agency in the vocation of
the body that responds to the melancholy of desire, marginalization, and
subjection. The relationship between the materiality of the body and language
is one in which the former calls upon the latter to make sense of it, to render
and grasp it, and to make it "real." The materiality of the body is a sublime limit
that exceeds language even as it demands language to name it. In this sense,
the dialectic between the sublime body and language echoes Cavell's notion of
becoming intelligible to oneself and the Emersonian idea of "the next self."[43]
Cavell identifies the inspiration for self-cultivation and the process of becoming intelligible to oneself with Emerson's grand refusal of conformity to authority and convention (which is in turn, so Cavell argues, a response to Kant's
insistence on conformity to the moral law).[44]

    There is an uncannily Emersonian note that Butler strikes in her recent
reflections on the political implications of performativity. I have already commented on the language of living with and through risk that Butler has in common with Emerson. Again, Butler is considerably less sanguine than Emerson
about what risk-taking entails. Even if one follows Cavell's reading of Emerson
as arguing along Kantian lines about the doubleness of the self, it remains
that Butler views the subject's entanglements under the constraints and re-
straints of gender and sexual identity, specifically, and all modes of difference,
generally, as more severe than the encumbrances Emerson identifies. Nonetheless, Butler shares Emerson's investment in the notion of possibility as a
moment and instance in which a self can thwart the power of conventions and
subsequently overcome the self called into being (interpellated) by power.
Butler is careful to qualify that she does not consider all identities to be oppressive. Instead, highlighting the forms of regulation that operate through
available norms of identity shows them to be "sites of ambivalence." As sites

of ambivalence, identities provoke "pleasure and pain" that speak to the anxiety of an identity being apt or not, as fitting and even enthralling, as well as potentially annulling and unstable. This means that both the "pleasure of and exhilaration of 'being' such and so are also haunted by a certain anxiety, a knowingness about the contingency of what we 'are.'"[45] Any foundationalist, essentialist, or narrative claims to identity are attempts to compensate for the inherent instability of identity. The instability of identity induces a paradox. It presents not simply a source of existential anxiety that presses one to become intelligible to oneself, but it also serves as a persistent reminder to be humble in the claims that one makes about oneself and others. In other words, it is a humility that folds the political imperatives of recognition over into the ethical demands of generosity. Presumably, Butler would be sympathetic to the Emersonian project of refusing conformity to convention, opinion, and authority; but the "high" Romantic self-reliance that Emerson posits appears too utopian to deal with the injunctions of the body and the psyche. Emerson resists authority and power by an appeal to self-reliance. Butler's project is, in large part, a query about how agency as the resistance to power can take place given the complicity of the self in its own subjection. If we are complicit in our subjection, Butler might ask Emerson, how can we trust ourselves to be self-reliant?

In contrast to the Emersonian ideal of perfectionism, I am arguing that the sublime plays a role in the prioritizations Butler discerns in the psychic life of power and agency. Recall that for Taylor the sublime is an indication of awe and even wonder, as well as reverence and commitment ("Achtung!"). The sublime as a framing epiphany, as Taylor would have it, also reveals the possibility of engaging a transcendent moral source (the good) that lies "beyond us" but with which we should aspire to (re)connect. Again, Taylor makes these conjectures about the sublime because of his faith in the inherent goodness of our moral sources. For Butler, the scenario is darker. There is an aspect of the sublime that exceeds our understanding, but it lies not in a transcendent source beyond life, but rather in the passionate attachments we have that are often oblique to our understanding. In other words, the desires we have that we cannot fully explain or understand—especially the desires that place us in conditions of submission and subjection—are paradoxically *and* ironically our best clues to the possibility of realizing agency and the self.[46]

My point here is that it is possible to find an analogous source to the unsettling, disciplining sublime that Taylor sees in the framing epiphanies of modernism in the passionate attachments that Butler identifies with the materiality of the body and the ambivalence of the psyche. The sublime body and psyche have similar effects to the ones Taylor identifies with framing epiphanies: namely, an unsettling that produces what seems like an inescapable ambivalence about what and who each of us desires. Furthermore, the sublime body and psyche reveal the problematic of trying to determine and comprehend why one desires what one desires at all. The inescapable melancholy that structures our desires, according to Butler, results from the ambivalence and uncertainty we feel toward desire—an ambivalence and uncertainty that is analogous to the mixture of awe and fear that Kant identifies with the sublime. And like the parallel instances of the sublime that Kant finds in nature (the mathematical and dynamic sublime of enormity and outsized phenomena that we cannot fully grasp in our understanding, such as the Swiss Alps, or perhaps Niagara Falls before the appearance of neon lights) as well as within the moral self (as in the *Critique of Practical Reason* in which Kant identifies the sublime with the moral law within us and the starry heavens above; which is to say, we are in possession of the sublime even as it remains, paradoxically, beyond our understanding and ability to fully explain), Butler identifies the failures and losses of melancholy as inspirations and sources of agency even as they force us to follow laws and norms not of our own devising. The sublime losses associated with melancholy are inspirations for the subversive and transgressive agency that contrasts with a sense of spiritual uplift or elevation. Indeed, the responses to melancholy that Butler identifies are expressions of anger, resentment, and even rage that can translate the psychic damage of subjection into "public" acts of political engagement, as well as hopes and aspirations for change.[47] Agency is born from the absence of freedom.

Thus, perhaps more like Emerson (and Cavell) and less like Taylor, Butler identifies agency's calling not with external sources but rather with the site(s) of the self: that is, the social conditions, context, and habitus shaped by history, the body, and, of course, the psyche. Thus, just as Emerson turned to himself, or rather within himself to help him understand the world, Butler turns to the production of the subject/self as the source of agency. *This* insight gives me an opportunity to elaborate on a conclusion I drew earlier: somewhat paradoxically Butler sets the stakes of nonconformity higher than Emerson did. For Emerson, the risk of nonconformity and refusal is acceptable, since the potential rewards have their own satisfactions (misunderstanding as the basis of greatness, for example). Butler casts nonconformity to norms and conventions as a defiance of the force of power. This defiance entails risks that include *social death*, that is, a denial of one's social existence.[48] As I showed in the last chapter in my discussion of Butler and melancholy, the desires of the abject of society—gays, lesbians, bisexuals, racial minorities, and so on—shape the passionate attachments to particular identities, as gendered, racialized, and the like. Deriding a concern for difference as "mere identity politics" is to disregard the pain and risks that come with fighting for social existence. Furthermore, as Cavell suggests, it overlooks the fundamental uncanniness of the ordinary, that is, the flow and flux between the familiar made strange and the strange becoming familiar: an insight revealed to us through performative, skeptical, and ironic ways of being in the world.[49]

On the Spiritual Aspirations of Melancholic Freedom

The Unfree Man

A. He stands and harks: what does he hear?
What sound is ringing in his ear?
What struck him down? What mortal fear?

B. Who once wore chains, will always think
That he is followed by their clink.
—Friedrich Nietzsche, from *The Gay Science*

Hopefully, it has become clear over the course of this interrogation of the religious dimensions of the contemporary discourse on agency that I view melancholy less as a lamentable condition of the spirit and more as an opportunity and occasion to realize the potential for freedom, possibility, and hope in complex and dark times. Agency as melancholic freedom begins with loss, and it presses on without assuming that any of us ever gets over the loss completely. Losses abound in our lives: losses of love, of moral sources, of a stable sense of self, of tradition, and of legitimacy. To wish a life without loss is a mark of immaturity.

The accounts of agency that Taylor and Butler provide are enormously rich, complex, and provocative, especially for an inquiry such as this one that seeks to uncover qualities of religious and spiritual life that often go unnoticed. The qualities of what I have been calling the religious imagination figure in both of their depictions of the conditions for the possibility of agency amidst fraught and fragile opportunities to express and realize hope. The religious imagination of melancholic freedom is paradoxical in its identification of fragility and ambivalence as preconditions for agency. Fragility attends to Taylor's aspirations to make strong evaluations in the context of moral pluralism and secular public life, as well as in Butler's claims for social existence eked out of the risks of social death and discursive vulnerability. Ambivalence arises as readily from Taylor's engagement with the modern balancing act of maintaining a commitment to political liberalism while also grasping onto the traditions that constitute our moral identities, as it does with Butler's aspiration to hold out for the possibility of agency and perhaps even freedom through the oppressive conditions that subject us to the forces of power. Despite the aspirations to move beyond the conditions that create melancholy, the subjective experience of loss *and* living with lost love is constitutive of being an agent—whether it takes the form of an aspiration to uncover the hidden love of the good that animates one's moral identity, or the longing to grieve and mourn the losses of social difference in order to love openly and freely. Thus, the sense that there is a lost love that stands at the center of one's moral identity proves to be a condition for the possibility of agency itself. In the end, contemporary agency is an expression of melancholic freedom.

I have marshaled the services of a range of thinkers to make the case that agency as melancholic freedom requires the deployment of the religious imagination to engage the aspirations to confront, transpire, and perhaps even transcend and transgress the limits that make the sources of the self obscure to us. The antiphony of Weber's fraught and at times embittered treatment of vocation brings into relief the sense in which the aspirations of agency require a call to love again despite melancholic losses. I have argued that the sublime serves as a conduit for the vocation of melancholic freedom, both in the form of Taylor's framing epiphanies and Butler's conjectures about the defiance that the body and the psyche pose to discourses and symbolic orders. Agency as a vocation requires wrestling with the unsettling effects of the sublime in order to disengage from the forces of dominant social imaginaries, whether these are manifest as a culture of secularism or as a political liberalism that obscures discrimination and hatred behind polite smiles and chatter.

As I have said throughout this book, the religious and spiritual significance of Taylor's and Butler's projects of regenerating agency is not to be found in the specific ends and aims of their respective projects but rather in the *qualities of aspiration and striving* they identify with melancholic freedom. These qualities signify a desire for transcendence, though not necessarily in the metaphysical sense of Taylor's moral sources (those sources are, after all, "beyond life"). Instead, this desire is more fully located in the immanent experience of yearning to move beyond the conditions of life as they currently affect us. This yearning and aspiration is tied to the work of the religious imagination: the faculty and ability to envision and, in Butler's case, to enact a new life, a next self.

It is this yearning for more—the aspiration for meaning, guidance, and the like—that characterizes the self as *active* in the regeneration of the conditions for the possibility of agency. And as an enterprise of seeking out agency—or at least seeking conditions that are conducive to the regeneration of agency, such as the cultivation of character, or greater attendance to the moral psychology of motivation, drives, and desires—melancholic freedom presses the religious imagination into the service of realizing these aspirations by invoking a sense of calling, that is, a vocation to do something and to be someone who feels that one's life is a necessary and worthy one to lead.

Melancholic freedom needs projects of regenerating agency in order to cultivate the sensibilities and dispositions that attune the self to possibilities and aspirations for transcendence: where transcendence covers a spectrum that ranges from the immanent concerns of political transcendence (as in overcoming oppression) all the way to the sense of being able to articulate and respond to a transcendent ideal or value. It is this mode of self-cultivation that maintains itself in often paradoxical forms (as in Butler's case) through an ideal of integrity and authenticity that is disciplining as well as fortifying, severe as well as enabling. It also speaks of a love that is denied, lost, or obscured. In sum, as an expression of love and as a severe yet enabling ideal, agency as melancholic freedom calls us into existence by instilling the aspiration to become a more genuine self. Melancholic freedom thus requires an attitude of piety and attunement: a piety to the ideals of integrity and an attunement to the conditions that enable possibility. As the faculty that enables vocation as well as projects of regenerating agency, the religious imagination is the capacity to engage in creative yet critical reflection on our states of being in the world. This means reflecting on what holds the self back and keeps it from flourishing. It is fair to characterize these features as forms of humanism, in the sense that the practices of self-transformation and cultivation aspire to the integrity of becoming more fully human. While the ideal of "becoming human" is problematic when applied to the poststructuralism of Butler's project of regenerating agency, I believe that the designs on resistance to regulatory practices imply a conviction to aspiring to do better and to *be* different. Agency as melancholic freedom aims to move beyond easy resolutions and readily available consolations. It is my hope that these reflections on melancholic freedom will open up avenues of dialogue for further explorations of the work of the religious imagination in regenerating agency, especially through the acknowledgment of the unavoidability of loss and the undeniable need for possibility and for hope.

Notes

CHAPTER I

I. Both theorists have been influential in shaping the work on agency and identity across a wide range of disciplines. As a major diagnostician and philosopher of modernity, Taylor has enjoyed critical appreciation, for example, by important contemporary social theorist such as Craig Jackson Calhoun and Hans Joas, and among political theorists such as Stephen K. White, Will Kymlicka, and William Connolly. See Craig Jackson Calhoun, "Imagining Solidarity: Cosmopolitanism, Constitutional Patriotism and the Public Sphere," *Public Culture* 14, no 1 (2002): 147–71; Hans Joas, *The Genesis of Values* (Chicago: University of Chicago Press, 2000); Stephen K. White, *Sustaining Affirmation: The Strength of Weak Ontology in Political Theory* (Princeton: Princeton University Press, 2000); Will Kymlicka, *Liberalism, Community, and Culture* (Oxford: Clarendon, 1989); and *Multicultural Citizenship: A Liberal Theory of Minority Rights* (Oxford: Oxford University Press, 1995); and William Connolly, *The Ethos of Pluralization* (Minneapolis: University of Minnesota Press, 1995).

Butler's work on performativity has been tremendously important for the development of gender and queer studies as well as for work in political theory, cultural studies, and critical theory. See, for example, Linda Alcoff, "Cultural Feminism versus Poststructuralism: The Identity Crisis in Feminist Theory," *Signs* 13 (Spring 1988): 405–36; Diana Fuss, *Identification Papers* (New York: Routledge, 1995); Elizabeth Grosz, "Experimental Desire: Rethinking Queer Subjectivity" in *Supposing the Subject*, ed. Joan Copjec (London and New York: Verso, 1994), 133–57; and Slavoj Zizek, *The Ticklish Subject: The Absent Centre of Political Ontology* (New York: Verso, 1999), 247–312.

2. Sigmund Freud, "Mourning and Melancholia," in *The Standard Edition of the Complete Psychological Works of Sigmund Freud*, ed. James Strachey (London: Hogarth Press, 1957), 14:243–60. Svetlana Boym argues

that, though there are elective affinities between nostalgia and melancholy, it is possible to distinguish between the two; the former has a greater public presence, and the latter is a more intensely personal phenomenon that runs the threat of associations with pathology. Svetlana Boym, *The Future of Nostalgia* (New York: Basic Books, 2001), 352–55, 358n.6. I take Boym's point about appearances, but in my estimation, nostalgia and melancholy share a great deal, both as phenomena as well as analytic categories. In fact, they do to such an extent that dissociating the two appears untenable and unconstructive. This is especially true in regard to what Boym calls "reflective nostalgia" and the "off-modern" possibilities that this form of nostalgia generates.

3. Robert Merrihew Adams, *Finite and Infinite Goods: A Framework for Ethics* (Oxford: Oxford University Press, 1999), 300–304. There is a great deal of overlap between the approaches that Adams and Taylor take, especially in the association they each identify between vocation and the love of the good.

4. For example, in the *Critique of Pure Reason*, a major turning point in Kant's interrogation into the conditions for the possibility of human cognition and knowledge occurs in the third antinomy, in which he examines how reason can spontaneously begin a series of causal relationships and *not* also, in turn, be an effect of a prior cause, such as God or some natural, prior phenomenon. In short, Kant concludes that we are, paradoxically, both free and not free. We are free through our capacity to be the first cause in a series of effects, and yet we are also encumbered by the conditions of nature, such as time, space, and other "forces"—laws of nature—that can determine our wills. The "solution" Kant comes upon serves as one of the bases for his arguments about our dual natures; that is, that we are both noumenal, in our ability to apply transcendental categories and ideas *freely*, and phenomenal, insofar as we are finite, encumbered beings. Immanuel Kant, *Critique of Pure Reason*, trans. Norman Kemp Smith (New York: St. Martin's, 1933), 464–79 (A532/B560–A559/B587).

5. For examples of the communitarian, analytic philosophical, and rational choice approaches to the problem of political participation as agency, see, respectively: Michael Sandel, *Democracy's Discontent: America in Search of a Public Philosophy* (Cambridge: Harvard/Belknap, 1996); Phillip Pettit, *A Theory of Freedom: From the Psychology to the Politics of Agency* (Oxford: Oxford University Press, 2001); and Dennis Chong, *Collective Action and the Civil Rights Movement* (Chicago: University of Chicago Press, 1991).

6. For this formulation of transcendence, I am indebted to Victor Kestenbaum's recent study of John Dewey, *The Grace and the Severity of the Ideal: John Dewey and the Transcendent* (Chicago: University of Chicago Press, 2002), 1–14 and 227n.1.

7. Clifford Geertz, "Religion as a Cultural System," in *Interpretation of Cultures* (New York: Basic Books, 1977), 87–125.

8. This is a phrase I borrow from Stanley Cavell's discussion of Emersonian perfectionism in his *Conditions Handsome and Unhandsome: The Constitution of Emersonian Perfectionism* (Chicago: University of Chicago Press, 1990), xxxvi–xxxvii.

9. More than thirty years after its initial publication, Rawls's *A Theory of Justice* (Cambridge: Harvard University Press, 1971) remains enormously influential. For Rawls's accommodation and response to his critics, see his *Political Liberalism* (New

York: Columbia University Press, 1995). For Habermas's touchstone texts, see *A Theory of Communicative Action*, vols. 1 and 2 (Boston: Beacon, 1984, 1987), and, more recently, *Between Facts and Norms: Contributions to a Discourse Theory of Law and Democracy* (Cambridge: MIT Press, 1998).

10. Calling it "the cultural studies approach" to political theory, Seyla Benhabib dismisses the advocates of the politics of difference as sacrificing political capital for the sake of cultural recognition. Seyla Benhabib, *Claims of Culture: Equality and Diversity in the Global Era* (Princeton: Princeton University Press, 2002).

11. For the communitarian side, see Michael Sandel, *Liberalism and the Limits of Justice*, 2nd ed. (Cambridge: Cambridge University Press, 1998), as well as *Democracy's Discontent*, and Michael Walzer, *Obligations: Essays on Disobedience, War, and Citizenship* (Cambridge: Harvard University Press, 1970). For a defense of the politics of difference, see Iris Marion Young, *Justice and the Politics of Difference* (Princeton: Princeton University Press, 1990).

12. For example, see Michael Walzer, *Thick and Thin: Moral Argument at Home and Abroad* (Notre Dame: University of Notre Dame Press, 1996).

13. The history of the contemporary feminist movement is instructive on this score. While there have been gains in initiatives such as pay equity between the genders that began, arguably, with the ethic that "the personal is political," gender inequality persists in the workplace. Nonetheless, the sense of urgency to remain politically active and engaged in a "feminist movement" has diminished severely. Barbara Epstein, "Feminist Consciousness after the Women's Movement," *Monthly Review* 54, no. 4 (September 2002): 31–37. For a discussion of the diminishing returns on participating in democratic political engagements, see Mark E. Warren, "What Can Democratic Participation Mean Today?" *Political Theory* 30, no. 5 (October 2002): 677–701.

14. This is a sentiment, I would argue, found throughout Michel Foucault's corpus. Foucault's work still stands as the gold standard of poststructuralism, even to his most vigorous critics. See, for example, Foucault's *Discipline and Punish: The Birth of the Prison*, trans. Alan Sheridan (New York: Vintage, 1979). In addition to Lacan's seminars themselves, for the Lacanian side, see Kaja Silverman, *The Acoustic Mirror: The Female Voice in Psychoanalysis and Cinema* (Bloomington: Indiana University Press, 1988). Perhaps the most vigorous and visible advocate for the Lacanian worldview is found in the work and person of Slavoj Zizek. See, for example, Zizek's *The Sublime Object of Ideology* (London: Verso, 1989). For a critique of what he considers to be the anemic political progressivism of literary theory and academic discourse, see Richard Rorty, *Achieving Our Country: Leftist Thought in Twentieth-Century America* (Cambridge: Harvard University Press, 1998).

15. Hardt and Negri's insistence that spontaneous yet coalescing groups will mobilize globally is a vivid contemporary example of the utopianism that often accompanies the rhetoric of agency. Michael Hardt and Antonio Negri, *Multitude: War and Democracy in the Age of Empire* (New York: Penguin Press, 2004). For a considerably less sanguine view of the limits to the effective possibilities of episodic political movements in our times, see Sheldon Wolin's "Fugitive Democracy" in *Identity and Difference*, ed. Seyla Benhabib (Princeton: Princeton University Press, 1996), 31–45.

16. Tu Weiming, *Centrality and Commonality: An Essay on Confucian Religiousness* (Albany: State University of New York Press, 1989).

17. Hannah Arendt, *The Human Condition* (Chicago: University of Chicago Press, 1958), see especially part II, "The Public and the Private Realm," 22–78.

18. Plato, *Republic*, 375b. For a thought-provoking commentary on this section of the *Republic*, see Catherine Zuckert, ed., *Understanding the Political Spirit: Philosophical Reflections from Socrates to Nietzsche* (New Haven: Yale University Press, 1988), 3.

19. Zuckert, *Understanding the Political Spirit*, 3.

20. Aristotle, *Nichomachean Ethics*, trans. Roger Crisp (Cambridge: Cambridge University Press, 2000), Book I, 13–14, 20–22/1098b–1110a, 1102a–1104s.

21. Zuckert, *Understanding the Political Spirit*, 3–4.

22. This division of spheres of life is reminiscent of Weber's diagnosis of modernity as having fallen into systems of rationalization and differentiation. The dominance of instrumental rationality, fortified by secularization, generates separate spheres of action; cf. Habermas, *A Theory of Communicative Action*, vol. I: *Reason and the Rationalization of Society*, trans. Thomas McCarthy (Boston: Beacon Press, 1984).

23. Zuckert, *Understanding Political Spirit*, 7–10.

24. Isaiah Berlin, "Two Concepts of Liberty" in *Four Essays on Liberty* (Oxford: Oxford University Press, 1969), 118–72. For a trenchant study of the early modern struggle with authority and tradition, see Jeffrey Stout, *Flight from Authority: Religion, Morality, and the Quest for Autonomy* (Notre Dame: University of Notre Dame Press, 1987).

25. Arendt, *Human Condition*, 248–56. Two notable critics of forms of political liberalism that seek to restrict and even exclude religious voices in liberal public discourse are the philosopher of religion Jeffrey Stout and the theologian Ronald Thiemann. See Jeffrey Stout, *Democracy and Tradition* (Princeton: Princeton University Press, 2003), and Ronald F. Thiemann, *Religion in Public Life: A Dilemma for Democracy* (Washington, D.C.: Georgetown University Press, 1996).

26. For an arresting presentation of this narrative about the fate of the self in modernity, see Harvie Ferguson, *Modernity and Subjectivity: Body, Soul, Spirit* (Charlottesville: University Press of Virginia, 2000), 1–19; cf. 136–65, 181–88.

27. Robert B. Pippin, "Nietzsche and the Melancholy of Modernity," *Social Research* 66, no. 2 (Summer 1999): 495–520.

28. James C. Edwards, *The Plain Sense of Things: The Fate of Religion in an Age of Normal Nihilism* (University Park: Pennsylvania State University Press, 1997), 1–58.

29. Max Weber, "Science as a Vocation" in *From Max Weber*, trans. H. H Gerth and C. Wright Mills (New York: Oxford University Press, 1946), 129–56.

30. For a fascinating study of Weber's critique of modernity and his preoccupation with the role of *Beruf*/vocation or calling, see Harvey Goldman, *Max Weber and Thomas Mann: Calling and the Shaping of the Self* (Berkeley: University of California Press, 1988).

31. Peter Homans, "Loss and Mourning in the Life and Thought of Max Weber: Toward a Theory of Symbolic Loss" in Peter Homans, ed., *Symbolic Loss: The Ambiguity of Mourning and Memory at Century's End* (Charlottesville: University Press of Virginia, 2000), 224–38; cf. Wendy Brown, "Wounded Attachments" in *States of Injury: Freedom and Power in Late Modernity* (Princeton: Princeton University Press, 1995), 52–76.

32. Freud, "Mourning and Melancholia." For Freud's views on desire for objects of love, see his "On Narcissism: An Introduction," in *Standard Edition*, 14:73–104; cf. Julia Kristeva's discussion of the inner tensions between the encumbrances of melancholia and the need for resolution in *Black Sun: Depression and Melancholia* (New York: Columbia University Press, 1989).

33. The most thorough sociological argument for rethinking the secularization thesis is found in José Casanova, *Public Religions in the Modern World* (Chicago: University of Chicago Press, 1994). On the relationship of Islamic fundamentalism to post-Enlightenment standards of public legitimation, see Roxanne L. Euben, *Enemy in the Mirror: Islamic Fundamentalism and the Limits of Modern Rationalism* (Princeton: Princeton University Press, 1999).

34. *Unlike*, say, Rawlsian political liberals, I maintain that there are no clear or adequate principles that distinguish the ethical ("the good") and the moral ("the right"). By framing the problem of agency in regard to loss and aspiration, my hope is to move beyond the narrow options of liberalism and communitarianism in order to explore a broader range of options and possibilities.

35. This is not to say that evil or freedom has simply become "ordinary" in our times. Instead, my claim is that we are lacking a moral and spiritual vocabulary that helps us to genuinely understand and appreciate the complexities of evil and freedom. In chapter 4, I elaborate on the analogy I am drawing between Arendt's thesis of the banality of evil and what I am calling the banality of freedom.

CHAPTER 2

1. Charles Taylor, *Sources of the Self: The Making of the Modern Identity* (Cambridge: Harvard University Press, 1989).

2. Immanuel Kant, *Groundwork of the Metaphysics of Morals*, trans. Mary Gregor (Cambridge: Cambridge University Press, 1998).

3. Taylor is, of course, offering up a caricature of deontological theories. It appears that R. M. Hare is a favored object of derision for Taylor. See Taylor, *Sources*, 53, 528n.3.

4. Ibid., 4.

5. This is Taylor's own characterization. See "Introduction," *Philosophical Papers 1: Human Agency and Language* (Cambridge: Cambridge University Press, 1985), 1–12. Hereafter *PP1*. Charles Taylor, *Philosophical Papers 2: Philosophy and the Human Sciences* (Cambridge: Cambridge University Press, 1985). Hereafter *PP2*.

6. Taylor, *Sources*, 4.

7. Taylor, *PP1*, 3.

8. Taylor, *Sources*, 93.

9. Ibid.

10. Ibid., 307.

11. For a discussion of the changes in the constitutive features of Taylor's theory of agency from his early essays, such as "What is human agency?" to the more robust formulations in *Sources of the Self*, see Owen Flanagan, "Identity and Strong and Weak Evaluation" in *Identity, Character, and Morality: Essays in Moral Psychology*, ed. O. Flanagan and A. O. Rorty (Cambridge: MIT, 1997), 37–66. Cf. Owen Flanagan,

Self Expressions: Mind, Morals, and the Meaning of Life (New York: Oxford University Press, 1996), 158–70.

12. Taylor, "What is human agency?" in *PP1*, 23f.

13. Ibid., 24f.

14. Throughout the text, I have, for the most part, avoided use of the universal "we," "our," and "us," with the exception of passages in which I am characterizing Taylor's arguments for a philosophical anthropology. In other words, "we," "our," and "us" appear in the text, mostly, in reference to Taylor's use of these terms.

15. Ibid., 25n.8.

16. Taylor, *Sources*, 20.

17. Ibid., 319.

18. Taylor, *PP1*, 33.

19. Ibid. Taylor develops a variation on this argument in his critique of Foucault and poststructuralist accounts of the limits of life possibilities for the self. See also Taylor, "Foucault on freedom and truth," in *PP2*, 152–84. For a precursor, of sorts, to the comparative work of this book, see the debate between Taylor and William Connolly on Foucault published in *Political Theory* as "Michel Foucault: An Exchange." William Connolly, "Taylor, Foucault, and Otherness," *Political Theory* 13, no. 3 (August 1985): 365–76; Charles Taylor, "Connolly, Foucault, and Truth," *Political Theory* 13 no. 3 (August 1985): 377–85.

20. Taylor, "What Is Human Agency?" 33–34.

21. See also Taylor, "Explanation and Practical Reason" in *Philosophical Arguments* (Cambridge: Harvard University Press, 1994), 34–60. Cf. Taylor, *Sources*, 72.

22. Compare Taylor's explanation of a practical reason that applies the "best account" principle of experience to William James's concluding remarks in his lecture "What Pragmatism Means." In relating how a pragmatist would account for belief in God, James writes:

> Her only text of probable truth is what works best in the way of leading us, what fits every part of life best and combines with the collectivity of experience's demands, nothing being omitted. If theological ideas should do this, if the notion of God, in particular, should prove to do it, how could pragmatism possibly deny God's existence? She could see no meaning in treating as "not true" a notion that was pragmatically so successful. What other kind of truth could there be, for her, than all this agreement with concrete reality?

William James, "What Pragmatism Means," in *Pragmatism and the Meaning of Truth* (Cambridge: Harvard University Press, 1978), 44. Taylor's focus on transitions in practical reason resonates with the disposition associated with the meliorism identified by James. Taylor does not invite the comparison to pragmatism, nor does he invoke it as a resource. It is a curious evasion in *Sources of the Self*, since a great deal of what Taylor has to say against epistemologically focused philosophy is consonant with pragmatist principles. Hans Joas criticizes Taylor on this count as well, underscoring that this as an obvious lacuna. For example, there are family resemblances between Taylor and Dewey in their respective phenomenological accounts of moral subjectivity, in their analyses of the role of ideals in the moral imagination, and even in the appeal to art as a form of cure or redemption. See Joas, *The Genesis of Value* (Chicago: University of Chicago Press, 2000), 142–44. It is plausible to read Taylor's most recent work, specifically his Gifford Lectures, as an attempt to rectify this situation. Taylor published portions of his Gifford Lectures as Charles Taylor, *Varieties of Religion Today: William James Revisited* (Cambridge: Harvard University Press, 2002).

23. In a genealogical project analogous to *Sources*, Taylor's recent work on the problem of "social imaginaries" speaks to this by attempting to determine how it is that secularism was able to capture the social imaginary of the west and why it continues to captivate. See Charles Taylor, "Modern Social Imaginaries," *Public Culture* 14, no. 1 (Winter 2002): 91–124.

24. Thomas Kuhn, *The Structure of Scientific Revolutions*, 2nd ed. (Chicago: University of Chicago Press, 1970).

25. Taylor's position here is one of the inspirations for the comparison I make in this book between his approach to the problem of agency and the work of Judith Butler.

26. Taylor, *Sources*, 27. Taylor makes a similar remark in "What is human agency?"

> The notion of identity refers us to certain evaluations that are essential because they are the indispensable horizon or foundation out of which we reflect and evaluate as persons. To lose this horizon, or not to have found it, is indeed a terrifying experience of disaggregation and loss. This is why we can speak of an "identity-crisis" when we have lost our grip on who we are. A self decides and acts out of certain fundamental evaluations.

Taylor, "What is human agency?" 35.

27. Taylor, *Sources*, 29. Taylor transposes this claim to the debates around multiculturalism in his classic essay "The Politics of Recognition," reprinted in Taylor, *Philosophical Arguments*, 225–56. See the exchange between Taylor and his critics in *Multiculturalism and "The Politics of Recognition,"* ed. Amy Gutmann (Princeton: Princeton University Press, 1992).

28. Taylor argues that "[t]he question at issue concerns which is a truer, more authentic, more illusion-free interpretation, and which on the other hand involves a distortion of the meanings things have for me. Resolving this issue is restoring commensurability." Taylor, *PP1*, 27. Cf. Taylor, *Sources*, 34–38.

29. See Charles Taylor, "Overcoming Epistemology," in *Philosophical Arguments*, 1–19.

30. Taylor, "What is human agency?" 35.

31. Taylor, *Sources*, 74–75.

32. Ibid., 53–55 and 62–65.

33. Taylor writes:

> [I]t is quite possible to conceive that the best theory of the good, that which gives the best account of the worth of things and lives as they are open to us to discern, may be a thoroughly realist one—indeed, that is the view I want to defend, without wanting to make a claim about how things stand for the universe "in itself" or for a universe in which the thesis that the

> boundaries of the good, as we can grasp it, are set by that space which is
> opened in the fact that the world is there for us, with all the meanings it has
> for us—what Heidegger called "the clearing" [Lichtung].

Ibid., 257. For an argument that religious ethics must necessarily take the form of
moral realism, see Franklin I. Gamwell, "Moral Realism and Religion," *Journal of
Religion* (1993): 475–95. For a moral realist position that does not rely on theism or
other religious beliefs, see Simon Blackburn, *Ruling Passions: A Theory of Practical
Reasoning* (Oxford: Oxford University Press, 1998).

34. Taylor, *Sources*, 53–62 and 256f.

35. Ibid., 27. See also Taylor, "What is human agency?" 33. See also Taylor's "Self-
interpreting animals" and "The concept of the person" in *PP1*, 45–76 and 97–114,
respectively.

36. Taylor, *Sources*, 77–80.

37. Ibid., 92–93. It is striking in a "post-ideological" era to have a notion such as
the love of the good reintroduced into moral discourse, in particular, at a time in which
moral philosophies that focus on obligation and duty are still dominant. Taylor is
not alone in this effort. Martha Nussbaum and Iris Murdoch are two notable fellow
travelers. In fact, Taylor's argument about the relation of the self to its moral sources is
deeply indebted to Murdoch's Platonism. Taylor does not adopt Murdoch's Platonic
view; instead he uses the idea of love of the good as paradigmatic for the bond between
the agent and her/his moral sources. See Iris Murdoch, *The Sovereignty of Good*
(London: Routledge, 1970); Martha Nussbaum, *The Fragility of Goodness: Luck and Ethics
in Greek Tragedy and Philosophy* (Cambridge: Cambridge University Press, 1986).

38. Ibid.

39. The picture here is clearly a vision drawn from Kant's portrayal of the king-
dom of ends.

40. The liberal theological tradition that began with Schleiermacher—an important interlocutor with the Romantics—situates the imagination at the heart of the
theological enterprise. Aside from Schleiermacher himself, other nineteenth century
figures that shaped this tradition include Dilthey, Schelling, and the Schlegel broth-
ers, among others. There are numerous twentieth-century theologians who employ the notion of the theological imagination as mediating between the human and
the divine, notably: Paul Tillich, *A Theology of Culture* (New York: Oxford University
Press, 1959); Ray L. Hart, *Unfinished Man and the Imagination* (Louisville: Westminster
John Knox Press, 2001 [1968]); Gordon D. Kaufman, *Theological Imagination: Constructing the Concept of God* (Louisville: Westminster John Knox Press, 1981); and
Mark C. Taylor, *Disfigurings: Art, Architecture, Religion* (Chicago: University of Chicago
Press, 1994).

41. Taylor, *Sources*, 211–33. On the one hand, it seems hardly coincidental that
Taylor's interpretation of the affirmation of the ordinary life is remarkably similar to
Weber's thesis in *The Protestant Ethic and the Spirit of Capitalism*. On the other
hand, Weber was seeking to divine the historical roots that infused capitalism with
the air of morality, while Taylor focuses on the moral elevation of everyday life itself.
Nonetheless, the two accounts come together in their critiques of modern rationalism, instrumentalism, and moral shallowness. I discuss this overlap between Taylor
and Weber in the final chapter.

42. Sheldon Wolin gives a similar account of the corollary effects of the ability of the new sciences to "master" nature and the creation of mechanisms of control and power in political institutions and practices. Wolin argues that the Baconian insights into the manipulation of the natural world find their way into efforts to marshal political power. Sheldon Wolin, *Politics and Vision: Continuity and Innovation in Western Political Thought*, expanded ed. (Princeton: Princeton University Press, 2004), see especially 214–56, 336–92, and 495–523.

43. Taylor, *Sources*, 358–59.

44. Ibid., 355.

45. The characterization of the "mainstream" Enlightenment is Taylor's. It is used, I believe, to set Kant's position in contradistinction to other Enlightenment thinkers, to Locke in particular.

46. It is noteworthy that Taylor follows Cassirer here in identifying the Cambridge Platonists as crucial precursors to Romanticism.

47. Taylor adopts the term "expressivism," on the suggestion of Isaiah Berlin, as a gloss on Berlin's discussion of Herder and "expressionism." See Taylor, *Hegel* (New York: Cambridge University Press, 1975), 13n.1. Expressivism is a tradition that Taylor reconstructs not only from Romanticism but also with post-Romantics such as Schelling, Hegel, Schopenhauer, Dostoyevsky, and Heidegger.

48. Taylor, *Sources*, 384.

49. Taylor, "Language and human nature," in *PP1*, 221.

50. Ibid., 226.

51. M. H. Abrams, *The Mirror and the Lamp: Romantic Theory and the Critical Tradition* (New York: Norton, 1958), 3ff.

52. Charles Taylor, "Irreducibly Social Goods," in Taylor, *Philosophical Arguments*, 127–45.

53. Taylor, "Theories of meaning," in *PP1*, 269.

54. Taylor, "Language and human nature," *PP1*, 230; cf. Taylor, "Theories of meaning," 263–69.

55. Ibid., 219.

56. Taylor, *Sources*, 376; emphasis added.

57. For example, see Charles Larmore's *The Romantic Legacy* (New York: Columbia, 1996).

58. For example, Taylor, *The Ethics of Authenticity* (Cambridge: Harvard University Press, 1992), 25–29.

59. Consider Taylor's concluding remarks to his massive commentary on Hegel:

> In a sense, the modern search for a situated subjectivity is the heir of that central aspiration of the Romantic period which Hegel thought to answer definitively—how to unite radical autonomy with the fullness of expressive unity with nature. Because nature cannot be for us what it was for that age, an expression of spiritual powers, the syntheses of the time can no longer command our allegiance.
>
> But the problem which concerned that generation, the opposition they attempted to reconcile, continues in different forms to our day. It seems ineradicable from modern civilization, which as heir to the Enlightenment

constantly re–awakens expressivist protest, and along with this, the claims of absolute freedom. The very urgency with which these claims are pressed makes the search for a situated subjectivity all the more vital. And the need grows more acute today under the impact of an ecological crisis which is being increasingly dramatized in the public consciousness. The fact that we are still trying to reconcile freedom and nature makes us still at home in the Romantic period. They speak to us, however bizarre their doctrines may appear to contemporary eyes.

And insofar as this search for a situated subjectivity takes philosophical form, Hegel's thought will be one of its indispensable points of reference. For although his ontological vision is not ours—indeed seems to deny the very problem as we now understand it—Hegel's writings provide one of the most profound and far–reaching attempts to work out a vision of em-bodied subjectivity, of thought and freedom emerging from the stream of life, finding expression in the forms of social existence, and discovering themselves in relation to nature and history. If the philosophical attempt to situate freedom is the attempt to gain a conception of man [sic.] in which free action is the response to what we are—or to a call which comes to us, from nature alone or a God who is also beyond nature—the debate will never cease—then it will always recur behind Hegel's conclusions to his strenuous and penetrating reflections on embodied spirit.

Taylor, *Hegel*, 570f.

60. Harold Bloom, *Ruin the Sacred Truths* (Cambridge: Harvard University Press, 1988).

61. Taylor, *Sources*, 378.

62. Ibid., 410–13. The paradigmatic form of the loss of this vision occurs in the philosophy and aesthetics of the post-Romantics that I will discuss later in this chapter.

63. Ibid., 449.

64. Ibid., 362.

65. Ibid., 372.

66. Ibid., 381.

67. Taylor makes his most succinct critique of contemporary appropriations of expressivism in *The Ethics of Authenticity*, 16–17 and 61–66.

68. Taylor, *Hegel*, 341.

69. Taylor, *Sources*, 419.

70. Quoted in ibid., 378.

71. Ibid., 479.

72. Ibid., 425–26; emphasis added.

73. Cf. David Tracy, "Fragments: The Spiritual Situation of Our Times," in *God, the Gift, and Postmodernism*, ed. John D. Caputo and Michael J. Scanlon (Bloomington: Indiana University Press, 1999), 170–81.

74. Taylor, *Sources*, 448.

75. Ibid.

76. Ibid., 462.

77. Ibid., 478.

78. Taylor captures well this experience of reading in his discussion Pound's poetry:

> The reality we are meant to report accurately on is not the bare scene, but the scene transfigured by emotion. And the emotion, in turn, is not simply personal or subjective; it is a response to a pattern of things which rightly commands this feeling. It is this pattern which is the "thing which has been clearly seen," and which the "precise interpretive metaphor" captures. The poetry which strives to be "accurate" is thus not simply mimetic. It liberates us from the constricting conventional ways of seeing, so we can grasp the patterns by which the world is transfigured. Pound's image, the "vortex" that he later took up along with Wyndham Lewis, his "ideogrammatic method" in the *Cantos*, all exhibit a poetry that makes something appear, brings it into our presence. But it doesn't work like the old epiphanies of being, where the object portrayed expresses a deeper reality. It doesn't come to us *in* the object or image or words presented; it would be better to say that it happens *between* them. It's as though the words or images set up between them a force field which can capture a more intense energy.

Ibid., 475.

79. Ibid., 588n.65.

80. Ibid., 315.

81. Ibid., 492.

82. Ibid., 446–49.

83. Ibid., 448–49.

CHAPTER 3

1. Charles Taylor, *The Ethics of Authenticity* (Cambridge: Harvard University Press, 1991), 25–29.

2. Charles Taylor, *Hegel* (Cambridge: Cambridge University Press, 1975), 3–50 and 537–71.

3. Taylor, *Ethics of Authenticity*, 13–24 and 55–70.

4. It is difficult to pinpoint the beginning of the contemporary revival of interest in the sublime. Arguably, as good a place to start as any is with Arendt's incomplete reflections on Kant and the role of the sublime in political judgment. Hannah Arendt, *Lectures on Kant's Political Philosophy*, ed. Ronald Beiner (Chicago: University of Chicago Press, 1989); see also her collection of essays, *Between Past and Future* (New York: Viking, 1968). For more recent treatments of the role of the sublime in political theory, see Stephen K. White's discussion of Burke in *Political Theory and Postmodernism* (Cambridge: Cambridge University Press, 1991); Jane Bennett's treatment of Schiller in "'How Is It, Then, That We Still Remain Barbarians?': Foucault, Schiller, and the Aestheticization of Ethics," *Political Theory* 24, no. 4 (November 1996): 653–72; and Bennett's recent book *The Enchantment of Modern Life: Attachments, Crossings, and Ethics* (Princeton: Princeton University Press, 2001). In literary

criticism, two central texts on the literary sublime are: Thomas Weiskel, *The Romantic Sublime: Studies in the Structure and Psychology of Transcendence* (Baltimore: Johns Hopkins University Press, 1976); and Neil Hertz, *The End of the Line* (New York: Columbia University Press, 1985). The philosophical literature on the sublime has focused largely, though not exclusively, on Kant's *Critique of Judgment*. Of particular note: Phillippe Lacoue-Labarthe and Jean-Luc Nancy, *The Literary Absolute: The Theory of Literature in German Romanticism*, trans. Philip Barnard and Cheryl Lester (Albany: State University of New York Press, 1988); Paul Crowther, *The Kantian Sublime: From Morality to Art* (Oxford: Oxford University Press, 1989); Paul Guyer, *Kant and the Claims of Taste*, 2nd ed. (Cambridge: Cambridge University Press, 1997); and Henry Allison, *Kant's Theory of Taste: A Reading of the Critique of Aesthetic Judgment* (Cambridge: Cambridge University Press, 2001). Not surprising, an especially engaging literature on the sublime is found in art criticism. See Bill Beckley, ed., *Sticky Sublime* (New York: Allworth Press, 2001); Bill Beckley and David Shapiro, eds., *Uncontrollable Beauty: Toward a New Aesthetics* (New York: Allworth Press, 2002); and Peter de Bolla, *Art Matters* (Cambridge: Harvard University Press, 2001).

5. Immanuel Kant, *Critique of Judgment*, trans. J. H. Bernard (New York: Hafner, 1951). See especially "Second Book," "The Analytic of the Sublime," §§ 23–54. The commentary literature on the third *Critique* is approaching Midrashic levels. A fascinating hermeneutical convergence of horizons has been taking place between philosophers and literary critics precisely through the invocation of Kant and the sublime. The common appeal here between philosophy and literary studies is in the mediating role Kant ascribes to judgment and the sublime: in which the sublime renders aesthetic judgment possible, specifically as taste, and subsequently forges a bridge between knowledge (or cognition) and morality (or freedom). In other words, judgment, by attending to the affective as well as the rational, synthesizes without reducing the conditions for the possibility of knowledge and freedom. In this regard, the third *Critique* not only connects the teleological projects of the first and second *Critiques*, but it also articulates a synthesis between reason and the affective that the Romantics would take as a fundamental imperative. It may appear contradictory, or at least ironic, that the Romantics would employ Kant to argue against Kant (that is, to use the third *Critique* to argue against the conclusions drawn in the first two *Critiques*), but such is the power and range of Kant's thought. This also speaks to the continuities that exist between authority (Kant) and revolutionaries (the Romantics). In the philosophical literature, in addition to the works I cited earlier, perhaps the clearest and most incisive work on Kant's aesthetics has been by Paul Guyer. For example, in addition to *Kant and the Claims of Taste*, see also Paul Guyer, *Kant and the Experience of Freedom: Essays on Aesthetics and Morality* (Cambridge: Cambridge University Press, 1993). On the theory and aesthetics side, Jean-François Lyotard's work on the avant-garde set the tone for the uses of the sublime in postmodern thought. See Lyotard's essays in *The Inhuman: Reflections on Time*, trans. Geoffrey Bennington and Rachel Bowlby (Stanford: Stanford University Press, 1991); also, Lyotard's lecture notes on the third *Critique* published as Jean-François Lyotard, *Lessons on the Analytic of the Sublime: Kant's Critique of Judgment*, trans. Elizabeth Rottenberg (Stanford: Stanford University Press, 1994).

6. Taylor, *Ethics of Authenticity*, 16–18, 25–30, and 45–69.

7. For a representative collection of essays on the analytic debate, see Gary Watson, ed., *Free Will* (Oxford: Oxford University Press, 1982).

8. Cf. Harry Frankfurt, *Necessity, Volition, and Love* (Cambridge: Cambridge University Press, 1999); see the essays in Owen Flanagan and Amélie Oksenberg Rorty, eds., *Identity, Character, and Morality: Essays in Moral Psychology* (Cambridge: MIT Press, 1990).

9. Robert Merrihew Adams, *Finite and Infinite Goods: A Framework for Ethics* (Oxford: Oxford University Press, 1999), 300–304. As Adams defines it, vocation or calling is the recognition of "who and what one ought to be."

10. Charles Taylor, "Iris Murdoch and Moral Philosophy" in *Iris Murdoch and the Search for Human Goodness*, ed. Maria Antonaccio and William Schweiker (Chicago: University of Chicago Press, 1996), 3–28. Murdoch was one of Taylor's teachers and had a major impact on his thought. Such is her influence that it is rather clarifying to read *Sources of the Self* in dialogue with Murdoch's *The Sovereignty of Good* (London: Routledge, 1970). Murdoch is quite elegant in the connections she draws between art and morality, particularly by highlighting the expression of "religious feeling or religious *perception*" she discerns in art, especially tragedy. See ibid, 85. See also her essay "The Sublime and the Good," in *Existentialists and Mystics: Writings on Philosophy and Literature*, ed. Peter Conradi (New York: Penguin Press, 1999), 205–20.

11. John Rawls's work is the major and most widely influential statement on this. See especially his *Political Liberalism* (New York: Columbia University Press, 1993).

12. Charles Taylor, *Sources of the Self* (Cambridge: Harvard University Press, 1989), 3.

13. I refer to "modern western identity" rather than simply "modern identity," as Taylor does, because it is clear, at least in texts such as his philosophical essays, *Hegel*, and *Sources of the Self*, that his arguments reflect a history of the development of the self in the modern west and not of global humanity. For example, one could contrast this depiction of modern western moral identity to east Asian Confucian ethical subjectivity that, in its ideal form, is deeply embedded in a tradition and requires location within not only a communal history but also a cosmological one. See Tu Weiming, *Centrality and Commonality: An Essay on Confucian Religiousness* (Albany: State University of New York Press, 1989). Nonetheless, given the global dominance of Western, specifically American and western European, "ways of life," an analysis of the kind of moral subjectivity and agency that Taylor undertakes is increasingly salient for "the rest" of the world. The historical account that Taylor provides is a story of supersessions of moral sources and the concomitant changes in the relationship of the self to these sources. As I mentioned above, Taylor's method of legitimating his philosophical anthropology is to tell the story of modern identity and moral agency on the level of individuals and also in terms of a collective consciousness, and thus puts the book in a vein similar to Hegel's *Phenomenology of Spirit*. Like the *Phenomenology*, *Sources of the Self* unfurls its narrative after a lengthy philosophical "preface." While both the *Phenomenology* and *Sources* focus heavily on the theme of overcoming alienation in its various forms, the morals of these two tales are not the same. The *Phenomenology* is a drama in which the protagonist, "Consciousness," wends its way dialectically to achieve self-consciousness *qua* freedom within history. It is also a story about the growth and development of rational, objective Spirit (*Geist*).

Sources is a different epic. It is a story not of a single protagonist but of two lovers—the self and the good/God/name-your-moral-source. Taylor's narrative is not a history of causal explanation but rather an extended meditation on the *idées fixes* that endure through the changes in the relationship between the self—the moral agent—and its moral sources and how these changes reflect larger historical and cultural sensibilities. Taylor's epic begins with the good as moral source, which is external to the self and yet the object of awe and love (Plato). As the relationship grows, the good becomes internal *and* external, cultivated through a reciprocation of love (*agape*) and grace (Augustine). Eventually the lovers demand intimacy and immediacy (Luther); have children (Deism); and then become solipsistic (Descartes). Soon, the lovers have rationalized their relationship (Locke) and develop lives independent of each other (Kant) and inevitably become estranged from each other (Locke again). There is a renewed passion in the relationship (Romantics) and an attempted reconciliation (Hegel) that leads to bitter separation and denunciation (Schopenhauer, Baudelaire). The story ends, or at least where we as contemporaries pick it up, with the self that has lost contact with its moral sources—its love—and is seeking for any way possible to reestablish the relationship and the possibility of hope (modernists).

14. The classic statement on negative freedom is found in Isaiah Berlin's "Two Concepts of Liberty" in his *Four Essays on Liberty* (London: Oxford University Press, 1969), 118–73.

15. Certainly, one can make the counterargument that a foundational example of moral psychology is found with Kant himself in his *Religion within the Boundaries of Mere Reason*. But even in the *Religion*, Kant formulates the problematic of moral psychology and motivation for ethical and moral agency in negative terms; that is, the agent is ethical and acts ethically only when she/he can constrain the natural existence of "radical evil" within. In other words, Kant still maintains that the agent is not naturally inclined toward the good and therefore requires a way of subjecting arbitrary wills/choice (*Willkür*) to the standard of ethical action posed by the ideal, ethical will (*Wille*). Immanuel Kant, *Religion within the Boundaries of Mere Reason and Other Writings*, trans. Allen Wood and George di Giovanni (Cambridge: Cambridge University Press, 1998), 33f./AK 6:4–6:5 and 61–70/AK 6:39–6:50.

16. Taylor, "What's wrong with negative liberty?" in *Philosophy and the Human Sciences: Philosophical Papers 2* (Cambridge: Cambridge University Press, 1985), 211–29.

17. For a nuanced discussion of the many faces—mythical and otherwise—of secularization and secularism, see José Casanova, *Public Religions in the Modern World* (Chicago: University of Chicago Press, 1994). For Coles's discussion of the secular, see his *The Secular Mind* (Princeton: Princeton University Press, 1999).

18. Taylor, *Sources*, 38–39.

19. Sophocles, *Antigone* in *The Three Theban Plays*, trans. Robert Fagles (New York: Penguin Press, 1984). For a remarkably poetic *and* poignantly political translation of *Antigone*, see Seamus Heaney, *The Burial at Thebes: A Version of Sophocles' Antigone* (New York: Farrar, Straus, and Giroux, 2004).

20. Mark Twain, *The Adventures of Huckleberry Finn* (New York: Chanticleer, 1950), chapter 31.

21. Emmanuel Levinas, "Time and the Other" and "Ethics as First Philosophy" in *The Levinas Reader*, ed. Sean Hand (Cambridge: Blackwell, 1990), 37–58 and 75–87.

22. To be fair, while Kant clearly identifies moral autonomy and responsibility with a binding force on the will of duty and obligation to the moral law, there is some overlap between the account of the changes in orientation and disposition I am describing here in the shift Huck makes from one moral world to another and the description of conversion that Kant provides early in the *Religion*. Kant, *Religion*, 67–68/AK 6:47.

23. William James, "The Will to Believe" in *The Will to Believe and Other Essays in Popular Philosophy, and Human Immortality* (New York: Dover, 1967), 1–31.

24. Taylor, *Sources*, 38f.

25. Robert B. Pippin, "Nietzsche and the Melancholy of Modernity," *Social Research* 66, no. 2 (Summer 1999): 495–520.

26. Harvey Goldman, *Max Weber and Thomas Mann: Calling and the Shaping of the Self* (Berkeley: University of California Press, 1988). Goldman's comparative study of Weber and Mann was enormously helpful in my consideration and reflections on the relationship between vocation and agency.

27. For surveys of this history, see, for example, Michael Allen Gillespie, *Nihilism before Nietzsche* (Chicago: University of Chicago Press, 1995); and James C. Edwards, *The Plain Sense of Things: The Fate of Religion in an Age of Normal Nihilism* (University Park: Pennsylvania State University Press, 1997).

28. Immanuel Kant, "An Answer to the Question: 'What Is Enlightenment?' " in *Kant: Political Writings*, ed. H. S. Reiss (Cambridge: Cambridge University Press, 1991), 54–60.

29. Taylor, "What's Wrong with Foundationalism? Knowledge, Agency, and World" in *Heidegger, Coping, and Cognitive Science: Essays in Honor of Hubert L. Dreyfus*, vol. 2, ed. Mark A. Wrathall and Jeff Malpas (Cambridge: MIT Press, 2000), 132.

30. Sigmund Freud, "Mourning and Melancholia," in *The Standard Edition of The Complete Psychological Works of Sigmund Freud*, trans. and ed. James Strachey (London: Hogarth Press, 1957): 14:243–60.

31. Svetlana Boym makes an effective argument that the persistent memories and experiences of exile and the like fall more aptly in the category of nostalgia rather than melancholy, since nostalgia derives more directly from experiences with memory and place than with melancholy. For my purposes, I do not draw an overly stark distinction between the function and place of the two categories, though I appreciate Boym's concern for the potentially pathological connotations of melancholy. Of course, nostalgia comes with its own "negative" associations, including sentimentality, weak-mindedness, and the like. Svetlana Boym, *The Future of Nostalgia* (New York: Basic Books, 2001), 5.

32. This is a standard theme among communitarians. For example, Michael Sandel makes a similar argument in *Liberalism and the Limits of Justice* when he contends that the self is never a self "prior" to its ends (values, goods, ideals) as Rawls insists. Instead, a self is only a self when it is in "possession of its ends." See Michael Sandel, *Liberalism and the Limits of Justice*, 2nd ed. (Cambridge: Cambridge University Press, 1998), 54–65.

33. Jürgen Habermas, *Postmetaphysical Thinking: Philosophical Essays*, trans. William Mark Hohengarten (Cambridge: MIT Press, 1993), 51, emphasis added. Stephen Mulhall makes a similar comparison between Taylor and Habermas in their respective appeals to the aesthetic. See Stephen Mulhall, "Sources of the Self's Senses

of Itself: The Making of a Theistic Reading of Modernity," in *Can Religion Be Explained Away?* ed. D. Z. Phillips (New York: Macmillan, 1996), 131–60.

34. It should be noted that Habermas is quite critical of Taylor's appeal to modern art as a source of moral inspiration. Habermas argues that conceding such a role to the aesthetic would reduce philosophy either to a form of aesthetics itself or to aesthetic criticism. In other words, philosophy would lose its discursive place amongst the "legitimate" disciplines. The quirkiness of the critique arises in the reversal made immediately following his criticism of Taylor's move to the aesthetic and Habermas's suggestion later in the essay that literature and art have the potential for producing "world-disclosing power." In my view, Habermas's contradiction here in invoking the Heideggerian/Arendtian idea of "world disclosure" is an illuminating example of how fraught so-called secular philosophers become when taking religion, the spiritual, and the metaphysical into serious consideration. Ibid; cf. Mulhall, "Sources of the Self's Senses of Itself," 131–60.

35. For example, the trajectory of the two volumes of *The Theory of Communicative Action* begins, in volume 1, with a Weberian analysis of the rationalization and differentiation of the life world, that is, the effects of secularization on the structure of experience, language, and so on. In volume 2, Habermas builds on the adoption of the secularization thesis and looks to the roots of the grammar of language games by invoking, among other sources, Durkheim's discussion of the "linguistification of the sacred." In short, the implicit argument in regard to the religious and the sacred is that rationalization and linguistification have not fully naturalized the metaphysical. Jürgen Habermas, *The Theory of Communicative Action*, vols. 1 and 2, trans. Thomas McCarthy (Boston: Beacon, 1984 and 1987, respectively).

36. See John Dewey, *Art as Experience* (New York: Perigree, 1959); Richard Rorty, *Contingency, Irony, and Solidarity* (Cambridge: Cambridge University Press, 1989); Stanley Cavell, *Disowning Knowledge: In Seven Plays of Shakespeare* (Cambridge: Cambridge University Press, 1987); Stanley Cavell, *Pursuits of Happiness: The Hollywood Comedy of Remarriage* (Cambridge: Harvard University Press, 1981); Martha Nussbaum, *Upheavals of Thought: The Intelligence of Emotions* (New York: Cambridge University Press, 2001); Cornel West, *Democracy Matters: Winning the Fight against Imperialism* (New York: Penguin Press, 2004). The movement is also in the other direction, which is to say, from the literary and aesthetic to the philosophical. George Steiner, Anthony Cascardi, Harold Bloom, Thomas Weiskel, and Gerald Bruns are just a few well-known examples of this genre.

37. For example, Taylor, *Sources*, 94. Cf. Murdoch, "The Sublime and the Good," 212.

38. Korsgaard affirms this point in regard to the question of normativity:

[W]e have normative concepts...because we have to figure out what to believe and what to do. Normative concepts exist because human beings have normative problems. And we have normative problems because we are self-conscious rational animals, capable of reflection about what we ought to believe and to do. That is why the normative question can be raised in the first place: because even when we are inclined to believe that something is right and to some extent feel ourselves moved to do it we can still *always* ask: but is this really true? And must I really do this?

Christine M. Korsgaard, *The Sources of Normativity* (Cambridge: Cambridge University Press, 1996), 46–47.

39. Immanuel Kant, *Groundwork of the Metaphysics of Morals*, trans. Mary Gregor (Cambridge: Cambridge University Press, 1997), 14 "note"/AK 4:400–401.

40. Cf. Jerome McGann, *Romantic Ideology: A Critical Investigation* (Chicago: University of Chicago Press, 1983). McGann's text is still a benchmark for critics of Romanticism. McGann's objections to Romanticism have become *de rigueur* for those who reject the tradition for its utopianism and subsequent desire for transcendence, its prioritization of the abstract over the particular and the social, the idealization of internal/inward concerns, and the subsequent valorization of the subjective. As I have noted, the primary reason Taylor distances himself from Romanticism has to do with the "ethics of authenticity," that is, a culture of self-fulfillment and subjectivism. In other words, Taylor's dismissal shares many of the features of McGann's critique. Part of the task I have set for this book is to join the spirited defense of the Romantic inheritance not for the sake of regress or even retrieval in the Taylorian sense of this term, but rather to tap into the aspects of Romanticism that contribute positively to projects of regenerating agency.

41. Richard Rorty, "Taylor on Self-Celebration and Gratitude," *Philosophy and Phenomenological Research* 54 (1994): 197–201; Quentin Skinner, "Modernity and disenchantment: Some historical reflections" in *Philosophy in an Age of Pluralism: The Philosophy of Charles Taylor in Question*, ed. James Tully (Cambridge: Cambridge University Press, 1994), 37–48.

42. Taylor, *Sources*, 75.

43. Both Rorty and Skinner make the point that Taylor's Catholicism has undue influence on his faith in moral realism. For both, the charge comes across as an *ad hominem* attack veiled in the guise of making a point about incommensurability. While it *might* count as a historicist point to say that Taylor's status as a Catholic has some play in his philosophy, it does not speak to the fact that he is quite assiduous in his genealogical and philosophical work, such as *Sources of the Self*, to present his arguments in a manner that does not bank on fideistic or dogmatic (Catholic) claims. Instead, Taylor includes "theism" as one of, but not the only, moral orientation that takes transcendent sources seriously.

44. Arendt lays out a similar set of conditions for the possibility of agency in *The Human Condition*, in which she identifies a series of correlations between action, speech, and identity. The public life of agency and the interpersonal engagements that it entails enable, according to Arendt, revelations and disclosures about who we are. Rather than appealing primarily to the sublimity of the aesthetic, Arendt makes the quasi-Hegelian point about the indispensable medium of public yet mutual recognition for meaningful agency; that is, that there is a "revelatory quality of speech and action [that] comes to the fore where people are *with* others and neither for nor against them—that is, in sheer human togetherness." Hannah Arendt, *The Human Condition*, 2nd ed. (Chicago: University of Chicago Press, 1998), 178–80.

45. Charles Taylor, "Language and human nature," in *Human Agency and Language: Philosophical Papers 1* (Cambridge: Cambridge University Press, 1985), 231.

46. Taylor, *Sources*, 92.

47. Ibid., 93. While Taylor makes a strong case for the necessity of moral sources as constitutive goods, the moral psychology that undergirds his theory of agency may not be obvious to all. Taylor acknowledges this in his reply to commentators in *A Catholic Modernity?*

> I was struck in some of the comments on *Sources [of the Self]* by how many people couldn't seem to grasp what question I was addressing. They took "moral sources" to be another name for the highest principles. They literally couldn't think outside the contemporary agenda.
>
> But, one wants to protest, don't you see that it *also matters* whether people can actually bring themselves to *do* the right thing? But then your interlocutor looks at you blankly and says: of course, but that's not *moral philosophy*; how people actually get motivated, that's in the domain of psychology, or sociology, or whatever.
>
> In other words, these two issues, what we should do and how we come to do it, which were unproblematically seen as part of the same inquiry by Plato, Augustine, and just about everybody else until the last three centuries, have been neatly sundered and placed in noncommunicating intellectual universes.

Charles Taylor, *A Catholic Modernity? Charles Taylor's Marianist Award Lecture* (New York: Oxford University Press, 1999), 120.

48. Taylor, *Sources*, 20.

49. Stephen K. White, *Sustaining Affirmation: The Strengths of Weak Ontology in Political Theory* (Princeton: Princeton University Press, 2000), 58–62. White makes a similar criticism of Taylor, namely, that his rejection of postmodern projects of identity as mere "works" serves to obscure the overlapping concerns he shares with theorists such as Derrida and Foucault.

50. Taylor, *Sources*, 92.

51. Ibid., 512.

52. Taylor, "Cross Purposes: The Liberal-Communitarian Debate" in his *Philosophical Arguments* (Cambridge: Harvard University Press, 1995), 181–203.

53. Cf. also Hans Joas, *The Genesis of Values* (Chicago: University of Chicago Press, 2000), 163.

54. Taylor, *Sources*, 17. Cf. Peter Berger, *The Sacred Canopy: Elements of a Sociological Theory of Religion* (New York: Anchor, 1969).

55. Taylor, *Sources*, 318–19.

CHAPTER 4

1. Hannah Arendt, *Eichmann in Jerusalem: A Report on the Banality of Evil* (New York: Viking, 1965). See also Daniel Jonah Goldhagen, *Hitler's Willing Executioners: Ordinary Germans and the Holocaust* (New York: Knopf, 1996).

2. Ward Connerly, "The Sweet Music of Equal Treatment" in *Affirmative Action: Social Justice or Reverse Discrimination?* ed. Francis J. Beckwith and Todd E. Jones (Amherst, N.Y.: Prometheus, 1997), 64–49; see also Ward Connerly, *Creating Equal: My Fight with Race Preferences* (San Francisco: Encounter Books, 2000).

3. The concern over the diminishing willingness to participate in public service, for example, has been sufficiently broad, such that both a Republican president (the first George Bush's "Thousand Points of Light") and a Democratic president (Clinton's creation of AmeriCorps) have made calls to the American citizenry to become more engaged in public life. For the academic laments over the flagging levels of civic engagement in American public life, see Robert Bellah et al., *Habits of the Heart: Individualism and Commitment in American Life* (Berkeley: University of California Press, 1985), and *The Good Society* (New York: Knopf, 1991); also Robert D. Putnam, *Bowling Alone: The Collapse and Revival of American Community* (New York: Simon & Schuster, 2000).

4. I address this turn to agency in the next section of this chapter in my discussion of the difference versus equality debate in feminist theory. I return to the theme of urgency, motivation, necessity, and agency in the last chapter, in which I discuss the idea of agency as a vocation.

5. Charles Taylor, "Leading a Life" in *Incommensurability, Incomparability, and Practical Reason,* ed. Ruth Change (Cambridge: Harvard University Press, 1997), 171–83.

6. Charles Taylor, "What's Wrong with Negative Liberty," in *The Idea of Freedom: Essays in Honor of Isaiah Berlin,* ed. Alan Ryan (Oxford: Oxford University Press, 1979), 175–93.

7. Charles Taylor, *The Ethics of Authenticity* (Cambridge: Harvard University Press, 1991), 13–24, 55–70, 109–121. See also Charles Taylor, "The Politics of Recognition" in his *Philosophical Arguments* (Cambridge: Harvard University Press, 1995), 225–56.

8. While I use "melancholy" and "melancholia" interchangeably, particularly in reference to Freud and Butler, I will predominantly use the English idiomatic terms "melancholy" and "the melancholic" throughout the text.

9. Stephen K. White, *Sustaining Affirmation: The Strengths of Weak Ontology in Political Theory* (Princeton: Princeton University Press, 2000), 69–71, 93–98.

10. The political theorists who fall under these hybrid categories are, somewhat ironically, also the ones most often called simply "communitarians," that is, theorists such as Will Kymlicka and Taylor himself. See Will Kymlicka, *Liberalism, Community, and Culture* (Oxford: Clarendon Press, 1989); and Michael Walzer, *Obligations: Essays on Disobedience, War, and Citizenship* (Cambridge: Harvard University Press, 1970). For Taylor, see his "Cross-Purposes: The Liberal-Communitarian Debate," in Taylor, *Philosophical Arguments,* 181–203.

11. There are a number of good discussions of this debate. See especially Joan W. Scott, "Deconstructing Equality-versus-Difference: or, the Uses of Post-structuralist Theory for Feminism," in *Feminist Studies* 14 (Spring 1988): 33–50; Linda Alcoff, "Cultural Feminism versus Poststructuralism: The Identity Crisis in Feminist Theory," in *Signs* 13 (Spring 1988): 405–36; Shane Phelan, "Specificity: Beyond Equality and Difference," in *differences* 5 (Spring 1991): 128–43; and Iris Marion Young, *Justice and the Politics of Difference* (Princeton: Princeton University Press, 1990).

12. In feminist theory, see Carol Gilligan's argument that there is a "female" ethics of care that is distinct from a "male" ethic of self-interest. In race theory, a similar set of claims is made for the singularity of black experience ("ontological blackness," as Victor Anderson calls it). Carol Gilligan, *In a Different Voice* (Cambridge: Harvard University Press, 1982). Victor Anderson, *Beyond Ontological Blackness: An Essay on African American Religious and Cultural Criticism* (New York: Continuum, 1995).

13. Susan Bordo, "Feminism, Postmodernism, and Gender-Skepticism" in *Feminism/ Postmodernism*, ed. Linda J. Nicholson (New York: Routledge, 1990), 150–53.

14. Charles Taylor, *Sources of the Self* (Cambridge: Harvard University Press, 1989), 488–99 and 508–18; see also Charles Taylor, *The Ethics of Authenticity* (Cambridge: Harvard University Press, 1994), 13–24, 43–54, and 109–22.

15. As DiStefano notes, it may be the case that the postmodern decentered self is a luxury only (white) men can enjoy. Christine DiStefano, "Dilemmas of Difference: Feminism, Modernity, and Postmodernism" in Nicholson, *Feminism/Postmodernism*, 73–77, esp. 76.

16. Seyla Benhabib, *The Claims of Culture: Equality and Diversity in the Global Era* (Princeton: Princeton University Press, 2002).

17. Michael Omi and Howard Winant, *Racial Formation in the United States* (New York: Routledge, 1986); bell hooks, *Feminist Theory: from Margin to Center* (Boston: South End Press, 1984).

18. Susan Moller Okin, "Is Multiculturalism Bad for Women?" *The Boston Review* (October/November 1997). Available: http://www.bostonreview.net/BR22.5/okin.html.

19. Benhabib, *Claims of Culture*, 1–48.

20. The increasingly problematic project of identifying categories for the U.S. census is a particularly good example of the dilemmas posed by a greater awareness of differences of identity and the structural lag in recognizing them. See, for example, Lawrence Wright, "One Drop of Blood," *The New Yorker* (25 July 1994): 46–55.

21. Martha Nussbaum, "The Professor of Parody: The Hip, Defeatist Feminism of Judith Butler," *The New Republic* (22 February 1999): 37–45.

22. Judith Butler, *Gender Trouble: Feminism and the Subversion of Identity* (New York: Routledge, 1990), 142.

23. The classic statement on social death is Orlando Patterson, *Slavery and Social Death: A Comparative Analysis* (Cambridge: Harvard University Press, 1982). I discuss the problematic of difference and social death in the next chapter on Butler and melancholy/melancholia.

24. The anger and fury of response to the consecration of Gene Robinson, an openly gay priest, as Episcopal Bishop of New Hampshire is a strikingly clear example.

25. J. L. Austin, *How to Do Things with Words*, ed. J. O. Urmson and Marina Sbisa (Cambridge: Harvard University Press, 1962); and Jacques Derrida, "Signature, Event, Context" in his *Margins of Philosophy*, trans. Alan Bass (Chicago: University of Chicago Press, 1982), 307–30.

26. Austin, *How to Do Things*, 26–32 and 53–59.

27. Butler, *Gender Trouble*, 89–120 and 143–47.

28. In actuality, Butler admits at the beginning of *Bodies that Matter* that she came to the notion of the performative through reading Derrida's "Signature, Event, Context." Judith Butler, *Bodies That Matter: On the Discursive Limits of "Sex"* (New York:

Routledge, 1993), 2. For an illuminating and incisive discussion of these texts, particularly as applied in the history of religion, see Amy Hollywood, "Performativity, Citationality, Ritualization," *History of Religions* 42, no. 2 (2002): 93–115.

29. Butler, *Bodies That Matter*, xi and 146.

30. Quoted in ibid, 13.

31. See Seyla Benhabib, "Feminism and Postmodernism" and Nancy Fraser, "False Antitheses" in Seyla Benhabib, Judith Butler, Drucilla Cornell, and Nancy Fraser, *Feminist Contentions: A Philosophical Exchange* (New York: Routledge, 1995), 20–25 and 67–69, respectively; also, Nussbaum, "Professor of Parody," 37–45.

32. Vicki Bell, "On Speech, Race and Melancholia: An Interview with Judith Butler," *Theory, Culture, & Society* 16, no. 2 (199): 170.

33. This is not to say that Butler ignores or does not discuss Lacan. She provides extensive commentaries on Lacan, especially in Judith Butler, *The Psychic Life of Power: Theories in Subjection* (Stanford: Stanford University Press, 1997), 83–131. Nonetheless, while she comments on Lacan and the influence of his approach to psychoanalysis, she seems more persuaded by the more "traditional" psychoanalysis of Freud as well as the Lacanian Marxist Althusser than by Lacan himself. The latter move is consonant with Butler's attempt to qualify her work as oriented toward the political rather than solely toward the cultural or the ethical. While the distinction of the political and the cultural is not always entirely clear in her writing, Butler's concern for the effects of power—rather than the play of the symbolic, "the Real," and the imaginary as Lacan describes it—makes the move to Althusser's treatment of ideology and subjection sound. I take up Butler's choice of Freud as a resource in my discussion of her treatment of melancholy. For criticism of Butler's reading of Lacan, see Slavoj Zizek, *The Ticklish Subject: The Absent Centre of Political Ontology* (New York: Verso, 1999), 247–312.

34. Bell, "Interview with Butler," 163–74.

35. Butler, *Bodies That Matter*, 229.

36. Ibid.

37. Ibid., 237.

38. Stanley Cavell, *Conditions Handsome and Unhandsome: The Constitution of Emersonian Perfectionism* (Chicago: University of Chicago Press, 1990), xxxvi–xxxvii.

39. David Hume, *Enquiries Concerning the Human Understanding and Concerning the Principles of Morals*, ed. L. Selby-Bigge (London: Oxford University Press, 1902), 162.

40. Charles Larmore, *The Romantic Legacy* (New York: Columbia University Press, 1996), 65–99.

41. Ibid., 82–83.

CHAPTER 5

1. For a Kantian argument that equates having obligations with being human, see Christine M. Korsgaard, *Sources of Normativity* (Cambridge: Cambridge University Press, 1996), 1–5 and 44–48.

2. Stanley Cavell, *Conditions Handsome and Unhandsome: The Constitution of Emersonian Perfectionism* (Chicago: University of Chicago Press, 1990), xxxv–xxxvii.

3. Immanuel Kant, *Groundwork of the Metaphysics of Morals*, ed. and trans. Mary Gregor (Cambridge: Cambridge University Press, 1997), 13–14/AK 4:400–401.

4. Ibid., 14–15/AK 4:402.

5. Judith Butler, *Psychic Life of Power: Theories in Subjection* (Stanford: Stanford University Press, 1997), 10–12 and 28–30.

6. Vicki Bell, "On Speech, Race and Melancholia: An Interview with Judith Butler," *Theory, Culture, & Society 16, no. 2 (199): 164.*

7. Judith Butler, *Gender Trouble: Feminism and the Subversion of Identity* (New York: Routledge, 1990), 143. It is noteworthy that Butler is hardly the first to introduce the metaphor of "negotiation" into the discourse of the self. Ervin Goffman, in *The Presentation of Self in Everyday Life* and in his work on frame alignment and symbolic interactionism, made use of the metaphor of negotiation to characterize the exchange between the self as the "actor" and what the actor perceives to be the expectations of a given audience or situation. In the sociology of knowledge tradition, Peter Berger and Thomas Luckmann suggested a similar negotiation of identity formation in the processes of socialization in *The Social Construction of Reality*. Nonetheless, Butler's work signifies an advance beyond Goffman and Berger and Luckmann insofar as she has put the discussion of negotiation within the context of a critique of power. Homi K. Bhabha makes an analogous set of moves with the notion of hybridity that he develops in postcolonial theory. See Ervin Goffman, *The Presentation of Self in Everyday Life* (New York: Doubleday, 1959); Peter Berger and Thomas Luckmann, *The Social Construction of Reality* (New York: Anchor, 1966); and Homi K. Bhabha, *The Location of Culture* (New York: Routledge, 1994), 25–26.

8. Louis Althusser, "Ideology and Ideological State Apparatuses (Notes Toward an Investigation)" in *Lenin and Philosophy and Other Essays*, trans. Ben Brewster (New York: Monthly Review Press, 1971), 127–88.

9. Ibid.

10. Bell, "Interview with Butler," 165.

11. Ibid., 170.

12. Charles Taylor, "Foreword" to Marcel Gauchet, *The Disenchantment of the World: A Political History of Religion*, trans. Oscar Burge (Princeton: Princeton, 1997), ix–xv. See also Taylor's "Two Theories of Modernity," *Public Culture*, 11:1 (1999): 153–174.

13. Sigmund Freud, "Mourning and Melancholia," in Sigmund Freud, *The Standard Edition of the Complete Psychological Works of Sigmund Freud*, vol. 14, trans. and ed. James Strachey (London: Hogarth Press, 1957), 237–58.

14. For example, see Julia Kristeva, *Black Sun: Depression and Melancholia*, trans. Leon S. Roudiez (New York: Columbia, 1989); Wendy Brown, "Resisting Left Melancholia," *boundary 2* 26, no. 3 (Fall 1999): 19–27.

15. Wendy Brown, "Resisting Left Melancholia," 19–21. Cf. Peter Homans, "Introduction" in *Symbolic Loss: The Ambiguity of Mourning and Memory at Century's End*, ed. Peter Homans (Charlottesville: University of Virginia Press, 2000), 1–40.

16. Quoted in Victor Kestenbaum, *The Grace and Severity of the Ideal: John Dewey and the Transcendent* (Chicago: University of Chicago Press, 2002), 209.

17. Freud, "Mourning and Melancholia," 245. See also Homans, *Symbolic Loss*, 36–38.

18. Freud, "Mourning and Melancholia," 245.

19. Bell "Interview with Butler," 172. See also, Peter Homans, *Symbolic Loss*, 1–42.

20. Homans, *Symbolic Loss*, 20.

21. For a commentary on the "sticky sublime," see the eponymous essay in Bill Beckley, ed., *Sticky Sublime* (New York: Allworth, 2001), 2–15.

22. The experience of melancholy is generalizable beyond gender and sexuality. For an argument on the losses and psychic condition of racial melancholy, see Anne Anlin Cheng, *The Melancholy of Race: Psychoanalysis, Assimilation, and Hidden Grief* (New York: Oxford University Press, 2001).

23. Kristeva, *Black Sun*, 53.

24. "The madman," from Friedrich Nietzsche, *The Gay Science: With a Prelude in Rhymes and an Appendix of Songs*, trans. Walter Kaufmann (New York: Vintage, 1974), 181–82.

25. Frederic Jameson, *The Political Unconscious: Narrative as a Socially Symbolic Act* (Ithaca: Cornell University Press, 1981), ix–xiv and 180–81.

26. Butler, *Psychic Life of Power*, 132–50.

27. Quoted in "Introduction" of Michel Foucault, *Ethics, Subjectivity, and Truth*, ed. Paul Rabinow (New York: Free Press, 1997), xxiv.

28. Walter Benjamin, "Theses on the Philosophy of History" in *Illuminations: Essays and Reflections*, ed. Hannah Arendt (New York: Schocken, 1969), 263.

29. E. M. Cioran, *The Temptation to Exist*, trans. Richard Howard (Chicago: University of Chicago Press, 1998); see also, Martha Minow, *Between Vengeance and Forgiveness: Facing History after Genocide and Mass Violence* (Boston: Beacon Press, 1998).

30. Wole Soyinka, *The Burden of Memory, the Muse of Forgiveness* (New York: Oxford University Press, 1999).

31. Butler, *Psychic Life of Power*, 18–19.

32. Ibid.

33. Jacques Derrida, *The Other Heading: Reflections on Today's Europe* (Bloomington: Indiana University Press, 1992), 18.The "anticipation of the unanticipatable" is Romand Coles's gloss on Derrida's discussion of the role of hope in the work of democracy. I am in strong agreement with Coles that the ethos of anticipating the unanticipatable should not become a fetish that allows agents to put off the hard work of democratic practices in favor of "messianic gestures toward 'the new' and 'possibility.' " Nonetheless, projects of regenerating agency need to proceed, as I have been arguing, by managing the dialectical tensions between "the is" and "the ought," between history and hope. See Romand Coles, *Beyond Gated Politics: Reflections for the Possibility of Democracy* (Minneapolis: University of Minnesota Press, 2005), 156–57.

34. Butler, *Psychic Life of Power*, 26–27.

35. Butler, *Bodies That Matter: On the Discursive Limits of "Sex"* (New York: Routledge, 1993), 241.

36. Bell "Interview with Butler," 176.

37. For example, see Richard Rorty, *Achieving Our Country: Leftist Thought in Twentieth-Century America* (Cambridge: Harvard University Press, 1998).

38. The shifts in the thought of Ernesto Laclau is an interesting comparative example of a "leftist" whose work has developed in a direction that makes him now read like a mainstream, political liberal of a Rawlsian stripe. As Jeffrey Isaacs has suggested, there has been a strange silence on the part of political theorists in response

the collapse of the Soviet Union and the apparent unviability of socialism. Democracy has been presented as a panacea, and yet few are engaging in a critical interrogation of the validity and viability of democracy in all political settings. The dominance of Rawlsian and Habermasian approaches in political theory represents, in my view, a remarkable narrowing of the political. In other words, Taylor is right to point out how political liberalism and naturalist philosophies have diminished and narrowed moral and ethical discourse, as well as the possibilities of political theory itself. For the shifts in Laclau's work, see his (with Chantal Mouffe) *Hegemony and Socialist Strategy: Towards a Radical Democratic Politics* (London: Verso, 1985; and his recent published exchange with Butler and Slavoj Zizek in Judith Butler, Ernesto Laclau, and Slavoj Zizek, *Contingency, Hegemony, Universality: Contemporary Dialogues on the Left* (London: Verso, 2000). See also Jeffrey C. Isaacs, *Democracy in Dark Times* (Ithaca: Cornell University Press, 1998). For a pointed response to Isaacs on the silence of political theory, see Sheldon Wolin, "What Time Is It?" *Theory & Event* (1997), 1, no.1.

39. I have borrowed this evocative phrase from the synthetic work of the anthropologist and political theorist James C. Scott. See his *Domination and the Arts of Resistance: Hidden Transcripts* (New Haven: Yale University Press, 1990).

40. For a discussion of Augustine on this form of self-inquiry, see Hannah Arendt, *The Human Condition*, 2nd ed. (Chicago: University of Chicago Press, 1998), 10–11.

41. bell hooks, *Yearning: Race, Gender, and Cultural Politics* (Boston: South End Press, 1996), 27. Cf. Rey Chow's remarks on "postmodern automatons" in her *Writing Diaspora: Tactics of Intervention in Contemporary Cultural Studies* (Bloomington: Indiana University Press, 1993), 55–72.

CHAPTER 6

1. Both essays appear in Max Weber, *From Max Weber: Essays in Sociology*, trans. and eds. H. H. Gerth and C. Wright Mills (New York: Oxford University Press, 1946), 77–156.

2. I am indebted to the discussion of calling and cultivation or *Bildung* found in Harvey Goldman, *Max Weber and Thomas Mann: Calling and the Shaping of the Self* (Berkeley: University of California Press, 1988). For a less sympathetic and subsequently more critical interpretation of Weber's vocation essays, see Dana Villa, *Socratic Citizenship* (Princeton: Princeton University Press, 2001), 186–245.

3. Max Weber, *The Protestant Ethic and the Spirit of Capitalism*, trans. Talcott Parsons (New York: Routledge, 1992 [1930]), 39–40.

4. Weber, "Science as a Vocation," 139; emphasis added.

5. Ibid., 143.

6. Weber, "Politics as a Vocation," 127.

7. Villa identifies Weber's preoccupation with the moral ideal of integrity as a theme that pervades his corpus. Villa, *Socratic Citizenship*, 213–26.

8. For a discussion of Weber's thesis as a meditation on the "demagification" of the world, see Goldman, *Max Weber and Thomas Mann*, 18–44.

9. Weber, "Science as a Vocation," 153.

10. For a collection of essays that take up this Weberian theme, see Asher Horowitz and Terry Maley, eds., *The Barbarism of Reason: Max Weber and the Twilight*

of Enlightenment (Toronto: University of Toronto Press, 1994). See especially the essays by Mark E. Warren, "Nietzsche and Weber: When Does Reason Become Power," 68–98; and Sheldon Wolin, "Max Weber: Legitimation, Method, and the Politics of Theory," 287–310.

11. Sheldon Wolin, "Fugitive Democracy" in *Democracy and Difference: Contesting the Boundaries of the Political*, ed. Seyla Benhabib (Princeton: Princeton University Press, 1996), 31–45. For Wolin's expansion on the fleeting and fugitive political possibilities of democracy, see Sheldon Wolin, *Politics and Vision*, expanded ed. (Princeton: Princeton University Press, 2004), 581–606.

12. Josiah Royce, *The Sources of Religious Insight* (New York: Scribners, 1912), 11.

13. John Dewey, *A Common Faith* (New Haven: Yale University Press, 1934), 1–28.

14. In regard to the idea of cultivation as linked both to spiritual practices as well as to political, ethical, and religious aspirations, I have in mind three sets of literature. Two of them are organically linked; the third is not connected to the other two but perhaps is closest to qualifying as articulating actual religious/spiritual practices. The first two literatures are exemplified in the works of Pierre Hadot and Alexander Nehamas. See Pierre Hadot, *Philosophy as a Way of Life* (Cambridge: Blackwell, 1995); and Alexander Nehamas, *The Art of Living: Socratic Reflections from Plato to Foucault* (Berkeley: University of California Press, 1998). Foucault's work on the "care of the self" found inspiration in Hadot's retrieval of ancient Greek Stoic philosophy and has been influential in fortifying Nehamas's project of philosophy as cultivation of the self. See Michel Foucault, *The Care of the Self, History of Sexuality*, vol. III, trans. Robert Hurley (New York: Pantheon, 1978). See also Michel Foucault, *Fearless Speech*, ed. Joseph Pearson (Cambridge: MIT Press, 2001), for Foucault's discussion of "parrhesia" or frank speech as a form of education and cultivation, esp. 89–166. Finally, from an entirely different tradition—Confucian humanism—there is Tu Wei-ming's enormously influential *Centrality and Commonality: An Essay on Confucian Religiousness (An Essay on Chung-yung)* (Albany: State University of New York Press, 1989), see esp. 89–121. It is certainly possible to read the continuation of the idea of philosophy and philosophical reflection as a form of spiritual practice beyond the point that Foucault identifies as the last historical "school" of this mode of western, philosophical cultivation of the self, namely, the appropriation of the ascetic and Stoic practices by fourth-century Christians. Foucault concludes that the idea of the care of the self or self-cultivation loses viability after Christianity takes it on; which is to say that these spiritual practices became, from that historical moment, overly circumscribed by the encroaching dogmatism of the Christian tradition—a dogmatism that Foucault identifies with the Nietzschean idea of slave morality and guilt. The critique is somewhat self-contradictory on Foucault's part, since he is, at least initially, interested in the care of the self because of the series of "techniques" that ancient philosophy offers for self-cultivation. See Foucault, *Fearless Speech*, 142–66. There is an argument to be made that the true, modern inheritors of this tradition were the Renaissance humanists, represented by figures such as Ficino, and later on by Erasmus and Vico. Anthony Grafton's work in this area is exemplary. For example, see his *Bring Out Your Dead: The Past as Revelation* (Cambridge: Harvard University Press, 2002).

15. Charles Taylor, *The Ethics of Authenticity* (Cambridge: Harvard University Press, 1992), 27–29.

16. Ibid. See also: Charles Larmore, *The Romantic Legacy* (New York: Columbia University Press, 1996); Richard Eldridge, *The Persistence of Romanticism: Essays in Philosophy and Literature* (Cambridge: Cambridge University Press, 2001); Stanley Cavell, *In Quest of the Ordinary: Lines of Skepticism and Romanticism* (Chicago: University of Chicago Press, 1988). I am especially indebted to Eldridge's book for convincing me of the centrality of the ideal of aspiration for the Romantic ethos, as well as for providing the arresting notion of "the persistence of romanticism."

17. Friedrich Schleiermacher, *On Religion: Speeches to its Cultured Despisers* (Cambridge: Cambridge University Press, 1996), 18–54.

18. The phrase "unattained but attainable self" is from Emerson's essay "History." Ralph Waldo Emerson, *Essays & Lectures* (New York: Library of America, 1983), 235–56. Stanley Cavell, *Conditions Handsome and Unhandsome: The Constitution of Emersonian Perfectionism* (Chicago: University of Chicago Press, 1990), xxxvi, 57. See also Stanley Cavell, *Cities of Words: Pedagogical Letters on a Register of the Moral Life* (Cambridge: Harvard University Press, 2004), 2–18.

19. Cavell, *Conditions*, xxxvi–xxxvii.

20. Hannah Arendt, *The Human Condition* (Chicago: University of Chicago Press, 1958), 192–93.

21. Cavell, *Conditions*, 3–4.

22. Ibid.

23. Stanley Bates, "Stanley Cavell and Ethics," in *Stanley Cavell*, ed. Richard Eldridge (Cambridge: Cambridge University Press, 2003), 36–43.

24. Ralph Waldo Emerson, "Self-Reliance" in *Essays & Lectures*, 257–82. Immanuel Kant, "An Answer to the Question: 'What Is Enlightenment?'" in H. S. Reiss, ed., *Kant: Political Writings* (Cambridge: Cambridge University Press, 1991), 54–61.

25. Cavell, *Cities of Words*, 24–26.

26. Harold Bloom, "Emerson and Whitman: The American Sublime" in Bill Beckley, ed., *Sticky Sublime* (New York: Allworth Press, 2001), 16–40.

27. Cavell, *Conditions Handsome and Unhandsome*, 16; cf. 18; Kant, "What Is Enlightenment?," 54–61.

28. In "Compensation," Emerson casts the problem as the soul's response to nature's unequal dispensation of abilities, opportunities, and fortunes among people—the differences between "Less" and "More." Death and calamity are constants of the cycle of life—Emerson calls it "growth"—that force each of us to adapt, cope, and keep moving forward. Ralph Waldo Emerson, "Compensation" in *Emerson: Essays & Lectures*, 300–302. Taylor's use of the narrative language of growth and maturity to describe agency as moral, practical reasoning in transitions is remarkably reminiscent of Emerson.

29. Emerson, "Self-Reliance," 271.

30. Ibid., 265.

31. Ibid., 269–73, especially 272.

32. Ibid., 271–72.

33. Ibid., 278–79.

34. Eagleton identifies this ethos as a species of the tragic and subsequently correlates the sublime with the melancholic disposition I have identified with contemporary experiences of freedom, especially the *sotto voce* quality that I associated with the banality of freedom in the last chapter. As Eagleton writes:

If tragedy has something of the melancholic joy of the sublime, it also displays for some critics a similar structure. The pain of the Kantian sublime springs from a recognition of finitude: we strive to measure up to some unfathomable Law or Reason, but inevitably fail. The sublime thus has an oedipal structure. But if our finitude is thus thrown into harsh relief, so by contrast is the august infinity which we crave; and in the very act of striving and failing to attain it, we act out a freedom in which we can hear a dim echo of the sublime power itself. In falling short of the Law or the Absolute, we acknowledge our affinity with it, recognizing that our only true dwelling place is within its eternal homelessness.

Terry Eagleton, *Sweet Violence: The Idea of the Tragic* (Malden, Mass.: Blackwell, 2003), 176–77.

35. Ruf makes a similar argument in his reading of William James insofar as he characterizes James as a religious thinker who was continuously struggling to find ways of maintaining an orientation of the self in the face of chaos. Frederick J. Ruf, *The Creation of Chaos: William James and the Stylistic Making of a Disorderly World* (Albany: State University of New York Press, 1991), xv–xviii and 123–40. Neville makes a similar argument in regard to the need for cultivating "poise" and "orientation" between the self and the ethical. Robert Cummings Neville, "A New Confucian Lament for Alienation" in *Loneliness*, ed. Leroy Rouner (Notre Dame: University of Notre Dame Press, 1998), 258–72.

36. Vikki Bell, "On Speech, Race and Melancholia: An Interview with Judith Butler," *Theory, Culture, & Society* 16, no. 2 (1999): 163–74.

37. Butler, *Psychic Life of Power*, 27–29; cf. 117–120.

38. Cavell, *Conditions Handsome and Unhandsome*, xxxvi. It is fascinating to read the parenthetical aside that follows this quote by Cavell as a précis for Butler's take on identity and agency:

The contention among voices may shift without settling once and for all. If voice is a predicate of a self, then the contention of voices suggests that, while a self has a world, the peculiar unity of the world of a self may express itself as a dissonance, a scene, say, of abdication, division, banishment, war, imprisonment.

Ibid., xxxvi–xxxvii.

39. Butler has in fact moved in this direction in her most recent work. Regrettably, the publication of her Spinoza lectures, in which she takes on problems of moral philosophy, appeared too late for me to give an adequate reading of her movement to the moral and the ethical in this book. See Judith Butler, *Giving an Account of Oneself* (New York: Fordham University Press, 2005).

40. Butler, *Psychic Life of Power*, 28–29; cf. Butler, *Bodies that Matter*, 10–11.

41. Butler, *Bodies That Matter*, 67.

42. Stephen K. White, *Sustaining Affirmation: The Strengths of Weak Ontology for Political Theory* (Princeton: Princeton University Press, 2000), 84.

43. Butler, *Psychic Life of Power*, 24; cf. Cavell, *Conditions Handsome and Unhandsome*, xxxv. Consider this excerpt from a recent interview with Butler, in which she

responds to critics who view her theory of gender identity as diminishing the possibility of making ethically relevant distinctions between identities:

> This view usually arrives at my door in the following form: Butler makes room for new possibilities of gender, but she fails to give us a criterion by which to distinguish between good and bad possibilities. Surely, Butler does not mean to condone or support the proliferation of all such possibilities, regardless of their ethical content. I think that the only way to answer this question is to take a few steps back and ask the following: under what political conditions does possibility itself emerge as a political good? And the answer to that is: under conditions in which gender has been constrained, in which certain sexual and gender minorities have felt their lives to be "impossible," unviable, unlivable, then "becoming possible" is a most certain political achievement. . . . That lives foreclosed now take themselves to be "possible" strikes me as a political good under conditions in which a certain heightened norm of compulsory heterosexuality works to make non-compliant lives into those which are impossible. . . . For me . . . an essential part of that generosity involves the suspension of the regime of truth that governs the elaboration and totalization of identities. If the identity we say we are cannot possibly capture us, and marks immediately an excess and opacity which falls outside the terms of identity itself, then any effort we make "to give an account of oneself" will have to fail in order to approach being true. And as we ask to know the other, or ask that the other say, finally, who he or she is, it will be important that we do not expect an answer that will ever satisfy. And by not pursuing satisfaction, we let the other live, offering a recognition that is not based on knowledge, but on its limits.

Judith Butler and William Connolly, "Politics, Power and Ethics: A Discussion Between Judith Butler and William Connolly," *Theory & Event* 4, no. 2 (2000), http://muse.jhu.edu/journals/theory_and_event/v004/4.2butler.html.

44. Cavell, *Conditions Handsome and Unhandsome*, xxxvii.

45. Ibid., cf. Butler, *Psychic Life of Power*, 10–11.

46. Cavell suggests a similar play between lacking and desiring, and between conformity and aversion. Cavell, *Cities of Words*, 22–24.

47. Butler, *Psychic Life of Power*, 10–11; cf. 195–98.

48. Ibid., 27–28; cf. 56, 60–62.

49. Stanley Cavell, *In Quest of the Ordinary*, 153–78. It is noteworthy that Cavell also highlights the features of loss and mourning that attend to the experience of the philosophers of skepticism, especially Hume and Thoreau.

Bibliography

Abrams, M. H. *The Mirror and the Lamp: Romantic Theory and the Critical Tradition*. New York: Norton, 1958.

Adams, Robert Merrihew. *Finite and Infinite Goods: A Framework for Ethics*. Oxford: Oxford University Press, 1999.

Alcoff, Linda. "Cultural Feminism versus Poststructuralism: The Identity Crisis in Feminist Theory." *Signs* 13 (Spring 1988): 405–36.

Allison, Henry. *Kant's Theory of Taste: A Reading of the Critique of Aesthetic Judgment*. Cambridge: Cambridge University Press, 2001.

Althusser, Louis. *Lenin and Philosophy and Other Essays*. Translated by Ben Brewster. New York: Monthly Review Press, 1971.

Anderson, Benedict. *Imagined Communities*. New York: Verso, 1991.

Anderson, Victor. *Beyond Ontological Blackness: An Essay on African American Religious and Cultural Criticism*. New York: Continuum, 1995.

Antonnaccio, Maria, and William Schweiker, eds. *Iris Murdoch and the Search for Human Goodness*. Chicago: University of Chicago Press, 1996.

Arendt, Hannah. *Between Past and Future*. New York: Vintage, 1968.

———. *Eichmann in Jerusalem: A Report on the Banality of Evil*. New York: Viking, 1965.

———. *The Human Condition*. Chicago: University of Chicago Press, 1958.

———. *Lectures on Kant's Political Philosophy*. Edited by Ronald Beiner. Chicago: University of Chicago Press, 1989.

Aristotle, *Nichomachean Ethics*. Translated by Roger Crisp. Cambridge: Cambridge University Press, 2000.

Austin, J. L. *How to Do Things with Words*. Cambridge: Harvard University Press, 1962.

Bates, Stanley, "Stanley Cavell and Ethics." In *Stanley Cavell*, edited by Richard Eldridge, 15–47. New York: Cambridge University Press, 2003.

Beckley, Bill, ed. *Sticky Sublime*. New York: Allworth Press, 2001.

Beckley, Bill, and David Shapiro, eds. *Uncontrollable Beauty: Toward a New Aesthetics.* New York: Allworth Press, 2002.

Beckwith Francis J., and Todd E. Jones. *Affirmative Action: Social Justice or Reverse Discrimination?* Amherst, N.Y.: Prometheus, 1997.

Bell, Vikki. "On Speech, Race and Melancholia: An Interview with Judith Butler." *Theory, Culture, & Society* 16, no. 2 (1999): 163–74.

Bellah, Robert N. *Beyond Belief: Essays on Religion in a Post-Traditional World.* Berkeley: University of California Press, 1970.

Bellah, Robert N., et al. *The Good Society.* New York: Knopf, 1991.

———. *Habits of the Heart: Individualism and Commitment in American Life.* Berkeley: University of California Press, 1985.

Benhabib, Seyla. *The Claims of Culture: Equality and Diversity in the Global Era.* Princeton: Princeton University Press, 2002.

———. *Situating the Self: Gender, Community, and Postmodernism in Contemporary Ethics.* New York: Routledge, 1992.

Benhabib, Seyla, Judith Butler, Drucilla Cornell, and Nancy Fraser. *Feminist Contentions: A Philosophical Exchange.* Edited by Linda Nicholson. New York: Routledge, 1995.

Benjamin, Walter. *Illuminations: Essays and Reflections.* Hannah Arendt, ed. New York: Schocken Books, 1969.

Bennett, Jane. *The Enchantment of Modern Life: Attachments, Crossings, and Ethics.* Princeton: Princeton University Press, 2001.

———. "'How Is It, Then, That We Still Remain Barbarians?' Foucault, Schiller, and the Aestheticization of Ethics." *Political Theory* 24, no. 4 (November 1996): 653–72.

Berger, Peter. *The Sacred Canopy.* Garden City, N.Y.: Anchor, 1969.

Berger, Peter, and Thomas Luckmann. *The Social Construction of Reality.* New York: Anchor, 1966.

Berlin, Isaiah. *Four Essays on Liberty.* London: Oxford University Press, 1969.

Bhabha, Homi K. *The Location of Culture.* New York: Routledge, 1994.

Blackburn, Simon. *Ruling Passions: A Theory of Practical Reasoning.* Oxford: Oxford University Press, 1998.

Bloom, Harold. "Emerson and Whitman: The American Sublime." In *Sticky Sublime,* edited by Bill Beckley, 16–40. New York: Allworth Press, 2001.

———. *Ruin the Sacred Truths: Poetry and Belief from the Bible to the Present.* Cambridge: Harvard University Press, 1989.

Bordo, Susan. "Feminism, Postmodernism, and Gender-Skepticism." In *Feminism/ Postmodernism,* edited by Linda J. Nicholson, 133–56. New York: Routledge, 1990.

Boym, Svetlana. *The Future of Nostalgia.* New York: Basic Books, 2001.

Brown, Wendy. "Resisting Left Melancholia." *boundary 2,* 26, no. 3 (Fall 1999): 19–27.

———. *States of Injury: Freedom and Power in Late Modernity.* Princeton: Princeton University Press, 1995.

Bruns, Gerald L. *Tragic Thoughts at the End of Philosophy: Language, Literature, and Ethical Theory.* Evanston: Northwestern University Press, 1999.

Butler, Judith. *Bodies That Matter: On the Discursive Limits of "Sex."* New York: Routledge, 1993.

————. *Excitable Speech: a Politics of the Performative*. New York: Routledge, 1997.
————. *Gender Trouble: Feminism and the Subversion of Identity*. New York: Routledge, 1990.
————. *Giving an Account of Oneself*. New York: Fordham University Press, 2005.
————. *The Psychic Life of Power: Theories in Subjection*. Stanford: Stanford University Press, 1997.
Butler, Judith, and William Connolly. "Politics, Power and Ethics: A Discussion Between Judith Butler and William Connolly." *Theory & Event* 4, no. 2 (2000), http://muse.jhu.edu/journals/theory_and_event/v004/4.2butler.html.
Butler, Judith, Ernesto Laclau, and Slavoj Zizek. *Contingency, Hegemony, Universality: Contemporary Dialogues on the Left*. London: Verso, 2000.
Calhoun, Craig Jackson. *Critical Social Theory*. Cambridge: Blackwell, 1995.
————. "Imagining Solidarity: Cosmopolitanism, Constitutional Patriotism and the Public Sphere." *Public Culture* 14, no. 1 (2002): 147–71.
————. "Morality, Identity, and Historical Explanation: Charles Taylor on the Sources of the Self." *Sociological Theory* 9, no. 2 (1991): 232–63.
Caputo, John D., and Michael J. Scanlon, eds. *God, the Gift, and Postmodernism*. Bloomington: Indiana University Press, 1999.
Casanova, José. *Public Religions in the Modern World*. Chicago: University of Chicago Press, 1994.
Cascardi, Anthony J. *The Subject of Modernity*. New York: Cambridge University Press, 1992.
Cavell, Stanley. *Cities of Words: Pedagogical Letters on a Register of the Moral Life*. Cambridge: Harvard University Press, 2004.
————. *Conditions Handsome and Unhandsome: The Constitution of Emersonian Perfectionism*. Chicago: University of Chicago Press, 1990.
————. *Disowning Knowledge: In Seven Plays of Shakespeare*. Cambridge: Cambridge University Press, 1987.
————. *In Quest of the Ordinary: Lines of Skepticism and Romanticism*. Chicago: University of Chicago Press, 1988.
————. *Pursuits of Happiness: The Hollywood Comedy of Remarriage*. Cambridge: Harvard University Press, 1981.
Cheng, Anne Anlin. *The Melancholy of Race: Psychoanalysis, Assimilation, and Hidden Grief*. New York: Oxford University Press, 2001.
Chong, Dennis. *Collective Action and the Civil Rights Movement*. Chicago: University of Chicago Press, 1991.
Chow, Rey. *Writing Diasporas: Tactics of Intervention in Contemporary Cultural Studies*. Bloomington: Indiana University Press, 1993.
Cioran, E. M. *The Temptation to Exist*. Translated by Richard Howard. Chicago: University of Chicago Press, 1998.
Coles, Robert. *The Secular Mind*. Princeton: Princeton University Press, 1999.
Coles, Romand. *Beyond Gated Politics: Reflections for the Possibility of Democracy*. Minneapolis: University of Minnesota Press, 2005.
Connerly, Ward. *Creating Equal: My Fight with Race Preferences*. San Francisco: Encounter Books, 2000.

————. "The Sweet Music of Equal Treatment." In *Affirmative Action: Social Justice or Reverse Discrimination?*, edited by Francis J. Beckwith and Todd E. Jones, 64–69. Amherst, N.Y.: Prometheus, 1997.

Connolly, William E. *The Ethos of Pluralization*. Minneapolis: University of Minnesota Press, 1995.

————. *Identity/Difference: Democratic Negotiations of Political Paradox*. Ithaca: Cornell University Press, 1992.

————. "Taylor, Foucault, and Otherness." *Political Theory* 13, no. 3 (August 1985): 365–76.

Crowther, Paul. *The Kantian Sublime: From Morality to Art*. Oxford: Oxford University Press, 1989.

De Bolla, Peter. *Art Matters*. Cambridge: Harvard University Press, 2001.

Derrida, Jacques. *Margins of Philosophy*. Translated by Alan Bass. Chicago: University of Chicago Press, 1982.

————. *The Other Heading: Reflections on Today's Europe*. Bloomington: Indiana University Press, 1992.

Dewey, John. *A Common Faith*. New Haven: Yale University Press, 1934.

Dews, Peter. "Disenchantment and the Persistence of Evil." IWM Working Paper No. 8. Vienna: IWM, 1997.

DiStefano, Christine. "Dilemmas of Difference: Feminism, Modernity, and Post-modernism." In *Feminism/Postmodernism*, edited by Linda J. Nicholson, 63–82. New York: Routledge, 1990.

Eagleton, Terry. *Sweet Violence: The Idea of the Tragic*. Malden, Mass.: Blackwell Publishing, 2005.

Edwards, James. C. *The Plain Sense of Things: The Fate of Religion in an Age of Normal Nihilism*. University Park: Pennsylvania State University Press, 1997.

Eldridge, Richard. *The Persistence of Romanticism: Essays in Philosophy and Literature*. Cambridge: Cambridge University Press, 2001.

Eldridge, Richard, ed. *Stanley Cavell*. New York: Cambridge University Press, 2003.

Emerson, Ralph Waldo. *Essays & Lectures*. New York: Library of America, 1983.

Epstein, Barbara. "Feminist Consciousness after the Women's Movement." *Monthly Review* 54, no. 4 (September 2002): 31–37.

Euben, Roxanne L. *Enemy in the Mirror: Islamic Fundamentalism and the Limits of Modern Rationalism*. Princeton: Princeton University Press, 1999.

Ferguson, Harvie. *Melancholy and the Critique of Modernity: Søren Kierkegaard's Religious Psychology*. London: Routledge, 1995.

————. *Modernity and Subjectivity: Body, Soul, Spirit*. Charlottesville: University Press of Virginia, 2000.

Ferguson, Russell et al., eds. *Out There: Marginalization and Contemporary Cultures*. Cambridge: MIT Press, 1990.

Flanagan, Owen. "Identity and Strong and Weak Evaluation." In *Identity, Character, and Morality: Essays in Moral Psychology*, edited by Owen Flanagan and Amélie Oksenberg Rorty, 37–66. Cambridge: MIT Press, 1993.

————. *Self Expressions: Mind, Morals, and the Meaning of Life*. New York: Oxford University Press, 1996.

Foucault, Michel. *The Archaeology of Knowledge and The Discourse on Language*. Translated by Alan M. Sheridan Smith. New York: Pantheon, 1972.

——. *The Care of the Self: History of Sexuality*, vol. III. Translated by Robert Hurley. New York: Pantheon, 1978.

——. *Discipline and Punish: The Birth of the Prison*. Translated by Alan M. Sheridan. New York: Vintage, 1979.

——. *Ethics, Subjectivity, and Truth*. Edited by Paul Rabinow. New York: Free Press, 1997.

——. *Fearless Speech*. Edited by Joseph Pearson. Los Angeles: Semiotext(e), 2001.

Frankfurt, Harry. "Freedom of the Will and the Concept of a Person." *Journal of Philosophy* 67, no. 1 (January 1971): 5–20.

——. *Necessity, Volition, and Love*. Cambridge: Cambridge University Press, 1999.

——. "On the Necessity of Ideals." In *The Moral Self*, edited by Thomas E. Wren and Gil G. Noam, 28–55. Cambridge: Cambridge University Press, 1993.

Freud, Sigmund. *Civilization and Its Discontents*. Translated by James Strachey. New York: W. W. Norton, 1989.

——. "Mourning and Melancholia." In *The Standard Edition of the Complete Psychological Works of Sigmund Freud*. Translated and edited by James Strachey. London: Hogarth Press, 1957, 14:243–60.

——. "On Narcissism." In *Standard Edition*, 14:73–104.

——. *Civilization and Its Discontents*. Translated by James Strachey. New York: W. W. Norton, 1989.

——. *The Uncanny*. Translated by David McLintock. New York: Penguin, 2003.

Fuss, Diana. *Identification Papers*. New York: Routledge, 1995.

Gauchet, Marcel. *The Disenchantment of the World: A Political History of Religion*. Translated by Oscar Burge. Princeton: Princeton University Press, 1997.

Geertz, Clifford. *The Interpretation of Cultures*. New York: Basic Books, 1977.

Giddens, Anthony. *Modernity and Self-Identity: Self and Society in the Late Modern Age*. Stanford: Stanford University Press, 1991.

Gilligan, Carol. *In a Different Voice*. Cambridge: Harvard University Press, 1982.

Gilroy, Paul. *The Black Atlantic: Modernity and Double Consciousness*. Cambridge: Harvard University Press, 1993.

Goffman, Ervin. *The Presentation of Self in Everyday Life*. New York: Doubleday, 1959.

Goldhagen, Daniel. *Hitler's Willing Executioners: Ordinary Germans and the Holocaust*. New York: Knopf, 1996.

Goldman, Harvey. *Max Weber and Thomas Mann: Calling and the Shaping of the Self*. Berkeley: University of California Press, 1988.

——. *Politics, Death, and the Devil: Self and Power in Max Weber and Thomas Mann*. Berkeley: University of California Press, 1992.

Grafton, Anthony. *Bring Out Your Dead: The Past as Revelation*. Cambridge: Harvard University Press, 2002.

Grosz, Elizabeth. "Experimental Desire: Rethinking Queer Subjectivity." In *Supposing the Subject*, edited by Joan Copjec, 133–57. London and New York: Verso, 1994.

——. *Volatile Bodies: Toward a Corporeal Feminism*. Bloomington and Indianapolis: Indiana University Press, 1994.

Gutting, Gary. *Pragmatic Liberalism and the Critique of Modernity*. Cambridge: Cambridge University Press, 1999.

Guyer, Paul. *Kant and the Claims of Taste*, 2nd ed. Cambridge: Cambridge University Press, 1997.

———. *Kant and the Experience of Freedom: Essays on Aesthetics and Morality.* Cambridge: Cambridge University Press, 1993.

Habermas, Jürgen. *Between Facts and Norms: Contributions to a Discourse Theory of Law and Democracy.* Translated by William Rehg. Cambridge: MIT Press, 1998.

———. *Postmetaphysical Thinking.* Cambridge: MIT Press, 1992.

———. *The Theory of Communicative Action, Volume One: Reason and the Rationalization of Society.* Translated by Thomas McCarthy. Boston: Beacon Press, 1984.

———. *The Theory of Communicative Action, Volume Two, Lifeworld and System: A Critique of Functionalist Reason.* Translated by Thomas McCarthy. Boston: Beacon Press, 1987.

Hadot, Pierre. *Philosophy as a Way of Life: Spiritual Exercises from Socrates to Foucault.* Translated by Michael Chase. Cambridge: Blackwell, 1995.

Hall, Stuart. "Cultural Identity and Diaspora." In *Identity, Community, Culture, Difference,* edited by J. Rutherford, 222–37. London: Lawrence & Wishart, 1990.

Hand, Sean, ed. *The Levinas Reader.* Cambridge: Blackwell, 1990.

Hardt, Michael, and Antonio Negri. *Multitude: War and Democracy in the Age of Empire.* New York: Penguin, 2004.

Hart, Ray L. *Unfinished Man and the Imagination.* Louisville: Westminster John Knox Press, 2001.

Heaney, Seamus. *The Burial at Thebes: A Version of Sophocles'* Antigone. New York: Farrar, Straus, and Giroux, 2004.

Hegel, G. W. F. *Hegel's Phenomenology of Spirit.* Translated by A. V. Miller. New York: Oxford University Press, 1977.

———. *Lectures on the Philosophy of Religion: One Volume Edition, The Lectures of 1827.* Translated by R. F. Brown, P. C. Hodgson, and J. M. Stewart. Berkeley: University of California Press, 1988.

Hobsbawm, Eric, and Terence Ranger, eds. *The Invention of Tradition.* Cambridge: Cambridge University Press, 1983.

Hollywood, Amy. "Performativity, Citationality, Ritualization." *History of Religions* 42, no. 2 (2002): 93–115.

Homans, Peter, ed. *Symbolic Loss: The Ambiguity of Mourning and Memory at Century's End.* Charlottesville: University Press of Virginia, 2000.

hooks, bell. *Yearning: Race, Gender, and Cultural Politics.* Boston: South End Press, 1990.

Horowitz, Asher, and Terry Maley, eds. *The Barbarism of Reason: Max Weber and the Twilight of Enlightenment.* Toronto: University of Toronto Press, 1994.

Huizinga, Johan. *Homo Ludens: A Study of the Play Element in Culture.* New York: J & J Harper, 1970.

Hume, David. *Enquiries Concerning the Human Understanding and Concerning the Principles of Morals.* Edited by L. Selby-Bigge. London: Oxford University Press, 1902.

Isaacs, Jeffrey C. *Democracy in Dark Times.* Ithaca: Cornell University Press, 1998.

James, William. *Pragmatism and the Meaning of Truth.* Cambridge: Harvard University Press, 1978.

———. *The Will to Believe and Other Essays in Popular Philosophy, and Human Immortality.* New York: Dover, 1967.

Jameson, Frederic. *The Political Unconscious: Narrative as a Socially Symbolic Act.* Ithaca: Cornell University Press, 1981.

Joas, Hans. *The Genesis of Values.* Chicago: University of Chicago Press, 2000.

Kant, Immanuel. *Critique of Judgment.* Translated by J. H. Bernard. New York: Hafner Press, 1951.

———. *Critique of Practical Reason.* Translated by Lewis White Beck. Indianapolis: Bobbs-Merrill, 1956.

———. *Critique of Pure Reason.* Translated by Norman Kemp Smith. New York: St. Martin's, 1933.

———. *Groundwork of the Metaphysics of Morals.* Translated by Mary Gregor. Cambridge: Cambridge University Press, 1998.

———. *Kant: Political Writings.* Edited by H. S. Reiss. Translated by H. B. Nisbet. Cambridge: Cambridge University Press, 1991.

———. *Religion within the Boundaries of Mere Reason and Other Writings.* Translated by Allen Wood and George di Giovanni. Cambridge: Cambridge University Press, 1998.

Kaufman, Gordon D. *Theological Imagination: Constructing the Concept of God.* Louisville: Westminster John Knox Press, 1981.

Kearney, Richard. *The Wake of Imagination: Toward a Postmodern Culture.* New York: Routledge, 1988.

Kestenbaum, Victor. *The Grace and the Severity of the Ideal: John Dewey and the Transcendent.* Chicago: University of Chicago Press, 2002.

Kierkegaard, Søren. *Repetition and Fear and Trembling.* Translated by Howard V. Hong and Edna H. Hong. Princeton: Princeton University Press, 1983.

Korsgaard, Christine. *Sources of Normativity.* Cambridge: Cambridge University Press, 1996.

Kristeva, Julia. *Black Sun: Depression and Melancholia.* Translated by Leon S. Roudiez. New York: Columbia University Press, 1989.

Kuhn, Thomas. *The Structure of Scientific Revolutions,* 2nd ed. Chicago: University of Chicago Press, 1970.

Kymlicka, Will. *Liberalism, Community, and Culture.* Oxford: Clarendon Press, 1989.

———. *Multicultural Citizenship: A Liberal Theory of Minority Rights.* Oxford: Oxford University Press, 1995.

Laclau, Ernesto, and Chantal Mouffe. *Hegemony and Socialist Strategy: Towards a Radical Democratic Politics.* London: Verso, 1985.

Lacoue-Labarthe, Phillippe, and Jean Luc Nancy. *The Literary Absolute: The Theory of Literature in German Romanticism.* Translated by Philip Barnard and Cheryl Lester. Albany: State University of New York Press, 1988.

Larmore, Charles. *The Romantic Legacy.* New York: Columbia University Press, 1996.

Lubiano, Waneema, ed. *The House that Race Built: Black Americans, U.S. Terrain.* New York: Pantheon, 1997.

Lyotard, Jean-François. *The Differend: Phrases in Dispute.* Translated by Georges Van Den Abeele. Minneapolis: University of Minnesota Press, 1988.

———. *The Inhuman: Reflections on Time.* Translated by Geoffrey Bennington and Rachel Bowlby. Stanford: Stanford University Press, 1991.

———. *Lessons on the Analytic of the Sublime: Kant's Critique of Judgment.* Translated by Elizabeth Rottenberg. Stanford: Stanford University Press, 1994.

————. *The Postmodern Condition: A Report on Knowledge*. Translated by Geoffrey
    Bennington and Brian Massumi. Minneapolis: University of Minnesota Press, 1984.
MacIntyre, Alasdair. *After Virtue*. Notre Dame: University of Notre Dame Press, 1984.
Minow, Martha. *Between Vengeance and Forgiveness: Facing History after Genocide
    and Mass Violence*. Boston: Beacon, 1998.
Mishra, Vijay. *The Gothic Sublime*. Albany: State University of New York Press, 1994.
Mol, Hans. 1976. *Identity and the Sacred: A Sketch for a New Social-Scientific Theory
    of Religion*. Oxford: Blackwell, 1976.
Morgan, Michael L. "Religion, History, and Moral Discourse." In *Philosophy in an Age
    of Pluralism: The Philosophy of Charles Taylor in Question*, edited by James Tully,
    49–66. Cambridge: Cambridge University Press, 1994.
Mulhall, Stephen. "Sources of the Self's Senses of Itself: The Making of a Theistic
    Reading of Modernity." In *Can Religion Be Explained Away?* edited by
    D. Z. Phillips, 131–60. New York: St. Martin's Press, 1996.
Murdoch, Iris. *Existentialists and Mystics: Writings on Philosophy and Literature*. Edited
    by Peter Conradi. New York: Penguin, 1998.
————. *The Sovereignty of Good*. London: Routledge, 1970.
Nehamas, Alexander. *The Art of Living: Socratic Reflections from Plato to Foucault*.
    Berkeley: University of California Press, 1998.
Neville, Robert Cummings. "A New Confucian Lament for Alienation." In *Loneliness*,
    edited by Leroy Rouner, 258–72. Notre Dame: University of Notre Dame Press,
    1998.
Nicholson, Linda J., ed. *Feminism/Postmodernism*. New York: Routledge, 1990.
Nietzsche, Friedrich. *The Birth of Tragedy and the Genealogy of Morals*. Translated by
    Francis Golffing. New York: Anchor Books, 1956.
————. *The Gay Science: With a Prelude in Rhymes and an Appendix of Songs*. Trans-
    lated by Walter Kaufmann. New York: Vintage, 1974.
Nussbaum, Martha. *The Fragility of Goodness: Luck and Ethics in Greek Tragedy and
    Philosophy*. Cambridge: Cambridge University Press, 1986.
————. "The Professor of Parody: The Hip, Defeatist Feminism of Judith Butler." *The
    New Republic* (22 February 1999): 37–45.
————. *Upheavals of Thought: The Intelligence of Emotions*. New York: Cambridge
    University Press, 2001.
Okihiro, Gary Y. *Margins and Mainstreams: Asians in American History and Culture*.
    Seattle: University of Washington Press, 1994.
Okin, Susan Moller, "Is Multiculturalism Bad for Women?" *The Boston Review*
    (October/November 1997): http://www.bostonreview.net/BR22.5/okin.html.
Omi, Michael, and Howard Winant. *Racial Formation in the United States: From the
    1960s to the 1980s*. New York: Routledge, 1986.
Pascal, Blaise. *Pensées*. Translated by A. J. Krailsheimer. New York: Penguin, 1995.
Patterson, Orlando. *Slavery and Social Death: A Comparative Analysis*. Cambridge:
    Harvard University Press, 1982.
Pettit, Phillip. *A Theory of Freedom: From the Psychology to the Politics of Agency*. Oxford:
    Oxford University Press, 2001.
Pippin, Robert B. "Nietzsche and the Melancholy of Modernity." *Social Research* 66,
    no. 2 (Summer 1999): 495–520.

Phillips, D. Z., ed. *Can Religion Be Explained Away?* New York: St. Martin's Press, 1996.
Putnam, Robert D. *Bowling Alone: The Collapse and Revival of American Community.* New York: Simon & Schuster, 2000.
Raposa, Michael L. *Boredom and the Religious Imagination.* Charlottesville: University Press of Virginia, 1999.
Rawls, John. *Political Liberalism.* New York: Columbia University Press, 1995.
———. *A Theory of Justice.* Cambridge: Belknap/Harvard University Press, 1971.
Reeve, C. D. C., trans. *Plato: Republic.* Indianapolis: Hackett, 1992.
Ricoeur, Paul. *Oneself as Another.* Translated by Kathleen Blamey. Chicago: University of Chicago Press, 1992.
Rorty, Amélie Oksenberg. "What It Takes to Be Good." In *The Moral Self*, edited by Thomas E. Wren and Gil G. Noam, 56–77. Cambridge: Cambridge University Press, 1993.
Rorty, Richard, *Achieving Our Country: Leftist Though in Twentieth-Century America.* Cambridge: Cambridge University Press, 1997.
———. *Contingency, Irony, and Solidarity.* Cambridge: Cambridge University Press, 1989.
———. "Taylor on Self-Celebration and Gratitude." *Philosophy and Phenomenological Research* 54 (1994): 197–201.
Rouner, Leroy, ed. *Loneliness.* Notre Dame: University of Notre Dame Press, 1998.
Royce, Josiah. *Sources of Religious Insight.* New York: Scribners, 1912.
Ruf, Frederick J. *The Creation of Chaos: William James and the Stylistic Making of a Disorderly World.* Albany: State University of New York Press, 1991.
Ruskin, John. *Modern Painters.* New York: Wiley & Halsted, 1856.
Said, Edward W. *Humanism and Democratic Criticism.* New York: Columbia University Press, 2004.
———. "Invention, Memory, and Place." *Critical Inquiry* 26 (2000): 175–92.
Sandel, Michael. *Democracy's Discontents: America in Search of a Public Philosophy.* Cambridge: Belknap Press of Harvard University Press, 1996.
———. *Liberalism and the Limits of Justice*, 2nd ed. Cambridge: Cambridge University Press, 1998.
Schleiermacher, Friedrich. *On Religion: Speeches to its Cultured Despisers.* Translated by Richard Crouter. Cambridge: Cambridge University Press, 1996.
Scott, James C. *Domination and the Arts of Resistance: Hidden Transcripts.* New Haven: Yale University Press, 1990.
Scott, Joan. "Deconstructing Equality-versus-Difference: Or the Uses of Post-structuralist Theory for Feminism." *Feminist Studies* 14 (Spring 1988): 33–50.
Shanks, Andrew. *"What Is Truth?" Towards a Theological Poetics.* London: Routledge, 2001.
Silverman, Kaja. *The Acoustic Mirror: The Female Voice in Psychoanalysis and Cinema.* Bloomington: Indiana University Press, 1988.
Skinner, Quentin. "Modernity and Disenchantment: Some Historical Reflections." In *Philosophy in an Age of Pluralism: The Philosophy of Charles Taylor in Question*, edited by James Tully, 37–48. Cambridge: Cambridge University Press, 1994.
Sophocles. *The Three Theban Plays.* Translated by Robert Fagles. New York: Penguin, 1984.

Soyinka, Wole. *The Burden of Memory, the Muse of Forgiveness*. New York: Oxford University Press, 1999.

Steiner, George. *Errata: An Examined Life*. New Haven: Yale University Press, 1999.

———. *Grammars of Creation*. New Haven: Yale University Press, 2001.

———. *Real Presences*. Chicago: University of Chicago Press, 1991.

Stevens, Wallace. *Wallace Stevens: Collected Poems and Prose*. New York: Library of America, 1997.

Stout, Jeffrey. *Democracy and Tradition*. Princeton: Princeton University Press, 2003.

———. *Ethics after Babel: The Languages of Morals and Their Discontents*. Boston: Beacon: 1988.

———. *Flight from Authority: Religion, Morality, and the Quest for Autonomy*. Notre Dame: University of Notre Dame Press, 1987.

Taylor, Charles. *A Catholic Modernity? Charles Taylor's Marianist Award Lecture*. Edited by J. L. Heft, S. M. New York: Oxford University Press, 1999.

———. "Connolly, Foucault, and Truth." *Political Theory* 13, no. 3 (August 1985): 377–85.

———. *The Ethics of Authenticity*. Cambridge: Harvard University Press, 1992.

———. "Forward." In *The Disenchantment of the World: A Political History of Religion*. Translated by Oscar Burge, ix–xv. Princeton: Princeton University Press, 1997.

———. *Hegel*. Cambridge: Cambridge University Press, 1975.

———. *Hegel and Modern Society*. Cambridge: Cambridge University Press, 1979.

———. "Iris Murdoch and Moral Philosophy." In *Iris Murdoch and the Search for Human Goodness*, edited by Maria Antonaccio and William Schweiker, 3–28. Chicago: University of Chicago Press, 1996.

———. "Leading a Life." In *Incommensurability, Incomparability, and Practical Reason*, edited by Ruth Chang, 171–83. Cambridge: Harvard University Press, 1997.

———. "Modern Social Imaginaries." *Public Culture* 14, no. 1 (Winter 2002): 91–124.

———. "Modernity and the Rise of the Public Sphere." Tanner Lecture, Stanford University, 1992.

———. *Philosophical Arguments*. Cambridge: Harvard University Press, 1995.

———. *Philosophical Papers 1: Human Agency and Language*. Cambridge: Cambridge University Press, 1985.

———. *Philosophical Papers 2: Philosophy and the Human Sciences*. Cambridge: Cambridge University Press, 1985.

———. *Sources of the Self: The Making of Modern Identity*. Cambridge: Harvard University Press, 1989.

———. "Two Theories of Modernity." *Public Culture* 11, no. 1 (1999): 153–74.

———. *Varieties of Religion Today: William James Revisited*. Cambridge: Harvard University Press, 2002.

———. "What's Wrong with Foundationalism? Knowing, Agency, and World." In *Heidegger, Coping, and Cognitive Science: Essays in Honor of Hubert L. Dreyfus*, vol. 2, edited by Mark Wrathall and Jeff Malpas 115–34. Cambridge: MIT Press, 2000.

Taylor, Charles et al. *Multiculturalism and "The Politics of Recognition."* Edited by Amy Gutmann. Princeton: Princeton University Press, 1992.

Taylor, Mark C. *Disfigurings: Art, Architecture, Religion*. Chicago: University of Chicago Press, 1994.

Thiemann, Ronald F. *Religion in Public Life: A Dilemma for Democracy.* Washington,
    D.C.: Georgetown University Press, 1996.
Thumma, Scott. "Negotiating a Religious Identity: The Case of the Gay Evangelical."
    Sociological Analysis 52, no. 4 (1991): 333–47.
Tillich, Paul. *A Theology of Culture.* New York: Oxford University Press, 1959.
Tracy, David. *The Analogical Imagination: Christian Theology and the Culture of
    Pluralism.* New York: Crossroad, 1981.
Trinh, T. Minh-ha. *Woman, Native, Other: Writing Postcoloniality and Feminism.*
    Bloomington: Indiana University Press, 1989.
Trilling, Lionel. *The Moral Obligation to be Intelligent: Selected Essays.* Edited by Leon
    Wieseltier. New York: Farrar, Straus, Giroux, 2000.
Twain, Mark. *The Adventures of Huckleberry Finn.* New York: Chanticleer Press, 1950.
Tu Wei-ming, *Centrality and Commonality: An Essay on Confucian Religiousness.* Albany:
    State University of New York Press, 1989.
———. *Way, Learning and Politics: Essays on the Confucian Intellectual.* Albany: State
    University of New York Press, 1993.
Tully, James, ed. *Philosophy in an Age of Pluralism: The Philosophy of Charles Taylor
    in Question.* Cambridge: Cambridge University Press, 1994.
Unger, Roberto Mangabeira. *Passion: An Essay on Personality.* New York: Free Press, 1984.
Villa, Dana. *Socratic Citizenship.* Princeton: Princeton University Press, 2001.
Walzer, Michael. *Obligations: Essays on Disobedience, War, and Citizenship.* Cambridge:
    Harvard University Press, 1970.
———. *Thick and Thin: Moral Argument at Home and Abroad.* Notre Dame: University
    of Notre Dame Press, 1996.
Warren, Mark E. "What Can Democratic Participation Mean Today?" *Political Theory*
    30, no. 5 (October 2002): 677–701.
Weber, Max. *From Max Weber: Essays in Sociology.* Translated and edited by H. H. Gerth
    and C. Wright Mills. New York: Oxford University Press, 1946.
———. *The Protestant Ethic and the Spirit of Capitalism.* Translated by Talcott Parsons.
    New York: Routledge, 1992 [1930].
Weiskel, Thomas. *The Romantic Sublime: Studies in the Structure and Psychology of
    Transcendence.* Baltimore: Johns Hopkins University Press, 1976.
West, Cornel. *Democracy Matters: Winning the Fight against Imperialism.* New York:
    Penguin, 2004.
———. *Keeping Faith: Philosophy and Race in America.* New York: Routledge, 1993.
White, Stephen K. *Political Theory and Postmodernism.* Cambridge: Cambridge
    University Press, 1991.
———. *Sustaining Affirmation: The Strength of Weak Ontology in Political Theory.*
    Princeton: Princeton University Press, 2000.
Wolin, Sheldon. "Fugitive Democracy." In *Democracy and Difference: Contesting the
    Boundaries of the Political,* edited by Seyla Benhabib, 31–45. Princeton: Princeton
    University Press, 1996.
———. *Politics and Vision: Continuity and Innovation in Western Political Thought.*
    Expanded Edition. Princeton: Princeton University Press, 2004.
Wrathall, Mark A., and Jeff Malpas, eds., *Heidegger, Coping, and Cognitive Science:
    Essays in Honor of Hubert L. Dreyfus,* vol. 2. Cambridge: MIT Press, 2000.

Wren, Thomas E., and Gil G. Noam, eds. *The Moral Self*. Cambridge: Cambridge University Press, 1993.

Wright, Lawrence. "One Drop of Blood." *The New Yorker* (25 June 1994): 46–55.

Yeats, W. B. *The Collected Poems of W. B. Yeats*. Edited by Richard J. Finneran. New York: Scribner, 1996.

Young, Iris Marion. *Justice and the Politics of Difference*. Princeton: Princeton University Press, 1990.

Zizek, Slavoj. *The Sublime Object of Ideology*. London: Verso, 1989.

———. *The Ticklish Subject: The Absent Centre of Political Ontology*. New York: Verso, 1999.

Zuckert, Catherine, ed., *Understanding the Political Spirit: Philosophical Reflections from Socrates to Nietzsche*. New Haven: Yale University Press, 1988.

Index

Abrams, M. H., 40
acknowledgment, 4, 16, 25, 32–33,
    57, 60, 65, 75, 80, 89, 102,
    108–09, 115–16, 128, 134, 145,
    173n.34
Adorno, Theodor, 110
agency
  alienation and, 19, 21, 31, 48–49,
    68, 73, 78, 86, 113, 117, 121, 132,
    159–60n.13
  as choice, 24–25, 58–60, 108–09,
    129, 137
  discourse on, 4–6, 10–12, 18, 57,
    72, 84–88, 125, 143
  as melancholic freedom, 5–7,
    19–21, 55, 58, 61–64, 80–82,
    86–88, 113, 120–21, 123, 137,
    143–45
  moral conversion and, 64, 82
  moral frameworks and, 25–33,
    35–37, 41–42, 52–53, 58,
    79–82
  motivation and, 5–8, 11, 27–28,
    35–37, 58–62, 69, 71, 77–78, 86,
    88, 94, 144, 160n.15, 164n.47,
    165n.4
  piety and, 64–65, 80–82, 105, 108,
    126, 138, 145

  as resistance and subversion,
    97–98, 101–03, 105, 109–10,
    112–13, 115, 119–21, 129, 133–34,
    139, 142, 145
  as spirit of politics, 13–14
  as strong evaluation, 24–34, 38,
    61–62, 65–66, 85–86, 130
  as vocation, 8, 20–21, 57, 59,
    64–65, 87, 103, 123–45
  See also projects of regenerating
    agency
  See also self/subject
alterity/otherness, 64, 74–75, 89,
    104–05, 119–20, 173–74n.43
  See also difference
Althusser, Louis, 100, 109–13,
    167n.33
  interpellation and, 112–13, 138
ambivalence, 75, 77, 87, 89, 99,
    105, 109–10, 112, 115–16, 118,
    123–26, 137–38, 140–43
Antigone, 63
Arendt, Hannah, 12, 38, 84, 151n.35,
    157n.4, 163n.44
aspiration, 3–5, 7–11, 14, 16, 19–21,
    39, 41, 43, 48, 56–57, 60–61,
    69, 77, 80, 86, 88, 93, 103–04,
    108, 113–15, 119, 121, 126–29,